Cambridge United
101 Golden Greats

CW00828690

CLUB HISTORIES

Aberdeen: A Centenary History 1903-2003	1-874287-49-X
Aberdeen: The European Era – A Complete Record	1-874287-11-2
Bristol City: The Modern Era – A Complete Record	1-874287-28-7
Cambridge United: The League Era – A Complete Record	1-874287-32-5
Cambridge United: 101 Golden Greats	1-874287-58-9
The Story of the Celtic 1888-1938	1-874287-15-5
Colchester United: Graham to Whitton – A Complete Record	1-874287-27-9
Coventry City: The Elite Era – A Complete Record	1-874287-51-1
Coventry City: An Illustrated History	1-874287-36-8
History of the Everton Football Club 1878-1928	1-874287-14-7
Halifax Town: From Ball to Lillis – A Complete Record	1-874287-26-0
Hereford United: The League Era – A Complete Record	1-874287-18-X
Ipswich Town: The Modern Era – A Complete Record	1-874287-43-0
Ipswich Town: Champions of England 1961-62	1-874287-56-2
Luton Town: The Modern Era – A Complete Record	1-874287-05-8
Luton Town: An Illustrated History	1-874287-37-6
Peterborough United: The Modern Era – A Complete Record	1-874287-33-3
Peterborough United: Who's Who?	1-874287-48-1
Plymouth Argyle: The Modern Era – A Complete Record	1-874287-54-6
Plymouth Argyle: 101 Golden Greats	1-874287-64-3
Portsmouth: From Tindall to Ball – A Complete Record	1-874287-25-2
Portsmouth: Champions of England – 1948-49 & 1949-50	1-874287-38-4
The Story of the Rangers 1873-1923	1-874287-16-3
The Romance of the Wednesday 1867-1926	1-874287-17-1
Stoke City: The Modern Era – A Complete Record	1-874287-39-2
Stoke City: 101 Golden Greats	1-874287-55-4
West Ham: From Greenwood to Redknapp	1-874287-19-8
West Ham: The Elite Era – A Complete Record	1-874287-31-7
Wimbledon: From Southern League to Premiership	1-874287-09-0
Wimbledon: From Wembley to Selhurst	1-874287-20-1
Wimbledon: The Premiership Years	1-874287-40-6
Wrexham: The European Era – A Complete Record	1-874287-52-X

WORLD CUP HISTORIES

England's Quest for the World Cup – A Complete Record	1-874287-61-9
Scotland: The Quest for the World Cup – A Complete Record	1-897850-50-6
Ireland: The Quest for the World Cup – A Complete Record	1-897850-80-8

MISCELLANEOUS

Red Dragons in Europe – A Complete Record	1-874287-01-5
The Book of Football: A History to 1905-06	1-874287-13-9

Cambridge United
101 Golden Greats

Series Editor: Clive Leatherdale
Series Consultant: Leigh Edwards

Kevin Palmer

Desert Island Books

First Published in 2002

DESERT ISLAND BOOKS LIMITED
89 Park Street, Westcliff-on-Sea, Essex SS0 7PD
United Kingdom
www.desertislandbooks.com

British Library Cataloguing-in-Publication Data
A catalogue record for this book is available from the British Library

ISBN 1-874287-58-9

Printed in Great Britain
by
Antony Rowe Ltd

Photographs in this book are reproduced by kind permission of:
The Cambridge *Evening News* and Cambridge United FC

~ Contents ~

~ *Preface* ~

I came to Cambridge United as a young boy from the sticks and was instantly made to feel welcome. United had not long come up from the Southern League and I was privileged to play a part in the club's roller coaster rise to playing on level terms with some of the country's biggest clubs like Chelsea, West Ham and Newcastle. I was fortunate enough to have Dave Stringer to help and guide me along, and thrilled to progress with young players of the ability of Steve Spriggs and Alan Biley to name but two. There is no better occupation for a lad in his late teens than to be a professional footballer.

Despite the club being located in a poor area – in the sense of attracting massive crowds – I feel that the supporters of Cambridge United are amongst the best in the country for their loyalty and dedication. They haven't always managed to witness success and the roller coaster has from time to time plummeted down some steep dips. But the management has often produced a good crop of youngsters, allied to an excellent scouting system that has helped to rebuild the club on a number of occasions. Many of these players are featured in this book and I am proud to be classed as one of them. At the time of writing this, John Taylor is occupied in lifting the club out of the doldrums once more and I fervently pray that United are at the start of something big once more.

STEVE FALLON

~ *Author's Note* ~

Cambridge United's Greatest Ever Players? Well, everyone can agree on the players like Fallon, Biley, Dublin and Taylor, and you only have to ask the old-timers to cement in names like Moore, Mannion and Murchison. When you get about two-thirds of the way through the list then things start to get blurred. What criteria do you use to fill in the gaps?

I whittled a rough list together with help from my colleague Leigh Edwards, then started the process of refining it with input from long-standing U's watchers like Dave Brown and Ken Moxham. Ex-United players and managers were invaluable in saying yea or nay to my suggestions and finally I got there with inevitable last-minute changes. If I had to do it again I would undoubtedly change the list slightly, but I'm not saying who would be dropped. Some players were very close to making the list and Harold Watson (1920s and 1930s) and Andy Fensome were on the fringes. I tried to erase any personal bias from the choice, leaving out some of my favourites like Tony Dennis, but an element of favouritism is inevitable. I'm sorry if any of your favourites have been left out, but nobody could ever do a list to please everybody. At least I didn't emulate the author of *Stoke City: 101 Golden Greats*, who omitted Peter Shilton on the grounds that he wasn't a good enough Stoke keeper, but the controversy generated certainly earned publicity for that book. I wouldn't dare omit a United legend from the list, but thank God it's a chronological list so I don't have to rank them.

This book has been put together with a great deal of input from the players, managers and fans who have been interviewed at length by me over the years. I have also pinched a little bit from other sources, so thank you to newspaper reporters (especially Randall Butt of the Cambridge *Evening News*) and internet writers everywhere. Congratulations to United Assistant Secretary Mark Johnson for sorting out the photos, but the biggest help of all has been Leigh Edwards. This guy has tracked down the most elusive of players and rounded up the families of the long-since departed. His knowledge of the game is encyclopaedic and without him I wouldn't have finished this book, so he gets the honour of having the book dedicated to him. Last but not least are the players themselves – all of them – even the ones who only played half a game in the Cambs League. They have all done their bit for Cambridge United and deserve congratulations.

KEVIN PALMER
October 2002

Chapter One

~ *Abbey Amateurs* ~

No 1. **WALLY WILSON**
Debut: v Abbey Crusaders, 27 August 1921
Farewell: v Histon, 11 May 1939

Wally was United's first goalscoring superstar, the only player to have scored five goals on three occasions. He also holds the record for most hat-tricks in a United career with fourteen.

Abbey United (as Cambridge United were known until 1951) began their competitive career in the Cambs League Division Three in 1921 and instantly dominated proceedings with Wally leading the line with athletic gusto. They played their home games at Stourbridge Common, which was a few hundred yards northwest of the present stadium, near to the River Cam. Wally's goalscoring prowess attracted the interest of Cambridge Town (the top club in the area) and he was loaned out to them for selected Southern Amateur League ties and FA Cup matches between October 1921 and January 1922. Despite these permitted absences, Wally easily topped United's goalscoring charts with 24 goals in their 24-game season.

For their Division Two campaign, Albert 'Twitter' Dring joined Wally up front, and the club strolled to another championship by winning twenty of their 22 games and scoring nearly five goals per game. Wally's medium-height, lean frame was housed in an amber and black striped shirt, which gave his team their early nickname of 'The Wasps' and it was Wally who provided the sting. He was fast and tricky in those early days and was unafraid to leap into situations were lesser players feared to tread. Mind you, that was a prerequisite for any good player in those rough-tough days. His reckless bravery (or stupidity) was proved by his heading ability. That uncompromisingly hard and heavy leather ball dissuaded many men from allowing it to come into contact with their heads, but Wally used to connect his noddle to the ball with a fearsome power that made bystanders wince. It was said that he could head a ball further than anyone else could kick it, which probably helps to explain why he lost nearly all of his hair over the course of his career and why he spent many hours of his life trying to soften up that hard leather cannonball in buckets of water.

United moved to a new ground in 1923, close to where the present stadium is located. It became known as the Celery Trenches, because of the furrows that stubbornly ran down the pitch, much to the chagrin of the frustrated groundsmen who vainly tried to remove them. Wally was one of four players who lived in nearby Stanley Road and on a matchday they would all meet up at the club's headquarters which was agreeably located in the old Dog and Pheasant pub in Newmarket Road. From there the players would emerge from their dressing room and lug the goalposts down the road to the ground. This procession of hard young men earned themselves the local nickname the 'Newmarket Road Roughs'. Sometimes, by way of a change, Wally would walk back to his house, change into his kit, and then cycle up to the Celery Trenches.

As the team was strengthened, and Wally got broader, heavier, older and slower, he was surprisingly converted into a winger and then a wing-half. His team captured the Cambs League Division One titles in 1925-26 and 1928-29, finishing as runners-up on five occasions and, along with the University Press, could lay claim to being the second-best club in Cambridge behind the mighty Town.

Abbey United moved to their present location in 1932, though it was known as the Abbey Ground in those days, because one tiny wooden stand hardly constituted a stadium. Wally was now becoming decidedly fat and was converted into a centre-half – 'the kingpin of the side,' as those old-fashioned stoppers were always known. He was also described as 'a great stumbling block to opposition forwards' and many a young dandy-boy striker would inwardly wince when confronted by this formidable, virtually bald, granite-like figure. His size also led to an endearing trait of him visibly drawing in his stomach when a long ball approached him, and using it to trap the ball and conveniently drop it at his feet. By this time Wally was clever enough to ensure that the younger defenders were assigned to any duties that involved heavy running, and after 1936 he tended not to venture far out of his area. By way of a swansong he managed a final hat-trick in April 1936. It had been seven years since his penultimate one, and nearly fifteen years since his first.

Wally worked for Cambridge Gasworks and used to play for the Gasworks' Married Men against the Single Men in matches played at the Abbey. He continued to play occasional games for the club during World War Two and was a familiar sight in the immediate post-war era, though he had now retired.

Magic Moment: *When Wilson was wrapping up his seventh and last United hat-trick in April 1936, a goat wandered onto the Abbey pitch. The animal had the good sense to take up a defensive role for United, keeping well out of our man's way.*

Worst Nightmare: *In a match against the University Press in February 1935 Wilson became the first United player ever to be sent off. He 'had words' with the referee. Presumably they were Anglo-Saxon in origin.*

CAMBRIDGE RECORD	Appearances	Goals
Cambs League	250+	78+
FA Cup		1

No 2. **GEORGE ALSOP**

Debut: v Abbey Crusaders, 27 August 1921
Final Farewell: v Soham, 8 May 1930

George Alsop led the defence in United's first ever season in the Cambs League Division Three in 1921-22 and if all good teams are built upon from the back, then George was the key element in the club's success.

He did so well in United's debut championship season that he was spotted by a sharp-eyed Chelsea scout who recommended him to manager David Calderhead. Alsop signed for Chelsea as a professional, and was on their books in 1922-23, but didn't play a League game for them, even though they were struggling in the First Division. He played for the reserves in the London Combination that season in an inside-right position, but couldn't displace the team's first-choice player in that position – Harry Ford – who had played in the 1915 FA Cup final. Sadly the dream never came off for George and he eventually returned to his old Abbey team.

One conundrum was George's position. He was used as a centre-half at the Abbey, even though he was only of medium height (5' 8"). He wasn't chunky either, weighing in at only 10st 7lb, but underneath that swept-back hairstyle and slight frame were a pair of sturdy legs. He had a hard shot, and long-distance, low drives were a speciality of his. He was also tricky enough to dribble round opponents. At Cambridge he was described as the starter of most of the team's good moves. With a description like that, it's hardly surprising that Chelsea experimented with him as an inside-forward, but United were happy to play him near the back, though it seems likely he was an early type of sweeper. My guess is he probably fulfilled a variety of roles – he certainly appears to be versatile enough. One thing is certain – his defensive partners would have towered above him.

George returned as captain – a very important position in those days when teams were selected by committee and there was no manager. In April 1925 George lifted the club's first cup – the Chatteris Engineering Works Cup – after a 5-0 tonking of Cottenham United, though he was sporting enough to call for 'three cheers for Cottenham'. Two days later he proudly held aloft the Cottenham Nursing Cup after a 2-1 victory over Girton United. A week after that came the really big prize in their parochial world. The Cambs Challenge Cup final ended in a overwhelming 6-1 victory over Girton, though the eventual destination of the trophy wasn't apparent until well into the second half. For George it was a dream come true – holding three trophies aloft in an eight-day period. A fortnight later he played in the final of the Creake Charity Shield, but this was a real toughie against United Cantabrians. After a goalless first game, the replay looked as though it was going to provide heartache for George. He hit the woodwork twice as the Abbey strove to equalise an early Cantabs goal. George's persistence paid off and he did indeed score an equaliser, but after four hours of football over the two ties there still wasn't a winner, so both clubs shared the trophy.

The following season (1925-26) United retained the Creake Charity Shield, with two goals from George helping them to a 4-1 win over RAF Duxford, sweet consolation for defeat in the Cambs Challenge Cup against the same opponents.

He scored over twenty goals in the 1927-28 season, bagging hat-tricks against Chatteris Town in the league and Great Shelford in the Creake Charity Shield (four goals). He scored twice in the Division One championship match against Chatteris Town in 1928-29 that ended 5-4, both goals coming in extra-time. United also won the Cambs Challenge Cup and Creake Charity Shield, the first time the 'treble' had been achieved. In addition, they garnered the Bury and District Cup, the Chatteris Engineering Works Cup and the Chatteris Nursing Cup to make it a clean sweep of five local cup competitions. Alsop left United in 1930, but continued to live in Cambridge until his death.

Magic Moment: *Alsop signed for the illustrious Chelsea – an astonishing leap from Cambs League Division Three, even if he never made their first team.*

Worst Nightmare: *In his last game for the Abbey, Alsop somehow shot over the bar from three yards. It's just as well they won the match 4-0 to cover his shame.*

CAMBRIDGE RECORD	Appearances	Goals
Cambs League	100+	31
FA Cup	unknown	–

No 3. **HARVEY CORNWELL**

Debut: v United Cantabs, 23 September 1922
Final Farewell: During the 1946-47 season

George Alsop may have flirted with Chelsea, but the greatest ever Cambridge-born footballer in history was Harvey Cornwall.

Known throughout the area as 'The Grand Old Master', Cornwell was born in 1895 and spent his early years working with his father picking mushrooms and selling them on Cambridge market. He was hooked on football and he turned out for his school teams at St George's and New Street, both in Cambridge. The last occasion he played for New Street generated some controversy. He had left school and intended to be just a spectator, when somebody thought it would be a good idea to have him in the team. After the match, a member of the opposition realised Cornwell was ineligible for the side and the game had to be replayed. Harvey also turned out every Thursday to play for New Chesterton Institute. He left school at fourteen and at the same time attracted the interest of Aston Villa, one of the most powerful clubs in the country, who wished to sign him. Sadly for Harvey, his father was not interested in football and insisted his son stayed in the mushroom-picking business with him – a decision that may well have rankled with Harvey all his life.

His dad didn't stop him from playing football though. Every Saturday and Thursday at noon he was given time off to pursue his first love. The only problem was that he could be anywhere in Cambridgeshire at the time and he would have to make his way back to Cambridge by any means available. The Cornwells didn't even have a horse – let alone a car.

Harvey was still in his teens when the Great War began in 1914. He enlisted in the Navy and ended up in Canada, where he promptly jumped ship and joined the Army. His second love was boxing and he finished as runner-up in the Canadian Forces featherweight championship, receiving an impressive cup for his troubles. Back home in Cambridge he was a regular at the old fairground booths, challenging the resident boxers and making himself a few shillings in the process.

After the war had finished he joined the Thursday Wanderers, but in the autumn of 1922 he started playing Saturday football for a team that had won the Cambs League Division Three in their first season – Abbey United. They were well on their way to promotion when Harvey joined, and with him in their side they cantered to the title.

For the first couple of seasons, Harvey was in the shadows of established stars like Wally Wilson, but from 1925 onwards he was untouchable, finishing as leading scorer on four consecutive occasions. He was undoubtedly helped by the change in the offside law, which reduced the number of defenders that had to be between attacker and goal from three to two. His first two hat-tricks were reserved for cup finals. He scored four as Cottenham United were beaten 5-1 in the Chatteris Engineering Works Cup in April 1925 and a week later bagged another three in the 6-1 win over Girton United in the Creake Charity Shield. Altogether, he scored nine hat-tricks in four seasons, his last one coming in the Creake Charity Shield semi-final victory over Cottenham United in March 1934, after a gap of six years.

As can be surmised from his featherweight boxing career, Cornwell was a lightweight, never going above 9½ stone, and small and wiry with it. He had a stooping figure, with a great shock of hair in a similar style to that worn by Stan Laurel. That boxing prowess also meant he was as hard as nails, but he was very, very fast. Although short, he used to delight in out-jumping six-foot defenders by a combination of perfect timing and an ability to defy gravity by hanging in the air. Although able to play in any of the forward positions, he revelled in the role of out and out goal-poacher, bewildering clod-hopping stoppers with neat ball control, and then scoring with either foot. He had the ability to swerve the big, heavy leather ball – no mean feat, though he was inclined to hang onto the ball for too long on occasions. Even when he was in his 30s he was still lightning fast.

By this time Harvey had started his own second-hand furniture business, delivering the furniture on a costermongers barrow, with which he won a number of barrow races against other tradesmen. As United played almost exclusively on a Saturday in those days, he was able to continue playing Thursday football for other clubs. He did leave United briefly in the 1930s and 40s to play for United Cantabs, Chesterton Victoria and Cambridge Town, but they were brief affairs and he could never leave his beloved Abbey United for long.

Harvey served in the Home Guard during World War Two, which enabled him to keep close tabs on his team. It was just as well. The club nearly went broke during that time and was only saved by the financial inputs of Harvey and an ice-cream man from Mill Road – Mr Sylvester.

It was soon after the war finished that Harvey played his last game for the club. He was then in his 50s, and this wonderful old amateur saw United through to the brink of semi-professionalism. He had spent 25 years with the club and had scored 185 recorded league and cup goals, though the true figure must be well in excess of 200. Not that he gave up his football – he loved it too much. He remained supremely fit and even at this age he was able to push a grand piano on his barrow five miles into Cambridge. One big regret was that he was never given a testimonial by anyone. He was due to receive one in March 1946, but for one reason or another it fell through. He passed away in September 1966, but will always remain as one of the greatest Abbey heroes of all time.

Magic Moment: *Cornwell played his final game for the Thursday Wanderers in April 1955 when he was almost 60, playing alongside his three sons – Harvey Junior, Jack, and Sam – all of whom had played for United at some time.*

Worst Nightmare: *Once, when Cornwell was out in the wilds of Cambridgeshire with his dad, mushroom picking, he was given time off to play football in Cambridge.*

He tried to hitch a lift with a horse and cart, but the driver said no and was astonished to see Harvey running behind him all the way to town in order to make the game.

CAMBRIDGE RECORD	Appearances	Goals
Cambs League	Approx 350	120+
FA Cup	Unknown	6

No 4. **RUSSELL CRANE**
Debut: v Cambridge Town reserves, 27 September 1941
Farewell: v Norwich City, 27 October 1958

Just coming into the side as Cornwell's Abbey career was ending, Russell Crane was the only U's player to appear in the Cambs, United Counties, Eastern Counties and Southern Leagues.

Russell was a Suffolk boy, born in Halesworth on 20 January 1926. He left school at the earliest opportunity, but that just happened to be in 1941 during World War Two. Too young at fifteen to enlist, the one thing that Russell wanted to do more than anything was play football. He got his chance at Abbey United. The club organised a series of friendly matches at the Abbey Ground, mostly against various RAF and Army sides, which had the dual benefit of keeping everyone's spirits up at the same time as ensuring that the ground wasn't requisitioned for war use. Because of his tender age, Russell was used sparingly, taking the field in every other game, as an inside-right, inside-left or centre-forward. His first recorded goal came in a 3-1 victory over Cambridge Town reserves on 27 September 1941 and over the next few seasons he became a regular entry in the goalscorers column, once netting four against village side Bourn in April 1943. As the Cambridge area had a high concentration of airfields, several famous footballing RAF members got to play against the Abbey. Russell came across such luminaries as Scottish wizard Alex James and Everton's goalscoring sensation Dixie Dean. What a fabulous way to gain a footballing education.

Russell joined the Navy in 1943, and could only turn out for his home club sporadically. His return to Cambridge in 1947 coincided with the restart of organised football and United now took a giant leap up from the Cambs League to the tougher world of the United Counties League. They were now coming up against stronger local outfits such as King's Lynn and Wisbech Town and, as a result, became more disciplined and stronger. The club became a limited company in 1948 and turned semi-professional the following year. Crane's role was now target man, and he finished as leading scorer in each of the four seasons United spent in the UCL, including an impressive haul of 40 league goals in 1948-49. In January 1949 he helped himself to eleven goals in just four games, which included consecutive hat-tricks against Northampton Town's 'A' (i.e. third) team and Bourne Town (four goals). In April he bagged a hat-trick against Boston United reserves at the Abbey to add to the four he had scored in the league game at Boston. With another three at Eynesbury, he became the first United player to grab five hat-tricks in a season.

Stockily built and strong, although quite small, he was noted for his fearsome shot, one hapless opponent breaking his hand in attempting to stop a Russell special. His prowess was also noted by the local paper, which proclaimed: 'It takes a Crane to lift United off the bottom.' His industriousness earned him the nickname of 'The Human Dynamo'.

Russell signed off United's UCL career in style with a hat-trick in the 6-0 League Cup final win against Symington's Market Harborough. Still hungry for advancement, the club joined the Eastern Counties League in 1951 as Cambridge United and appointed Bill Whittaker as their first full-time manager. Russell himself turned down the chance to join Peterborough United of the Midland League, even though it would have meant a significant pay rise – he simply loved his club too much. He remained overall top scorer in the first season, but was brought down a peg by taskmaster Whittaker after having scored both goals in a sensational Cambs Invitation Cup victory over Cambridge's top team – Cambridge Town. Russell was expecting praise off his boss; instead he got nitpicking criticism off a man who wanted to keep his players' feet firmly on the ground. That season Russell grabbed his eighth and final hat-trick, which puts him third on the list of the players with the most three-goal hauls.

Whittaker soon converted Crane into an attacking left-back. Russell found the transformation easy, as he could watch the play unfold in front of his eyes and he no longer had to continually swivel his head to see what was behind him. The defence was now one of the meanest in the ECL, no easy feat when they were coming up against the 'third' teams of clubs like Arsenal and Spurs, with players who would soon be First Division regulars. Russell was required to play triangle balls, rushing forward to be on the receiving end of Whittaker's probing passes.

A benefit was played for Crane on 16 April 1956 to mark his fifteen years' service. Russell Crane's XI took on a Combined XI in front of 1,500 who witnessed a 2-2 draw. His undying loyalty to the cause was also noted when he turned down the chance of a trial with Ipswich town, preferring to guide his club into the heady heights of the Southern League. This was a world away from the parochial Cambs League, which he rejoined in 1958 with Soham Town, and then in 1960 with Sawston, where he started coaching. He worked for BICC, then the world's biggest cable manufacturers, and, now retired, still lives just round the corner from the ground.

Magic Moment: *In an East Anglian Cup semi-final against Ipswich in 1951, Russell was required to take a penalty. The mud was so glutinous that he had to sit on the ball to wipe his boots clean before scoring it. United won 6-4 in extra-time.*

Worst Nightmare: *Russell 'scored' at Spalding by charging the goalkeeper over the line. This did not endear him to the home crowd and it was only the bravery and size of future U's chairman Geoff Proctor that guaranteed him a safe escort off the pitch.*

CAMBRIDGE RECORD	Appearances	Goals
Cambs League	unknown	unknown
United Counties League	141	83
Eastern Counties League	181	46
Southern League	12	–
FA Cup	unknown	9

No 5. **BOB BISHOP**
Debut: v Rushden, 23 August 1947
Final Farewell: v Eynesbury, 5 May 1955

Whereas Russell Crane was a 'local lad made good', the signing of 'outsider' Bob Bishop in 1947 was the first indication that Abbey United weren't just joining the United Counties League for fun.

Bob hails from Southminster in Essex, and he is a 1921 model. He played village football until the outbreak of World War One, also turning out as an amateur with Southend United for the odd game. He joined the Army and also had a trial at Luton Town, impressing them enough to sign professional terms in 1942. He played for the club occasionally when he wasn't engaged in active service.

After he was demobbed in 1946, Bishop moved to Cambridge – the home town of his wife. He sneakily turned out for Cambridge Town for a few games, which wasn't permitted as they were strictly an amateur side, but Bob somehow neglected to mention the fact that he was a professional. His presence was duly noted by Abbey United, who under the progressive chairmanship of Bill Taverner had decided to take the bull by the horns and push the club forward into the semi-professional United Counties League. With Bob as the first ex-professional player to sign for them, they backed up their intentions with deeds as they filled the right-back berth.

The huge step upwards proved difficult for the club, and they struggled at the bottom end of the table in that first season, after which Bob left the club and moved to Bury Town of the Eastern Counties League for three seasons.

In 1951 Abbey United changed their name to Cambridge United, appointed Bill Whittaker as their first proper manager, and moved into the Eastern Counties League. This presented a higher standard of football than the UCL, because United were coming up against the 'A' (third) teams of League clubs, and therefore playing regularly against First Division players. Whittaker was impressed with Bob – who had many tricks up his sleeve that the average right-back didn't possess. He was a genuine two-footed player, comfortable with either foot, and he was also good in the air – a trait that is definitely not shared with most full-backs. Though he was only of average height, he was well-built and fit, which compensated for the fact that he looked much older than his 30 years, with his smart swept-back hair setting him apart from the boyish looks or rough-hewn features of his team-mates. These patrician looks were also at odds with his playing style, which was decidedly tough – some say as a result of him being an admirer of Arsenal.

After four years in the first team, he hung up his playing boots in 1955 and donned a pair of trainer's boots instead. His four-year stint on the training pitch safely saw his team establish a foothold in the Southern League. In March 1959 he was granted a testimonial against an All-Stars XI, including ex-internationals Wilf Mannion, Jimmy Hagan and Eddie Baily.

Bob quit football and concentrated on his other job. He had originally been a manager at the Regal Cinema and New Theatre, but after a couple of years had gone into accountancy. He joined Pye Unicam and worked his way up to be chief accountant. He is now retired and is living in Felixstowe.

Magic Moment: *In one of his first games for Luton during the war, Bishop played against the awesome figures of Bill Shankly and Eddie Hapgood – a remarkable situation for a young man fresh from playing against village sides.*

Worst Nightmare: *Bishop scored an own-goal in Russell Crane's benefit match when he attempted to an intercept a ball on the line and succeeded in kicking it into his own net.*

CAMBRIDGE RECORD	Appearances	Goals
United Counties League	26	3
Eastern Counties League	135	2
FA Cup	Unknown	–

No 6. **ALBERT GEORGE**
Debut: v Rushden, 23 August 1947
Final Farewell: v Chelmsford City reserves, 6 September 1956

Whereas Bishop was something of an outsider, Albert George was one of the Cambridge-born lads who naturally endeared themselves to the fans who had grown up with them.

George was born on 5 January 1925 and played for Chesterton Boys and Cambridge Juniors around the time that World War Two broke out. He earned county honours, but was unable to progress further at the time because of the more urgent need to defeat the Germans. He joined the Navy in 1943 and didn't return to the football field until he was demobbed in 1946.

In 1946-47 he played for Saxons, whose home 'ground' was Parker's Piece – the famous expanse of grass in Cambridge's city centre that also housed the homeless Abbey United in the early 1930s. Both Saxons and Abbey United competed in the Cambs League that season and Albert's abilities were utilised for the Abbey the following season when the lure of United Counties League football proved too strong for him.

He was originally played at left-half, but proved to be such an effective goalscorer in that position that he was moved to inside-forward, then into the centre-forward role under Bill Whittaker's managership. Albert was only 5' 7½" tall and weighed just 10½ stone, but he was supremely fit and very quick. A genuine two-footed player, he confounded the critics who doubted his ability to play up front by becoming a goal-poacher alongside Jack Thomas, who looked and played like a conventional centre-forward. Albert relied on good timing and acute positional sense which, harnessed with his speed, saw him prove a useful foil to Thomas as a chance-taker in the six-yard box. He was also a brave player and wasn't afraid to throw himself amongst flying boots in the penalty area. In the early days Albert used to take penalties, preferring to place the ball rather than blast it, as he didn't have a powerful shot.

In 1954 he joined Exning United of the Peterborough and District League, but two years later rejoined Cambridge at the behest of Bert Johnson, ostensibly to coach the reserves who were in the same league as Exning. The coaching never materialised, but Albert played several games for the reserves and five for the first team. He then rejoined Exning for a season before moving on to Camden United and the University Press.

It was hardly surprising that he played for the University Press, because he worked as a printer for them for 50 years. Although now retired, he has maintained a commendable fitness level by swimming three times a week and cycling regularly. He lives in Cherry Hinton, near Cambridge.

Magic Moment: *In January 1954 Albert George demonstrated his goal-poaching abilities by bagging two first-half goals against Gillingham reserves. A spectator called out 'give us a hat-trick', and he obliged in the second half by scoring a further two goals.*

Worst Nightmare: *Albert George prides himself on being a clean player, but blotted his copybook by receiving his only booking in his early days with Saxons. He was 'over-enthusiastic' with a tackle.*

CAMBRIDGE RECORD	Appearances	Goals
United Counties League	136	45
Eastern Counties League	46	27
FA Cup	unknown	7

No 7. STAN THURSTON
Debut: v Charlton Athletic reserves, 3 September 1949
Farewell: v Charlton Athletic, 30 April 1956

Another player who represented his county and endeavoured to always play the game in the correct spirit was Stan Thurston.

Footballers in the 1950s were considered to be much tougher than their modern counterparts, but several exceptions can be found to this generalisation and Stan is a prime example of a gentleman footballer. Stepping onto the pitch into his favourite right-wing position with not a hair out of place, he invariably ended the match with a clean kit and perfectly coiffured, swept-backed hair. You could guarantee that he would scarcely commit any fouls and that he would go about his business in a quiet and unassuming manner. Though he did communicate whilst on the pitch, off it he was a reserved man who would rarely initiate any conversations.

This makes it sound as though he was ineffective, but this is far from the case. Stan was a fast winger, with a pronounced body swerve to take him past his left-back. He faced hot competition for his place in the form of Teddy Bowd, who relied more on trickery to compensate for a slower playing style.

Stan's pace and skill meant that he usually ended up in a perfect position to either cross the ball or shoot, and he often chose the latter option, which explains his goalscoring ratio of a goal every three games – an excellent figure for an out and out winger. He seemed to have had a pathological loathing of heading the ball, probably because it would have ruined the immaculate hairstyle. In many respects he is similar to another winger who would shine 40 years later, but Lee Philpott preferred the left wing.

Stan was yet another man who was born within Cambridge's boundaries, a breed which seemed to have died out in the 1960s. He was born in

1922 and after excelling as a schoolboy and county player he joined Cambridge Town. The advent of war interrupted his Town career and he ended up enduring the jungles of Burma – which he hated. He received shrapnel wounds in his legs (whilst running away, he joked) and was always first on the train when any leave came up.

When the war ended he carried on playing for Town, but when Abbey United offered him semi-professional terms in the summer of 1949, it was enough to tempt him away from the strictly amateur Town. He became one of the few professionals on United's books and received £3 10s a week to supplement his main job at the Cambridge Gasworks.

He was 34 by the time he left United, and went on to play for a few more clubs, including Stowmarket Town. He also became player-coach at Milton, which must have challenged his communication skills. He got a job working in a golf shop in Great Shelford, joining the Co-op bakery in later years. He died in 1998, but he has grandchildren and great-grandchildren who all support Cambridge United. Maybe one day another Thurston will tear down the wing at the Abbey protecting an immaculate hairstyle.

Magic Moment: *In an FA Cup second qualifying round replay at Wisbech Town in October 1952, United were deadlocked at 2-2 when Thurston raced through in the last minute of extra-time to snatch a dramatic victory.*

Worst Nightmare: *Thurston's war career began in Britain, but he was always late returning to his barracks after appearing for Cambridge Town, which prompted the authorities to post him abroad to Burma, so he believed.*

CAMBRIDGE RECORD	Appearances	Goals
United Counties League	71	25
Eastern Counties League	79	32
FA Cup	unknown	3

No 8. **HARRY BULLEN**
Debut: v Eynesbury, 26 December 1949
Farewell: v Eynesbury, 5 May 1955

Also joining Abbey United from Cambridge Town was left-back Harry Bullen.

Harry was born in Cambridge in September 1919 and played for Cambridge schoolboys and the county team. He signed for Cambridge Town (then easily the top club in the City) in 1936, becoming one of their youngest ever players at seventeen. He played for them for the three years prior to the war, in his preferred left-back role, returning to them once hostilities had finished. (During the war he had played for the 8th Army side). Despite being strictly amateur, Town became the first club team from Cambridge to reach the FA Cup first round, when they succumbed to Swindon Town in 1946. Cambridge University had been semi-finalists in 1876-77.

In the middle of the 1949-50 season he switched to Abbey United, now established firmly as the number two club in Cambridge. Although the war had robbed him of many valuable playing years, at 30 he was still one of the most experienced men at the club, a fact that was obvious when his appearance was taken into consideration. He wasn't huge, but he was solid, and with his balding pate actually looked much older than he was. It was no surprise when he was awarded the captaincy immediately.

Perhaps the greatest compliment I can pay Harry is to say that he was the sort of player that the fans would barely notice during a game. He went about his business quietly and efficiently and with the minimum of fuss. He was as hard as nails and he was certainly not going to be forced off the ball. His wife well remembers him coming home every Saturday with a collection of bruises all over his face and body, as well as the overpowering smell of liniment which Harry would apply at night. His lack of goals accurately reflects that he was a defensively-minded full-back, and was too old and slow to be bothered with any left-wing raids into the opposition half. The solid back line of that era was enough to keep United in the top four of every ECL season that he played in.

By the end of the 1954-55 season he was aged 35 and ready for retirement. A benefit match was played in May 1955 against a Combined XI in front of 3,000. To the crowd's joy, Harry had a go at being a centre-forward, but despite the crowd roaring 'Give it to Harry', he couldn't break the habit of a lifetime and score a goal.

One overlooked aspect of football is the strain it puts on family life. Football was played every Christmas Day and Boxing Day, every Easter and every Bank Holiday. Harry had felt guilty about neglecting his wife and two young daughters for so long, and now he vowed to make it up to them. On Christmas Day 1955 he was able to sit down and enjoy a proper Christmas dinner for the first time in his adult life.

Harry also loved tennis, and he worked for Grey's in Cambridge, manufacturing tennis racquets. He wasn't a cricket lover, though (Grey's also made bats). The game was far too slow and genteel for him – not like the rough and tumble of football in Cambridge. He was still living in his home town when he died in March 1992.

Magic Moment: *Both Harry Bullen and Bob Bishop became fathers on the same day, with both children being born in the same nursing home.*

Worst Nightmare: *United were unbeaten for the first nine games of 1951-52 and were top of the ECL, but injury to Bullen against Chelsea 'A' on 17 November meant he was a passenger for over an hour. United lost 1-2, and lost their next four games.*

CAMBRIDGE RECORD	Appearances	Goals
United Counties League	57	–
Eastern Counties League	121	–
FA Cup	unknown	–

No 9. **RAY RUFFETT**
Debut: v Stamford, 19 August 1950
Farewell: v Harwich & Parkeston, 23 April 1955

Raymond Douglas Ruffett also had a vested interest in stopping the opposition from scoring, though he wasn't a local lad like Harry Bullen, being born in Luton on 20 July 1924.

Ruffett began his career with his local club, Luton Town, as a 15-year-old apprentice, playing for half-a-crown a week tea money (equivalent to 12½p in decimal currency). Unfortunately, that was also the year that war broke out, so he was playing in a wartime league when he turned professional in October 1941.

There were more pressing matters than football, so Ray joined the 6th Airborne Division. He later fought in the Battle of the Ardennes, and finally ended up spending a year fighting in Greece.

He was demobbed in 1946 and played for the reserves in the Football Combination against the top London reserve sides. He finally got a crack in the first team in April 1949, playing at wing-half. Cruelly, he was crocked by a player who came 'over the ball' and rearranged his knee ligaments for him. In those pre-substitute days, he was forced to remain in the middle of the pitch, which was covered in mud, not even being allowed to hobble on the wing like most injured players. When he eventually returned to fitness, he was effectively sacked by the hard Scottish manager Dally Duncan, who brutally informed him that he'd 'had his chance'.

Ruffett joined Abbey United at the start of the 1950-51 season, but still lived in Luton, which meant catching a bus to Hitchin, then taking the train to Cambridge, and a bus to the ground. He became friends with the licensees of The Globe pub, opposite the ground, and they would make him a coffee when he arrived.

Ray was a right-half – a calm, unruffled player, who played at a pace to suit himself, but he wasn't slow. Alongside Percival and Whittaker he formed one of the strongest half-back lines in the Eastern Counties League, one that opposition players had a great deal of trouble penetrating. Many League clubs would have wanted a defence that strong. His forte was in his acute positional strength, which made it relatively easy for him to snuff out the faster forwards he came across. He was a dead-ball specialist, and was capable of whipping in corners and free-kicks with either foot. He was also good in the air. The beginning of the end for Ray came in a match against Gorleston, when he went up for a high ball with an inside forward. Johnny Percival came up behind him, and attempted to use Ray as a stepladder, accidentally kneeing him in the back. The trainer did his bucket and sponge routine, but soon afterwards Ray was flattened by a high velocity leather ball. Although he later returned to action, he was diagnosed as having 'fibrositis affecting the sciatica nerve'. This hampered him enough to eventually end his career. Unfortunately, he retired just after manager Bill Whittaker resigned, so received no benefit match.

Ruffett returned to Luton, and eventually got a job at Vauxhall Motors on the sub-assembly line. He is now retired, and still lives in Luton.

Magic Moment: *It was Ruffett's superb free-kick at Newport which was headed in by Saward. It sealed United's only non-League giantkilling.*

Worst Nightmare: *Ruffett was made captain from 1951-54, but could never get a word in edgeways because of the vociferous outpourings of player-boss Bill Whittaker.*

CAMBRIDGE RECORD	Appearances	Goals
United Counties League	28	–
Eastern Counties League	125	2
FA Cup	unknown	1

No 3. Harvey Cornwell (second from right) watches as the club president's daughter kicks off the first fixture at the Abbey v University Press, on 31 August 1932

No 19. Fred Howell

No 21. Roy Kirk

No 26. Rodney Slack

No 22. Sammy McCrory

No 32. Bud Houghton

No 34. Robin Hardy

No 39. Jimmy Thompson

No 40. Terry Eades

No 42. Trevor Roberts

No 43. Peter Vasper

Chapter Two

~ *Fifties Rockers* ~

No 10. **LEN CROWE**
Debut: v Great Yarmouth, 18 August 1951
Farewell: v Harwich & Parkeston, 5 May 1956

Len Crowe was one of a host of players who joined the club in Ray Ruffett's second United season.

Len was born in Farnborough on April Fool's Day 1928. He was playing for Farnborough after the war, when he was spotted by a scout for Crystal Palace who promptly signed him in 1948. Crowe played for Palace reserves but failed to make the first team, though it must be remembered that even in the reserve eleven he was coming across England internationals and crowds of 15,000 when they played at places like Highbury. He did impress one first-teamer at Selhurst Park, and when Bill Whittaker was appointed Cambridge manager at the start of the 1951-52 season he brought the 23-year-old Len with him.

Crowe was an inside-right mostly, although he could also fill in at right-half. He was well named, because he had sharp, bird-like features and used to swoop onto the ball during the game just like a crow after a grain of corn. He had no pace whatsoever, so had to rely on his brain to compensate. As Pele once said: 'I can run much faster than those who run without thinking.' This leisurely way of going about things fooled some people into thinking he was lazy, but more astute observers were aware that he got through much work during a game: it's just that he did it without drawing attention to himself. He did get noticed when he struck a dead ball though. He would stroll up casually and dispense it like a rocket. He didn't score a great number of goals for an inside-forward, but he created many more.

The signing of Wilf Mannion effectively ended Len's United career at the relatively young age of 28. Mannion, although ten years older, had more pace than Len and certainly possessed more skill, but that is more a reflection on Mannion's abilities rather than any shortcomings in Len's game. Nevertheless, he was disillusioned enough to walk out on football for a while and concentrated on his job at Marshall's. It was Den Smith at Newmarket Town who was persuasive enough to get Len back onto the football field, and for a while his presence once more graced the Eastern Counties League as it had done for the best part of a decade.

Len left Marshall's and joined Turner and Hall as a tiler. He didn't know anything about tiling, but that quick brain enabled him to pick it up as he went along. He also made a footballing swansong alongside Alan Moore and Russell Crane by turning out for ex-Cambridge United versus ex-Cambridge City in a benefit match for Ron Simpson in May 1967. All three old-timers fittingly scored in a 4-4 draw. It seems that there really is no substitute for experience.

Magic Moment: *In United's first competitive game against a League side, Crowe was recalled from the reserves for the FA Cup home tie with Newport in November 1953. United trailed 1-2, but the 7,500 crowd saw Len rise above three players to head a dramatic equaliser. United won the replay 2-1 five days later in Monmouthshire.*

Worst Nightmare: *Crowe was unable to repeat his magic in the second round home tie with Bradford Park Avenue in front of 10,000. United lost 1-2.*

CAMBRIDGE RECORD	Appearances	Goals
Eastern Counties League	100	21
FA Cup	unknown	3

No 11. **JOE GALLEGO**
Debut: v Great Yarmouth, 18 August 1951
Farewell: v Harwich & Parkeston, 5 May 1956

Joe Gallego and his brother Tony provided an unusual slice of Spanish flair in the English-dominated Cambridge United team.

The year was 1937: the place was San Sebastian. The Spanish Civil War was erupting all around. A mother and her two sons and three daughters were fleeing from place to place to find somewhere safe to stay. There was nowhere. Salvation eventually came from England, when a charitable society offered to provide refuge for 2,000 boys and girls. All these were shipped to Southampton, from where they would be billeted to addresses across the country. The Gallego children ended up in Cambridge, ostensibly for three months. They've been there ever since. As the Spanish Civil War ended, so World War Two started, meaning that they were separated from their mother for ten years.

The two boys – Jose (born in April 1923) and Antonio (June 1924) – had their names anglicised to Joe and Tony, and both indulged their passion for football. Joe played for Cambridge Town from 1941, playing various friendly games against local and military opposition, including Abbey United, for whom his brother played in goal.

Joe carried on playing for the Town until January 1947, by which time the number of scouts watching him was cause for embarrassment. Town were a strictly amateur club, playing for the love of the game, and they certainly didn't want the professional teams luring away their best players. They couldn't compete with the likes of Brentford, though, and Joe left for Griffin Park, whilst Tony (who was also playing for Town at this time) moved to Norwich a couple of months later, though the 5' 10" keeper only played one League game for the Canaries.

Joe, not unnaturally, thought he was bettering himself by moving into the world of professional football, but he was in for a rude awakening. Suddenly everything was money-orientated, and the players treated more like commodities than human beings. He had one, otherwise enjoyable season at Brentford, when he played most of his six League games. But he then contracted pleurisy, which kept him out for three months, followed by a bad ankle injury, which cost him more time out. By the time he had recovered, Brentford didn't want him and sold him to Southampton in May 1948.

Joe did well enough for the reserves to make the first team, but on his Second Division debut he chipped a bone in his ankle and again fell out of favour. Southampton hoped to sell him to Exeter City, but by this time he hankered after the more enjoyable world of non-League football.

He went to Colchester United – then in the Southern League – and the contrast compared to the League clubs couldn't have been greater. The club genuinely cared about their players and ensured they were well looked after, and Joe was able to really enjoy himself. Colchester did well enough in 1950 to earn themselves League status, when it was expanded from 88 to 92 clubs. Although Joe played briefly for them in the League, he badly wanted to come back to Cambridge.

He joined Cambridge United as they entered the semi-professional world of the United Counties League – a good compromise that enabled him to enjoy his football as well as play at a decent level. His brother Tony was already back at the Abbey.

Joe was a left-winger, but because he was genuinely two-footed, was able to play on the opposite wing if required. He was fast, even at the end of his career, and had a sprinkling of continental flair to bamboozle the full-backs. He was an attacking winger, with a hard, accurate shot, which can be surmised from his goals total of 31 from 113 league games. He also was described as 'unpredictable', which was a compliment, as so many lesser players made it all too obvious as to what they were going to do. He was athletic, with a smart hairstyle, which, together with those Latin looks, must have made the few lady supporters swoon.

He left Cambridge at the end of the 1955-56 season, and once more reunited with his brother, who was at Biggleswade Town. Joe then joined Exning United, Milton, and Camden United. He carried on playing (and coaching) till he was 50, but by this time (the early 1970s) the youngsters were being 'inspired' by Don Revie's cynical Leeds side and the tackles were getting downright dangerous, especially when they found out Joe was an ex-professional.

Joe had worked for the Gas Board all his working life, but his health deteriorated and he had a series of eight heart attacks and had to retire at 59. Thankfully, as a result of a triple heart bypass, he is now fit and healthy, apart from the ex-footballer's standard complaint of bad knees. His brother Tony also lives in Cambridge.

Magic Moment: *Well OK, it was a magic moment for Tony and not Joe. Cambridge Town were the elite club, but in December 1943 the Abbey put the Town to the sword by winning 7-2 at the City Ground – a result Tony will never let his brother forget.*

Worst Nightmare: *On his Brentford debut, Gallego got a ticking-off from his manager for sportingly retrieving the ball and handing it to the opposition goalkeeper. This was an example of the cynical attitude of professional football that Joe hated so much.*

CAMBRIDGE RECORD	Appearances	Goals
Eastern Counties League	113	31
FA Cup	unknown	2

No 12. **JOHNNY PERCIVAL**
Debut: v Great Yarmouth, 18 August 1951
Farewell: v Sudbury, 14 April 1956.

Unlike the Gallegos, flair wasn't a word you would normally associate with Johnny Percival, as he was a good old-fashioned English stopper.

He was born in Norwood on 19 April 1924, and was christened Ronald Frederick John Percival, though he became variously known as Jack, John or Johnny.

Village football was where Johnny's career began and it wasn't until a mate of his signed for Tunbridge Wells just after the war, that he was inspired to follow him. The trainer at Tunbridge was an ex-Huddersfield Town player, and through his intervention he was offered a trial with the Terriers. He impressed enough as a wing-half to win a professional contract in February 1948.

Huddersfield had been the best club in the country during the 1920s, but had struggled to fight off relegation in the years either side of the war. Their side was made up of useful players like Northern Ireland international Peter Doherty and record goalscorer Jimmy Glazzard, but George Stephenson's team were not good enough to pull themselves out of trouble. Johnny made his debut at Burnley in a 1-2 defeat in May 1948, but it was a big step up from minor-club football and Johnny only made eight League appearances for the Terriers, spread over three seasons. His lack of action was largely due to a debilitating attack of jaundice, which kept him out of contention for a year. Though he was enjoying himself, it became apparent that he wasn't destined to become a regular, particularly as he was playing second fiddle to George Hepplewhite, so in May 1950 Percival moved to Chesterfield, then a useful Second Division outfit.

His time at the Recreation Ground was an unhappy one and he only played in half a dozen League games, at left-half. After the Spireites were relegated from the Second Division, Jack looked for an escape route. And it was Cambridge manager Bill Whittaker who provided it.

Bill was at Huddersfield at the same time as Johnny and signed his ex-colleague on professional terms in the summer of 1951. With United operating on a semi-professional basis, it caused problems with training. Though the full-timers could train together, those players with outside jobs were effectively unable to train with them. These mostly local players often found their best coaching came on the field of play, when the experienced heads like Johnny would put them right if they made a mistake, even if it was his fearsome boss and defensive partner Bill Whittaker who cocked up.

Johnny was a centre-half, though, as mentioned, he had also played wing-half in his earlier days. He did not provide a huge physical presence, being lumbered with skinny legs that looked too thin to support his weight, but he still managed to play like a good old-fashioned stopper. He was reminiscent in style of England international Neil Franklin. Physically, Johnny was 6ft 2in, with a tough-looking face and swept-back hair. He looked similar to Vinnie Jones in some photographs, but in comparison Jones appeared angelic.

It was a daunting sight for any opposition forward to face Percival and Whittaker, and anyone who lacked courage and confidence was going to suffer the consequences. Johnny was prepared to go in hard against any-one, and under today's refereeing standards he'd probably be sent off long before half-time. He was excellent in the air and a powerful header of the ball, and Jack reminds us that they really did play with balls in those days, not the balloons that modern-day footballers use. So far, his description would fit virtually that of any central defender in the Eastern Counties League, but the difference was that Johnny could play a bit too. He was comfortable on the ball and this led to him being described as 'one of the best pivots in the ECL'. 'Pivot' was a popular term to describe a centre-half in the 1950s – the solid point on which the success of the team revolved. In the five seasons that Johnny played for United, only Totten-ham's 'A' side could boast a substantially meaner defence in the ECL.

Johnny became captain in his last season at the Abbey, and the club held a benefit match in April 1956, which was billed as 'Jack Percival's XI v Roddy Munro's XI'. This was effectively a Cambridge derby between United and City. Jack's side won 6-0, with the help of two ex-Spurs players, Eddie Baily and John Woodward.

Percival left Cambridge in August 1956 to join Bexleyheath and Welling, managed by the old Charlton and Portsmouth striker Charlie Vaughan. Johnny helped them escape from the Kent League and into the Southern League Division One in 1959, the same season Cambridge first appeared there. That was where Johnny's playing career ended, and he took up a post on the coaching staff. He worked for an oil company for a while, before becoming a warehouse foreman. He lives near Saxmundham.

Magic Moment: *Well, this has to be Percival's only goal in 159 League matches. It came in a 3-3 draw at Lowestoft in March 1954.*

Worst Nightmare: *Percival's time at Chesterfield. Though it's stretching the point to describe them as a northern club, Johnny found a clique which excluded Southerners.*

CAMBRIDGE RECORD	Appearances	Goals
Eastern Counties League	159	1
FA Cup	unknown	–

No 13. **BILL WHITTAKER**
Debut: v Great Yarmouth, 18 August 1951
Farewell: v Histon, 19 March 1955

Percival's central defensive partner was Bill Whittaker, who in addition to being a superlative player was also the first professional manager in the club's history.

William Paul Whittaker was born in Charlton on 20 December 1922, but it was with Arsenal that he first appeared, being part of their ground-staff. Although promising enough to play in a schoolboy international, he only stayed a year in north London. In July 1938 he signed for Charlton Athletic, originally turning out for their nursery club – Bexleyheath and Welling. By 1939 he had broken through to Charlton reserves and was earning the princely sum of £1 10s a week (£1.50).

During the war, he was a rear-gunner in a bomber, a task which shattered his nerves for the rest of his life, making him sweat profusely, turning him prematurely grey, and making him appear much older than he was. He also had a stint in the Navy, but managed to find time to play football for Dartford, and guest for Watford and Plymouth.

Bill made his Charlton debut as a wing-half in September 1946, but was standing in the shadows of Charlie Revell, who went on to play in every FA Cup game of the 1946-47 season up to and including the 4-0 semi-final win over Newcastle. Charlton were desperate to make amends for the 1-4 defeat they had suffered against Derby in the final the season before, so the fans were astonished when Bill was chosen for the 1947 final in place of the injured Revell and second-choice Bert Johnson (who also went on to manage Cambridge United). Bill hadn't played in the first team for five months and had never played in an FA Cup-tie before. Charlton overcame Burnley 1-0, and Bill turned in a solid performance, which justified manager Jimmy Seed's faith. Indeed, nobody could claim to have done any better in what is now regarded as one of the worst ever finals.

Despite his winner's medal, Bill was still only third choice and he only made 29 appearances for Charlton over three seasons (never playing another FA Cup-tie for them). His club had turned down an offer from Exeter City, but when Huddersfield offered a massive £10,000 fee for him in November 1948 he moved up north and made 43 League appearances for them in a season and a half. In June 1950 he moved back down to the big smoke, and joined Crystal Palace, also for £10,000 (a Palace record). He played 35 times for them in 1950-51 and scored the only League goal of his career as well.

Cambridge United were looking for a manager to kick off their debut in the Eastern Counties League in 1951-52, and they delighted the fans by capturing Bill as player-manager. He was still only 28 and had recently been sold for two massive transfer fees (the equivalent of several million pounds today). He instilled a disciplined and professional attitude within the club, and encouraged his team to play well, with his edict of 'football all the time'. This was a revelation when so many teams played variations on the theme of 'kick and rush', but that's not to say he was a namby-pamby manager. Even in training he would dish out some meaty tackles on his men, a trait which didn't always endear him to them. On the pitch he was a commanding presence in stature and character, forever shouting and convincing his men that they were world-beaters.

He led by example and was incredibly hard-working on the pitch. He read the game well, and was a tough tackler, but one who was guaranteed to win most 50-50 balls fairly. When he had the ball, he would often be able to split defences asunder with a clinical pass. He was also a mean finisher, scoring with a 30-yard corker on his United debut and scoring a hat-trick in a 7-1 win over Newmarket Town in April 1952.

Under Bill, United never finished outside the top four in the League and he also led them to the FA Cup first round for the first time in 1953-54 and 1954-55. His managerial contract was extended by three years after the 2-1 FA Cup giantkilling at Third Division Newport County in November 1953, but he suddenly resigned in March 1955, stating that he wanted to concentrate on football without having to manage. This was obviously a smokescreen because he went on to player-manage Newmarket soon afterwards. Although perhaps the real reason will never be known, there has to be a suspicion that the refusal of the board to allow him to take on an outside job to bolster his wages may be the most likely factor.

Whittaker didn't stay at Newmarket long, moving back to his roots at Blackheath, and working as a porter at Covent Garden's fruit and vegetable market. He was a 60-a-day cigarette smoker and, perhaps inevitably, died of long cancer in 1977 aged just 54.

Magic Moment: *In a Cambs Invitation Cup semi-final against Histon in March 1955, Whittaker took a penalty. He tapped the ball forward and Peter Dobson ran on to score. This is legal as the ball had travelled the length of its own circumference.*

Worst Nightmare: *Whittaker wasn't always successful in the FA Cup. In his first tie for Cambridge United in October 1951 they lost 3-4 at home to March Town.*

CAMBRIDGE RECORD	Appearances	Goals
Eastern Counties League	128	23
FA Cup	unknown	2

No 14. **LEN SAWARD**
Debut: v Stowmarket Town, 2 October 1952
Final Farewell: v Clacton, 7 May 1958

The player who Whittaker displaced at Crystal Palace was Len Saward, though he made amends by signing Len to Cambridge United later on.

Len's father was in the Royal Artillery, which explains why Leonard Roderick Saward was born in Aldershot on 6 July 1927, whilst his brother Pat was born in Ireland a year later. Len was an amateur with Beddington Town after the war and was playing in a kickabout when the Crystal Palace scout spotted him. He joined the ground staff in 1947, signing professional terms two years later. He played mostly for the reserves in the Football Combination, but did play nine League games at inside-forward, scoring one goal for Palace. A move to Arsenal looked to be on the cards, until Len got involved in a punch-up with a QPR player that changed their minds. He became disenchanted with the Eagles and moved to Tonbridge in 1951 after turning down Notts County who would not offer him enough. He moved to Cambridge United in the autumn of 1952 for £750, which was less than a third of his original valuation.

United gained an inside-right who was unusually tall, at a shade under six feet, and was memorably described as being eel-like, as he wriggled his way through the opposition's defence. Despite this dexterity he wasn't fast, but was forced to rely on good positional sense to ensure he wasn't required to extend himself unduly. This cat-like desire not to walk an unnecessary step led to sniping criticism that he took things too easy – a synopsis Len would probably agree with – but he compensated by having a decent heading ability and a strong shot with either foot.

He starred in United's giantkilling of Newport County in December 1953, scoring the crucial second goal in the 2-1 victory in south Wales. Newport were sufficiently impressed and the following month they signed him for £750. Len was desperate for League football and played 25 League games for County over two seasons, scoring four goals, until he broke a rib at Watford. He played for Brentford briefly and was told if he could stop Jimmy Hill from scoring in a London Challenge Cup match against Fulham, they would sign him up. But Hill scored two minutes from the end.

Saward rejoined Cambridge in March 1955, but was moved out on to the right wing when Wilf Mannion arrived. Len actually played in all the forward positions for United, bar outside-left and wing-half. His abilities improved noticeably under the tutelage of Mannion and they formed a close understanding on the field of play. Mannion told Len he was as good a player as he'd ever played with, which, coming from a regular international, was quite some compliment.

Len remained in the shadow of his younger brother Pat (who died in 2002). Pat didn't share Len's laid-back attitude to footballand went on to build a distinguished career at wing-half with Millwall, Aston Villa and Huddersfield and won a total of eighteen caps for the Republic of Ireland. Many say that it was Len who was actually the better player, which just goes to show how important hard graft is, if you wish to succeed.

In October 1957 Len was granted a benefit game against an Invitation XI, the quality of which can be judged by the fact that international players Jackie Sewell and Peter McParland were used as linesmen. The match was played under United's first set of floodlights, which were acquired by Len and sold to the club. They were mounted on telegraph poles, but their 32,000-watt output wasn't going to turn night into day.

Len joined Sudbury Town in July 1958 and then went on to Newmarket Town, before becoming player-coach (and later manager) at Soham Town Rangers between 1961 and 1967. He rejoined Cambridge United and worked in the commercial department between 1965 and 1987 and later became a porter at Magdalene College Cambridge as well as working for the social services.

Magic Moment: *Len Saward sealed United's only non-league giantkilling when, at the far post, he headed in Ray Ruffett's free-kick for the vital second goal in a 2-1 win.*

Worst Nightmare: *In September 1955, United (who had reached the first round the two previous seasons), were beaten in the preliminary round by lowly Chatteris. The club scapegoated Len, accused him of being drunk, and suspended him for a fortnight.*

CAMBRIDGE RECORD	Appearances	Goals
Eastern Counties League	125	33
FA Cup	unknown	2

No 15. **LES STEVENS**
Debut: v Clacton, 22 August 1953
Final Farewell: v Bury Town, 17 October 1956

The other scorer in that FA Cup win at Newport was winger Les Stevens.

Leslie William George Stevens (born in Croydon on 15 August 1920) was an amateur with Tottenham Hotspur from May 1937. He had a spell with their nursery club, Northfleet, before signed professional terms for Spurs in January 1940. He made his debut against Fulham in May 1942 in the London War League, scoring twice from his favourite inside-right position. He played throughout the war years, not only for Spurs, but also for several guest clubs (Aldershot, Arsenal, Charlton, Chelsea, Crystal Palace and Millwall). When the war ended he switched to outside-left, making his Football League debut at West Brom in Division Two in September 1946. By the following season, he was no longer an automatic choice, fighting for his place alongside Welsh international Ernie Jones.

In February 1949, after having played 54 League games for Spurs, and scoring five goals, he transferred to Bradford Park Avenue for the scarcely believable sum of £10,000. Park Avenue were desperately trying to retain their Second Division status, an attempt that failed in 1949-50 when they finished bottom (Spurs were top). At the end of the season, Park Avenue cut their losses and sold Les to Crystal Palace.

After twenty League games at Palace, who were bottom of Division Three (South), he dropped into the Southern League with Tonbridge, before moving across to Kent League sides Snowdown Colliery Welfare and Ashford United. It was in the summer of 1953 that Bill Whittaker lured him to Cambridge – both having been at Palace together.

Stevens cut quite a dash at Cambridge, being a slightly built, baby-faced man, with an impeccable taste for hand-made suits. Somebody once likened him to a tailor's dummy, and the flashiness helped to convince the locals that he was a typical Cockney – though strictly speaking he wasn't.

Being of frail composition, it was natural that Les should be a winger. He was used mostly on the left, but was versatile enough to be able to switch to the right if required. Even though he was in his mid-30s at Cambridge, he still possessed explosive acceleration and once he had used this pace to dispose of his full-back he was able to flight the ball beautifully onto the striker's head with consistency and accuracy. He also had a wicked shot, which was demonstrated with a hat-trick against Stowmarket Town in August 1954, but he was unable to head a ball to save his life, and had a marked reluctance to tackle, which shows the strong survival instinct in him.

Stevens left the U's in 1955 and went back to the Kent League, this time with Canterbury. He made a brief comeback with Cambridge the following season, but left finally in October 1956. He ran an off licence in New Cross and died in Wickford, Essex, in February 1991.

Magic Moment: *Stevens set United on the way to beating Newport, weaving past four defenders to score the opener. His reward was a home tie with his old club, Bradford.*

Worst Nightmare: *Stevens visited the cinema once, with Les Medley of Spurs. They ended up facing one another, as one was deaf in his right ear and the other in the left.*

CAMBRIDGE RECORD	Appearances	Goals
Eastern Counties League	63	16
FA Cup	unknown	5

No 16. **RON MURCHISON**
Debut: v Lowestoft, 20 August 1955
Farewell: v Clacton, 7 May 1958

Another wonderful goal-creator of this period was right-half Ronald Angus Murchison, one of the magical three Ms (along with Wilf Mannion and Brian Moore) who created pandemonium in opposition defences almost everywhere they played.

Ronald Angus Murchison was born in the Scottish county of Ayrshire on 12 February 1927. He played when he was in the Army and was picked four times to play for South Palestine in the Middle East. On returning to Scotland he played junior (i.e. non-league) football for Auchterader Primrose. He went through a lean spell for a few weeks, but returned to top form in a cup game that happily for him was observed by a scout from Southend United, who was meant to be looking at another player. The other player was forgotten, but Ron was offered a trial, which was hastily cancelled when Southend embarked on an overseas tour.

Soon afterwards a letter came from Ipswich manager Scott Duncan, and in June 1950 Ron signed for the Third Division (South) outfit. At first he was perpetual twelfth man (in those pre-substitute days), but in December 1950 he made his debut at inside-left at Northampton Town and went on to make 38 consecutive games at wing-half during the 1951-52 season, alongside Doug Rees and Tommy Parker. Throughout his time at Ipswich Ron was in competition for his place with Scottish wing-half Neil Myles, but by the start of 1952-53 it was the latter who had gained a stranglehold on the first-team spot so, in his last couple of years at Portman Road, Ron was in the reserves, who played in the London Combination. It was still a high standard of football, as he was coming across international players from the likes of Spurs and Arsenal. One consequence of the maximum wage was that Ipswich could afford a massive squad of nearly 40 players, so competition for places even at this level was red-hot. Ron made his final appearance for Ipswich's first team in April 1955, moving to Cambridge in the close season, when another ex-Ipswich player recommended him to manager Gerald Williams. Shortly afterwards, the inexperienced Williams was sacked after an embarrassing FA Cup defeat by Chatteris Town, despite the club topping the ECL at the time.

Murchison made his debut on a stiflingly hot August afternoon, which prompted a physical collapse, then an attack of the shivers in the dressing room. The trainer (definitely not a physio) put it down to a slight attack of malaria – a misdiagnosis that was faithfully reported in the local paper.

When Wilf Mannion arrived, Ron found his perfect ally. They often resorted to planning strategies on the centre-circle prior to kick-off, a conspiracy that led to a proliferation of first-minute goals. Ron was a refined, steady player, who was careful never to waste a pass. He was an excellent defender and he seemed to be able to read the minds of his opponents to cancel out any threat they posed. Once the ball was safely in his possession, the United attackers could prepare themselves, because Ron excelled in long crossfield balls which never left the grass, but which usually found their target. In emergencies, he was sometimes called upon as a striker, though it wasn't his best position.

He worked at Pye Telecommunications as an inspector for thirteen years, but spent the 1961-62 season playing for Bexleyheath and Welling in the Kent League. Later he got a job as a representative for a firm selling sports equipment. Now retired, he is another who lives close to the Abbey Stadium. Close enough for one of those long-range raking passes in fact.

Magic Moment: *For Ipswich against Gillingham, Murchison scored a first-half goal that bobbled before creeping in, then conceded a late own-goal when the ball bounced in off his head under a challenge. The 1-1 draw gave a fellow Scot a big pools win.*

Worst Nightmare: *After each game for Bexleyheath, Murchison often caught the milk train home to Cambridge at 2am, then started work at Pye's a few hours later.*

CAMBRIDGE RECORD	Appearances	Goals
Eastern Counties League	94	12
FA Cup	unknown	2

No. 17. **WILF MANNION**
Debut: v Holbeach, 18 August 1956
Farewell: v Norwich City 'A', 21 April 1958

Murchison's co-conspirator on the centre-circle was Wilf Mannion, undoubtedly the most skilful player ever to have played for United and, perhaps, the finest inside-forward England has ever produced. Possessing a greater variety of tricks than Billy Smart's Circus, he dazzled the foot-balling world for 25 years.

Wilf was born in May 1918 and went to his local school in South Bank in Yorkshire, and at the age of seven was good enough to be playing with kids twice his age. His first club was South Bank St Peters and whilst there he attracted the interest of Middlesbrough on the other side of the River Tees. They signed him up in August 1936 and by January 1937 he had broken into the first team as an 18-year-old inside-forward. He became a star turn at Ayresome Park, gaining the nickname 'Golden Boy', which was a reflection on his ability as much as his blond hair. Both Wilf and Boro seemed poised on the edge of greatness by 1939, but we all know what happened in that year. He fought with the 7th Battalion (The Green Howards) and for a while was reported 'missing in action' whilst in France. Thankfully he was 'found', and returned to England in the Dunkirk evacuation, before heading off to fight in the Middle East. He also played as a guest for Bournemouth and Tottenham.

In September 1946 Mannion was selected for England's first post-war international, and he made a dramatic impact by destroying Northern Ireland with a hat-trick in the 7-2 win. The new England set-up revolved around Wilf, Stanley Matthews, Tom Finney and Stan Mortensen, at a time when England could lay claim to being the most powerful football nation in the world. They slaughtered Portugal 10-0 in Lisbon and humbled Italy 4-0 in Turin. With Mannion on board, England won fifteen out of nineteen matches until June 1950. In May 1947 he represented Great Britain against a 'Rest of Europe' side in a match that was billed as 'The Match of the Century'. Half a million hopefuls applied for the 134,000 tickets at Hampden Park, and Wilf, who had been stung by criticisms that Raich Carter should have taken his place, treated them to a wonderful performance. He scored twice and the headline in this over-hyped game was 'Matthews and Mannion mesmerise Europe'.

With so many colleagues of comparable standard around Mannion, it was no wonder England enjoyed a superiority complex. The real test for England came in their first World Cup, in 1950, when they were given a slap in the face by the United States with that infamous 0-1 reverse. Wilf's final England cap came against France in October 1951, so he avoided being part of the Hungarian humiliation of 1953. His 26 caps would have been far higher if not for the war.

By 1948 Wilf had been in conversation with American baseball legend Babe Ruth, who opened his eyes to the vast wages that could be earned in sport. Even though Middlesbrough were regularly attracting over 50,000 to Ayresome Park, they were only paying Wilf a fraction of his true worth, thanks to the £12 'maximum wage' that the footballing authorities had instigated to artificially cap players' earnings. Wilf was unhappy about this situation and was also angered at the jealousy of his team-mates when he was provided with a club house. He demanded to leave, but although Oldham and Leeds made bids of £15,000, and Aston Villa were prepared to pay £25,000 (well in excess of the British record), Middlesbrough steadfastly refused to let him go. Unfortunately, they retained his registration, and without their permission he was unable to leave the club. In desperation he went on strike for several months, but the club refused to back down, and Wilf reluctantly rejoined them as he was struggling to support his pregnant wife. He carried on playing until April 1954, confirming his status as Boro's greatest ever player, then announced he would not be signing a new contract.

Mannion's 'retirement' lasted until Christmas, when he signed for Hull City for £5,000, after Boro finally relented and let the 36-year-old go. He also started writing for the *Sunday People*, exposing in his column the corruption that was rife within football. Wilf stated that he had refused a 'bribe' by a top club. The Football League demanded to know the name of the club and, when Wilf refused, they banned him from playing in the League from April 1955.

As the FA weren't a party to the ban, he joined non-league Poole Town. He played there for six months before his old friend Bert Johnson persuaded him to join Cambridge United in August 1956. It is almost impossible to convey the excitement that swept through the club, and indeed, through the whole of the Eastern Counties League, and attendances doubled and tripled wherever he appeared.

Wilf was 38, an age where most top-class footballers are pale shadows of their former selves. Wilf was different. He maintained a full repertoire of feints, swerves and dummies that meant he was still able to bewitch and hypnotise opponents. He also was supremely fit and had surprising acceleration off the mark, so even players half his age could be beaten, often without Wilf needing to even touch the ball. His age meant that long surging runs were a thing of the past, but other players obliged and awaited that killer pass into the space ahead of them. Although he was short and slightly built, he did a remarkable imitation of a jack-in-the-box, and a fair proportion of his 22 League and Cup goals came via that golden head.

Although that famous hair was receding, Wilf maintained a boyish twinkle in his eyes. He was a quiet, modest man, who used to enjoy a tot of whisky in the Supporters Club before a game. At half-time he would be asked teasingly what the team should do in the second half, and he always replied that they should 'push it about a bit'. His one indulgence was to come back from away games by taxi, but he certainly wasn't a prima donna, and on a Sunday he would often be found behind a pulpit in church.

He left Cambridge in May 1958, just before his 40th birthday, and joined King's Lynn but, due to his taking on a pub in Stevenage, he never kicked a ball for them. He appeared briefly for Haverhill Rovers, and also returned to the Abbey in March 1959 for Bob Bishop's testimonial. He tried his hand as player-manager with Earlestown in Lancashire in 1960, but they went bankrupt two years later. He moved back to his roots and got various odd jobs, before finally Middlesbrough were shamed into giving him a joint testimonial with his Boro colleague George Hardwick. He became a matchday host at the new Riverside Stadium and died in April 2000. His biography is called *Golden Boy* and is written by Nick Varley.

Magic Moment: *In November 1947 Mannion persuaded his new girlfriend (and future wife) Bernadette to watch him against Blackpool. He entertained her (and the Boro crowd) with a display of dummies, juggling and keepy-uppy. Boro also won 7-0.*

Worst Nightmare: *During his first footballing strike, Mannion was forced to take a job selling chicken coops in Oldham to make ends meet.*

CAMBRIDGE RECORD	Appearances	Goals
Eastern Counties League	56	16
FA Cup	unknown	2

No 18. **BRIAN MOORE**
Debut: v Sudbury, 10 November 1956
Farewell: v Wisbech Town, 6 May 1960

Completing the triumvirate of M's is Brian Moore, who was the recipient of most of Murchison and Mannion's through passes. He is the most prolific goalscorer in United's history, but is not related to the late ITV commentator of the same name.

Brian McGowan Moore hails from Belfast, entering the world on 29 December 1933. He began his career in Glentoran's junior team, working his way through the reserves, until by the end of his second season he managed ten consecutive games in the first team. Brian was still an amateur, but all Glentoran were willing to offer him was the chance to sign for the reserves so, disillusioned, he quit football for a year. That might have been the end of his career, but out of the blue he was offered the chance to play in Distillery's first team, which he jumped at. He did so well he was selected to play for the Irish League against the English League in October 1954 at Anfield, and was marked by 18-year-old Busby babe Duncan Edwards. The end of the game launched big Irish celebrations, as they reckoned that losing 2-4 was as good a result as they could have wished for.

His big break in English football came at the end of his second season at Distillery. Whilst playing in a cup final at Coleraine, the West Ham manager Ted Fenton, who was there to check up on another player, spotted him. It was Brian who got the chance to sign for West Ham in February 1955 for £4,500, which he gratefully took.

West Ham later became known as the 'Academy Club', due to the production line of their players who went on to become top coaches and managers. One of these was Malcolm Allison, then top dog amongst the players. Brian used to go greyhound racing with Malc and his mates, which drew concern from his manager, who thought they were 'too forward' for an impressionable Irish lad. Fenton gave him his debut in the last match of that season at Nottingham Forest, and in 1955-56 he occasionally partnered Billy Dare and John Dick, scoring his only Hammers goal in a 2-3 defeat at Rotherham in December 1955.

On Boxing Day 1955 Moore was playing at Middlesbrough when a full-back's clearance sent the heavy leather ball smashing into his right eye. Brian eventually got to his feet, convinced he had got mud in his eye, though the trainer could find none. In those pre-substitute days he was forced to remain on the pitch, though he was staggering around in a daze. It was on the train on the way home that he collapsed and was rushed into hospital. Then came the shock diagnosis – Brian's retina was irreparably damaged and he was virtually blind in that eye.

West Ham said he would be silly to play on, and a year later granted him a testimonial along with Geoff Hallas, who had suffered a similar fate. In the meantime the footballer's union – the PFA – had given Moore £500 to compensate him for the fact that he wouldn't play again. Soon afterwards though, Brian signed for Cambridge United, because his boyhood hero Wilf Mannion was there.

Originally Brian had been a schoolboy centre-half, but seeing Wilf work his magic in the inside-right position in an international match had led Brian to switch positions to emulate him. Unfortunately, the PFA were concerned by the possible implications of a player receiving compensation and then carrying on playing, so they issued legal proceedings against him. United originally agreed to provide him with a solicitor, but at the last minute they baulked at the cost, and Brian was forced to defend himself, a prospect he found daunting. Nonetheless, he won his case, only to find the PFA had brought another against him. This time the PFA won, but they were only interested in the judgment, not the £500 that Brian had given to his parents for a new television set.

You might wonder how a one-eyed man could play football. Certainly at first, his impaired vision had caused Brian problems, and he was continually bumping into people in the street, and pulling out in front of cars on his bicycle. Over time though, his brain had started to compensate for the loss and he began to find it easier to judge the speed and distance of the ball, something you really need two eyes to do. Moore was also helped by the brilliance of Mannion and Ron Murchison, who formed a three-man gang to terrorise ECL defences. Brian had been switched to outside-right at Mannion's insistence, and by the start of the 1957-58 season their tactics had been honed to perfection. Mannion and Murchinson would feed the ball through to the galloping Moore, using their voices to tell him when the ball was coming on what was literally his blind side. Because the passes were so precise, and Brian had that happy combination of blistering pace and an ability to score from any angle or distance, the unsophisticated defenders he came across didn't have a hope. Brian wasn't a particularly good header of the ball, but on the ground he was unsurpassed, being blessed with a lean, yet muscular physique which was the envy of many. Brian scored an astounding 68 goals that season, including 49 in the league – a figure that comfortably exceeded Crane's figures of 40 in the league and 43 overall in 1948-49. Brian scored five hat-tricks that season, which included a five-goal haul against Sudbury Town in the opening 39 minutes in April 1958. Any centre-forward would be thrilled at those figures, but for a player operating behind the striker it was truly astonishing.

Finishing runners-up to Spurs 'A' was enough to earn United an invitation into the Southern League, but a combination of the higher standard of football and the departure of Mannion meant that Brian was never going to match the goalscoring exploits of the previous season. He stayed at United until July 1960, when he moved across the Cam to Cambridge City. He had fallen out with new player-manager Alan Moore, partly over a dispute about Brian's house (which United had subsidised), partly because Brian, as captain, was continually telling his boss off for being so slow on the pitch. Moore didn't get on so well at City, largely because it was their chairman – Mr Ridgeon – who had signed him, not the manager. Because the players around him weren't as understanding of his poor eyesight, a player would sometimes dispossess him on his right side, which would cause a shout of 'Wake up, Moorey' from the fans. Nevertheless, he remained with City for four seasons before moving to Wisbech Town, where he had the dubious privilege of taking part in a 1-10 FA Cup debacle by Brighton. He played briefly for Boston United and Newmarket Town before becoming player-manager with Pye's, where he also worked. He is usually to be found on the local golf course and, even now, retains his superb physique.

Magic Moment: *In one ECL game, an opposition player was continually chopping Moore down. Brian complained loudly, but Mannion told him to just get on with it. Mannion soon 'innocently' crocked the assailant's ankle. 'See', said Mannion, 'if you keep on fouling, you'll always come off worse'.*

Worst Nightmare: *At hospital, Moore received little sympathy about his eye. A lady doctor told him it had cleared up. 'But I can't see out of it', protested Brian. 'Oh you won't', she replied, 'the retina's damaged, but the eye's healed up splendidly.'*

CAMBRIDGE RECORD	Appearances	Goals
Eastern Counties League	52	59
Southern League	67	21
FA Cup	unknown	4

No 19. **FRED HOWELL**
Debut: v Tonbridge, 23 August 1958
Farewell: v Wellington, 6 May 1963

The first player to be recruited for the assault on the Southern League was wing-half Fred Howell.

Fred was born in Great Yarmouth on 6 June 1933 and, as a youth, captained Yarmouth Boys. When he left school he went into Yarmouth's 'A' team, before doing his stint of National Service by joining the RAF at eighteen. On his return he was rapidly promoted from Yarmouth reserves into the first team, where he impressed Cambridge manager Bert Johnson playing against his Cambridge United side in the Eastern Counties League. He signed just in time for the big step up into the Southern League, but chose to remain in Yarmouth and commute to Cambridge when required.

Howell was a chunky, ginger-haired wing-half, but at an inch under six feet, he wasn't short. He was soon to become a darling of the Abbey, because he was just the sort of player that the fans love. He was credited with doing the work of three men and went about his business with a totally committed, no-nonsense attitude. He was an enthusiastic tackler, which gave some observers the impression that he was a dirty player, but Fred is adamant that he always tried to tackle cleanly, citing the fact that going in clumsily against your opponent is just as likely to injure yourself as well as him.

His five seasons at United illustrated the rapid progress that the club made during that era. After a mediocre first season in the Southern League's South Eastern Section in 1958-59, they failed to finish in the top eleven by one place, which meant they had to join the First Division the following season, instead of joining their rivals Cambridge City in the new Premier Division. Another average season followed as Bill Craig had an unhappy five-month reign as United manager, but the appointment of Alan Moore as United boss was one of the most significant in United's history. The players all became full-time professionals, instead of just some of them, and they achieved promotion to the Premier in 1960-61 by finishing as runners-up to Kettering Town. After a flirtation with the relegation zone in 1961-62, they survived to mount an exciting race for the title in Fred's last United season of 1962-63. Their big rivals were City, who just pipped them for the title, and Fred experienced more disappointment when they lost in the first round of the FA Cup at Bedford Town 1-2, despite Fred's goal sparking hopes of a revival.

Howell signed for Wisbech Town in the summer of 1963, under Jesse Pye, the ex-Wolves centre-forward who had won a solitary England cap in 1950 (alongside Wilf Mannion). Pye recruited a lot of top players as they briefly challenged the two Cambridge clubs for the honour of being the top club in the county. (Peterborough didn't qualify, because they were then in Huntingdonshire). Fred played for three seasons before taking a break from the stresses of football.

After his rest, he rejoined Great Yarmouth Town as a player-coach, before moving next door to rivals Gorleston. By then he had stopped playing, but coached them as they won the Eastern Counties League title for the first time in twenty years in 1972-73. He lives in Gorleston to this day.

Magic Moment: *In the Hunts Premier Cup semi-final replay in April 1960, Howell unleashed two thunderbolts to sink Peterborough United, who had dominated the Midland League for five years and were on the verge of entering the Football League.*

Worst Nightmare: *Fred was so careful when tackling, that he would get upset if he thought he'd injured an opponent. Even in the heat of a derby with Cambridge City he was concerned when a clumsy tackle resulted in an injury to City's Eddie Robinson.*

CAMBRIDGE RECORD	Appearances	Goals
Southern League	195	23
FA Cup	unknown	7

No 20. **PHIL HAYES**

Debut: v Weymouth, 11 April 1959
Farewell: v Clacton, 16 December 1961

Another player who was never stationary on the pitch (or anywhere else for that matter) was Phil Hayes – a striker whose thirst for goals is only exceeded by Brian Moore's.

Philip Henry Hayes was born in Chiswick on 23 December 1935 and was part of Brentford's youth team until 1955, with a break in 1953 as he completed his National Service for the Army. His military career took him to Wales, where he briefly turned out for Brecon Corinthians in the Welsh League.

In 1955 Hayes started playing for Slough Town, then in the Corinthian League, and after a couple of seasons there he was spotted by a Millwall scout by the name of Dusty Miller in December 1956, who recommended him to manager Ron Gray.

Like Brentford, Hayes was also on amateur terms with Millwall, and a spell in the reserves followed, until he took part in the London Challenge Cup final of 1957. Though Millwall lost 1-3 to West Ham at Upton Park, Phil scored and this prompted a call up into the League side. His strongest position was always centre-forward, but hot competition for places meant that he was shunted between all the five forward positions, never being able to settle into one role. This, and a bad knee injury which kept him out for three months at a critical time in his career, meant he only played in sixteen League games for the club, scoring once, at Brighton. Then a new manager came in and there was the inevitable mass clearout of unwanted players.

Cambridge United manager Bert Johnson had gone to Millwall to sign the Scottish defender Bill Craig, but he took the opportunity of bringing Phil to the Abbey as well. Johnson's intention was to deploy him on the wing and that was where he was playing when he made his memorable debut at Weymouth in the Southern League's South-East Section. United's 0-7 thrashing and an identical score at King's Lynn four days later prompted Johnson to reassemble his side and heed Phil's advice to play him at centre-forward alongside Brian Moore. The change was dramatic. Just a week after the Lynn debacle, Phil ran riot at their neighbours Wisbech and grabbed himself four goals in the Cambs Professional Cup final first leg. Suddenly, an attack that had put too much responsibility onto Brian Moore had a new outlet to exploit. Sadly, it was too late to lift the club into the top eleven, where they needed to finish to take their place in the new Premier Division that would commence the following season.

With a prolific strike force in place, promotion from the new First Division was hoped for, but an inconsistent start under new boss Bill Craig cost United dearly. Though Phil finished the season as top scorer with 30 goals, his team could only finish in mid-table. Brian Moore had left the club by the next season, so it was. Phil who had to bear the heavy burden of goal-getter, virtually single-handed. With new manager Alan Moore beefing up the rest of the team, Phil's impressive tally of 34 league goals was good enough this time to clinch promotion.

Phil would be the first to admit he was not the most skilful of players, but he had the biggest heart of any of them. He would run forever and never give up, even if the game was lost. He would chase lost causes, bang in a goal, then the next minute be racing back to help out the defence. He was one of those players who it was impossible to leave out of the side, not that the crowd would have forgiven any manager who dared to do it. He was slim (with that work-rate he could never have eaten enough to be anything else) and was unafraid to throw himself into the most dangerous of penalty areas. He was an opportunist striker, waiting to pounce on any-thing that presented itself, and was the epitome of Cambridge. His strike-rate of 70 goals in 100 league games speaks for itself. The fact that he man-aged to fill Brian Moore's boots without the team suffering is as much praise as anyone could have asked for.

Alan Moore's route to promotion success was to make all the players full-time professionals, but Phil didn't want that as he was still living in London at the time. In December 1961 he transferred to Yiewsley, who later became known as Hillingdon Borough. He had six seasons there and for a while played alongside the legendary Jackie Milburn, who was player-manager. He then played for Kent sides Ramsgate and Folkestone before returning to Cambridge in the late 1960s to join Tommy Bickerstaffe's City. He played a part in the last truly great City side, which finished as runners-up in the Southern League Premier Division in 1970-71.

Hayes then had a spell as player-manager at Stotfield in the South Midlands League, not hanging up his boots till the age of 40. He was in charge of the play facilities in Crawley for many years, but in retirement he still busies himself coaching youngsters. Even now he can't stand still.

Magic Moment: *Hayes's goal in the 3-2 win over Bury Town in the FA Cup third qualifying round in October 1961 meant that he had scored in United's last nine FA Cup-ties. His FA Cup goals total of twelve puts him one ahead of John Taylor in United's all-time list.*

Worst Nightmare: *Hayes could never keep still for one minute, even in the changing room. Anybody ear-wigging at the door wouldn't have to wait long before they heard the inevitable 'For goodness sake, sit down Phil'.*

CAMBRIDGE RECORD	Appearances	Goals
Southern League	100	70
FA Cup	unknown	12

No 44. Vic Akers

No 45. Brian Greenhalgh

No 46. David Lill

No 47. Willie Watson

No 48. Brendon Batson is far left. The player taking evasive action is Dave Moyes

Chapter Three

The Professionals

No 21. **ROY KIRK**
Debut: v Hinckley, 20 August 1960
Farewell: v King's Lynn, 11 September 1963

If Phil Hayes was all skin and bones, then Roy Kirk was probably all fat and muscle. His appearance belied his ability though, and his vast experience made him a natural choice for manager after the resignation of Alan Moore.

Roy was born in Shuttlewood, near Bolsover, on 11 June 1929. As Bolsover was a coal-mining town, it was hardly a shock that he began his footballing career playing for the Colliery's side.

He escaped the hard work of pit life by joining Second Division Leeds United in October 1948, initially as understudy to the monumental figure of John Charles. Kirk made his debut in February 1951 and went on to make 34 League appearances in his two seasons there. Although basically a centre-half, he was tried as a No 9 in the 1951-52 season. Indeed, he played in just about every position bar goalkeeper for Leeds, but failed to make any one position his own, though Charles was moved permanently up front as Roy and his colleagues had taken good care of the defence. Roy's rounded face and shock of dark hair had become familiar to the scouts at Coventry City who were desperately seeking a centre-half to try to maintain their club's precarious Division Two status. Kirk was transferred to them in March 1952 for a hefty £10,000, and though he couldn't keep them up, he became their first-choice centre-half for the next eight years as they languished in Division Three (South) and Division Four. He stayed around long enough to enjoy their promotion season of 1958-59 and ended his time there, after a total of 330 League appearances, when they finished fourth in the Third Division.

Cambridge United's manager, Alan Moore, had spent three seasons playing alongside Roy, so he knew that he was just the man to become the heart of his new defensive line-up. Although a massive presence on the pitch at 6ft tall and 14½ stone, he was signed for more than his bulk. He had a neat trick of trapping the ball quickly and hitting it first time to a winger with either foot. Kirk surprised many people by covering a great deal of ground very quickly and was a dominant presence in the air as well. He was as hard as nails and there was no forward who could ever intimidate him.

Roy was also given a spell at centre-forward and his finest game in that position came against Lowestoft Town in October 1962, when he bagged a couple of goals to put his side into the FA Cup first round for the first time in eight years.

With such massive experience under his belt, Roy became captain and then player-coach. When Alan Moore unexpectedly resigned in October 1963, Roy was appointed as caretaker manager. His first task was to hang up his boots to concentrate on the job in hand. He was a well-respected figure amongst the players, getting his points across without needing to bawl at them. He motivated the team brilliantly and a good run of results led to his permanent appointment in February 1964.

He had mixed success as a manager. He did win the Southern League Cup in 1965, but it was in the Southern League that the club wanted to perform as they were now openly pursuing the long-term goal of Football League membership. Roy was unable to lift the team higher than mid-table and, after a bad start to the 1966-67 season, he resigned his position.

Kirk became landlord at the Royal Oak and New Inn pubs in Peterborough, but died in November 1984 aged 55.

Magic Moment: *In an FA Cup-tie for Coventry v Northampton in November 1954, Kirk scored with an 80-yard clearance – the goalie trying to avoid the missile.*

Worst Nightmare: *That spectacular goal made up for Kirk's painful game against Orient two months earlier, when he scored both goals for the opposition in the 2-2 draw.*

CAMBRIDGE RECORD	Appearances	Goals
Southern League	89	4
FA Cup	unknown	2

No 22. **SAM McCRORY**
Debut: v Hinckley, 20 August 1960
Farewell: Gravesend & Northfleet, 2 May 1962

Another old-timer who still managed to prove that age wasn't a barrier to ability was inside-forward Sam McCrory.

Samuel McKee McCrory was a Belfast boy, born on 11 October 1924. This was a bad time to be born as World War Two straddled his teenage years, but after it had finished he played for Linfield. He was transferred across the Irish Sea to Swansea Town in October 1946 and became one of their finest inside-forwards, bagging 46 goals in 103 League games. Although the Swans were relegated from the Second Division in his first season, he was there when they won the Third Division (South) title in

1948-49 on the back of an incredible home record that featured twenty wins and one draw in their 21 games.

In March 1950 he dropped back down to Division Three (South) to join struggling Ipswich Town, making his debut that month in the hot-house of a local derby with Norwich. He was the leading scorer for Town in 1950-51 with 21 League goals, including a hat-trick at Crystal Palace in November 1950. The following season he once more topped the League goalscoring charts and ended his Town career with a useful record of 39 League goals in 97 appearances.

In August 1952 he went to Plymouth Argyle, newly promoted from Ipswich's division and he helped to guide them to their equal highest-ever finishing position of fourth in the Second Division. From then on it was a case of relegation struggles and after 50 League games and eleven goals he was on his way again.

In June 1955 he joined Southend United of (yes, you've guessed it) Division Three (South). They had been seeking promotion out of there for 34 years, and Sam was seen as a big hope for elevation. They sort of achieved a promotion. In 1957-58 Sam stuck away 31 League goals to equal Jim Shankly's 29-year record and by finishing in the top half they earned themselves a place in the new Third Division, whilst teams such as Crystal Palace and Coventry formed the Fourth Division. McCrory stayed at Roots Hall until the end of the 1959-60 season, by which time he had racked up 91 League goals in 205 games.

He had already represented Northern Ireland at 'B' level and went on to make his only full international appearance on 4 October 1958 in a 3-3 home draw against England. He even managed to score a goal, though he was almost 34 years old. By then he was looking far older than he was, his hair having receded markedly, and he was mocked by the English as being 'an old man'.

McCrory was certainly venerable by the time he joined Alan Moore's Cambridge United in the summer of 1960 but, like many veterans, he possessed the brains to compensate for the lack of speed. In Jimmy's case, his main trick was to shield the ball, rendering it almost invisible to his opponents. Once he had the ball, he would only surrender it on his terms. He was a creative player and both Phil Hayes and Jimmy Gibson were able to make a good living from goals scored, fed to them by the master. Alan Moore considers him to be the crucial factor in United's elevation into the Southern League Premier. Sam didn't only make goals, either. In September 1960 he gave March Town United a lesson in top-class finishing by scoring four goals in a 7-3 FA Cup qualifying round thrashing.

Sam was a quiet, gentle man, both on and off the pitch, living just round the corner from the ground in Elfleda Road in a club house. He lasted two seasons at United, but by then his age was really starting to take its toll on his body and his contract wasn't renewed. In May 1962 he was granted a testimonial against an All-Star XI featuring Cliff Holton (who had once scored two hat-tricks in two days for Watford) and Roy Smith (a former Cambridge City man, now at Portsmouth). The All-Stars lived up to their billing by winning 6-2.

McCrory returned to Northern Ireland to play for and manage Crusaders, before retiring and running a pub in Donaghee, County Down.

Magic Moment: B*efore an East Anglian Cup-tie against Norwich in November 1961, the Norwich chairman boasted 'once more the East Anglian Cup will grace the boardroom at Norwich City.' After Sam had scored the winner (3-2) at Carrow Road, Alan Moore crowed 'once more the East Anglian Cup will* not *grace the boardroom at Norwich City.' In fact it came to the Abbey. United won the final 2-1 v Hitchin.*

Worst Nightmare: *In April 1950, during a 0-5 defeat at Aldershot, McCrory became the first ever Ipswich Town player to be sent off in a League game.*

CAMBRIDGE RECORD	Appearances	Goals
Southern League	74	14
FA Cup	unknown	7

No 23. **BILLY WELSH**
Debut: v Hinckley, 20 August 1960
Farewell: After 22 February 1965

Another 'foreigner' in United's ranks was Billy Welsh, who wasn't Welsh at all, but Scottish, having been born in Kilsyth in 1936. With a half-back line comprising Welsh, Kirk, and Howell, United had a solid wall of six-footers to demoralise opposing strikers.

Billy played for his local side Kilsyth Juniors, before moving on to a more famous junior outfit called Rob Roy, before finally finishing up at Glencairn Juniors with Jim Sharkey (more of whom later). Billy went on to play for Airdrieonians, then a firmly established top-division side in Scotland. He had a trial with Leeds United, but it was Cambridge United who made a firm offer for him. Manager Alan Moore always made a point of studying the Scottish PFA lists to see who was available and often made lengthy journeys to try and capture the better players.

And this boy could play. He was a left wing-half, and although a long-striding player, he also managed the difficult knack of combining it with excellent ball control. He had done plenty of running and playing football in the RAF during his National Service and this had helped to maintain a high fitness level. Welsh was a big man at 6ft 2in, with 'footballer's legs' that made it a nightmare when he was shopping for trousers. He would find a pair that were long enough, with the correct waist measurement, but invariably they wouldn't fit over his muscular thighs and calves. Although physically built as a defender, his auburn-haired frame was often spotted helping out the attack, but sadly his goals tally seems to suggest that he was reluctant to shoot on goal as much as he should have done, because he couldn't half whack the ball when he wanted to. All in all he was a polished performer who could always be relied on to perform consistently. Indeed, his playing style never varied from the time he was playing in Scottish junior football, according to his colleague Jim Sharkey.

Although he was a huge physical presence in the flesh, he was a dapper man, immaculately dressed and a true gentleman. He wore black driving gloves as he drove around in his beloved 2.4 litre Jaguar saloon in British Racing Green. He was known either as 'Squire' or as 'The Baron' (after a character in a 1960s TV programme). He was famous in the dressing room for never swearing. If something really upset him, the strongest phrase he would utter was 'blast it!' His wife noticed that this reluctance to use bad language would often go to pot on the football field and that even Billy could resort to using words that were proscribed in polite company.

In November 1964 his wife went into labour (eventually producing a daughter) on the same morning as United were playing in an FA Cup first round tie at Barnet. United only made the FA Cup proper on a few occasions and, although he played, Billy took the brunt of the blame for a 1-2 defeat as everyone said his mind was elsewhere. That was the beginning of the end. He left Cambridge in 1965 after falling out with manager Roy Kirk and joined Bath City, then managed by Malcolm Allison. After a year he joined Manor Athletic (now known as Brentwood) in the Olympian League.

Billy moved back to Scotland and tried to become an amateur once more, which proved to be a bureaucratic nightmare. Sneakily he broke the rules to play a few games for Troon. He ran his own heating and ventilation business and a couple of years before retiring went on a hillwalking holiday in the Lake District with friends and family. He wandered off on his own and accidentally fell to his death off a 300-foot cliff. In life Billy was just like he was on the pitch – loving a challenge and fearing nothing.

Magic Moment: *At Bath City, the Welsh family took over Malcolm Allison's house where they welcomed a stream of bailiffs and debt collectors searching for Big Mal.*

Worst Nightmare: *In a match against Yeovil, Welsh took an ankle injury in a vicious tackle. Billy ignored the trainer's request to check it out and hobbled off after the* *match to go dancing with his wife. It was only when the dance was over that he deigned to visit Addenbrookes Hospital. He had gone dancing on a broken ankle.*

CAMBRIDGE RECORD	Appearances	Goals
Southern League	178	11
FA Cup	unknown	2

No 24. **BRIAN BOGGIS**

Debut: v Clacton, 19 August 1961
Farewell: v Weymouth, 18 September 1965

Another attack-minded defender was Brian Boggis, one of the greatest wing-backs in United's history.

Although Brian was born in Wisbech in 1941, he was brought up in Great Yarmouth. He used to play for his school team on a Saturday morning, and then turn out for Gorleston in the afternoon. His football was helped along by appearing in a fine Gorleston side whose presence was graced by players of the calibre of Dave Stringer (see No 56) and Peter Simpson, who went on to be a stalwart at Arsenal for fifteen years.

It looked as though Brian was destined for the First Division when he was spotted by Bert 'Sailor' Brown, a scout with Aston Villa. He signed for them at sixteen but didn't make the grade and soon afterwards went to Crystal Palace, which was similarly unproductive.

Boggis was playing as a left-back in a practice match for Chelmsford when he caught the eye of Cambridge manager Alan Moore. Though small, Brian was quick and sharp and it was obvious that he had an abundance of skill. At the end of the match Moore rushed over too him and urged him to come to Cambridge as a professional, though he eventually supplemented his money by taking a second job at Marshall's.

He signed just in time for United's assault on the Southern League Premier and quickly established himself as a truly great left-back. Not that it was possible to hold him back, because he was forever tearing down the line, looking to deliver a killer cross into the area. Sometimes this would mean swapping positions with the man on the left-wing – a nightmare for opposing right-backs, confronted with two wingers racing down the left touchline. His pace and trickery also made him a formidable defender and opposing right-backs would sometimes beat him, only to be confronted by him once more as he raced past them and challenged them again. It was said that if you wanted to take the ball past him, you would have to do it six times. He wasn't a great header of the ball, largely due to his diminished stature, but such was his consistency and ability to avoid injuries, that he didn't miss a League game until well into his fourth season. He lived opposite the ground and was a popular participant in the Thursday night drinking sessions that the players would enjoy in the local pubs.

Boggis moved to Wisbech Town during the 1965-66 season, becoming player-manager at Fenland Park a couple of years later. When Wisbech announced they were dropping out of the Southern League, he quit to join Stevenage to stay at that higher level. He stayed there for two years, and then got a job with Geoff Proctor at the Abbey Sports and Social Club (Rex Club). Alan Moore (ever persuasive) lured him to Histon for a while, but when the Rex closed down he took over a pub in Gorleston. Brian has now run fourteen pubs in 30 years, plus one nightclub. He is currently host at a 62-seater pub-restaurant in Aldeburgh, Suffolk, called the Victoria, where he would welcome a visit from any U's fans. Presumably he is a master at nipping in and out of the tables and avoiding collisions.

Magic Moment: *Boggis was ever present in the League during his first three seasons, setting a record for consecutive appearances that was only beaten by Jamie Murray.*

Worst Nightmare: *0-0 in one match at half-time, Boggis had been playing well whilst Johnny Haasz hadn't. Yet Boggis was subjected to a barrage of abuse from manager Alan Moore, whilst Haasz was praised. It was psychology from Moore, who knew Brian would relax and under-perform unless geed up, whilst Haasz was the opposite.*

CAMBRIDGE RECORD	Appearances	Goals
Southern League	159	2
FA Cup	unknown	–

No 25. **JIMMY GIBSON**
Debut: v Clacton, 19 August 1961
Farewell: v Peterborough United, 1 February 1965

The main outlet for Boggis's crosses was Jimmy Gibson, who continued the strong line of fearsome United attackers that terrorised Southern League defences in the late 1950s and early 60s.

James Gibson was a Belfast boy and was born during the London blitz on 4 September 1940. He was a teenage striking sensation with Linfield and attracted the attention of Newcastle's legendary striker Jackie Milburn, who recommended him to the Magpies' manager Charlie Mitten. No manager was going to turn down that kind of endorsement and Jimmy was signed in January 1959 for the not-inconsiderable sum of £6,000.

He made his Division One debut in a 3-1 win over West Ham in March 1959, but then was shunted into the reserves for eighteen months, on account of being third choice behind the long-serving duo of Bill Curry and Len White. In September 1960 Gibson made a comeback, but despite scoring in the 2-0 win over Nottingham Forest it proved to be his last game for Newcastle. Although a powerful striker in the Milburn mould, it was said that he lacked guile. Perhaps Newcastle would have been better served if they had converted him into a central defender, because they were relegated that season having conceded 109 goals. Jimmy was versatile enough to play in that role, but that would only become apparent later on.

Cambridge United's Alan Moore travelled to Ireland to capture Jimmy's signature on a contract in the summer of 1961 and offered him a club house as a further inducement to sign. Gibson rapidly established himself in the side, effectively pushing aside Phil Hayes and became the leading scorer for two consecutive seasons, scoring twice as many League and Cup goals as his nearest challengers.

Although powerful, he was slim, with a fashionable early-1960s short haircut and a typically Irish lop-sided grin. He seemed to have a never-ending supply of energy and any central defender that tried to keep tabs on him would be a physical wreck after the 90 minutes were up. Jimmy was brave and had a prodigious leap that meant he could claim almost any ball, even if it was as high as the crossbar. He formed a variety of striking partnerships with players of the ilk of Matt McVittie and Norman Bleanch, but by scoring five hat-tricks between February 1962 and November 1963 he wasn't going to be outdone by anyone.

I have already alluded to the fact that Gibson might have been converted to a central defender whilst at Newcastle, and he was sometimes used in this position at the Abbey, though he was too valuable as a striker to extend this experiment for very long.

In February 1965, struggling Luton Town – who were about to drop into the Fourth Division – signed Jimmy. They converted him into a wing-half and he made 32 League appearances for them in two seasons, although the Hatters never witnessed any of his magical goals.

Afterwards he went across to the United States to become a coach. He is still there, showing Americans how to bang in the goals like Wor Jackie.

Magic Moment: *In January 1963, Gibson became the first ever Cambridge United goalscorer on Anglia Television's pioneering Match of the Week programme in a 1-1 draw at Bedford Town. The commentator was Trevor Bailey, better known for his cricket broadcasts on Test Match Special.*

Worst Nightmare: *Not so much a nightmare for Gibson, but definitely one for the other players. They would all go drinking on a Tuesday night and as they staggered round the training pitch on Wednesday morning would be greeted by the ultra-fast figure of Jimmy who appeared to suffer no ill-effects from the previous night's activities.*

CAMBRIDGE RECORD	Appearances	Goals
Southern League	145	65
FA Cup	unknown	7

No 26. **RODNEY SLACK**

Debut: v Clacton, 18 August 1962
Farewell: v Margate, 2 May 1970

Easily the most popular player to have turned out for United in the 1960s, Rodney Slack was undoubtedly the greatest goalkeeper United had in their non-League era.

Slack was born in Peterborough on 11 April 1940 and brought up in the nearby village of Farcet. He joined Leicester City in the mid-1950s in the days when the maximum wage was still in force. This enabled the club to have a massive squad, with five or six teams made up of varying ages and grades of players. It was a long hard slog for Rodney to work his way through all these teams, but he did well enough to sign professional terms in September 1958. He found a friend in Scottish international goalkeeper Johnny Anderson, who had been first-choice keeper for several years, but was on the verge of being frozen out by a new talent (unfortunately that wasn't Rodney). Anderson spent many hours on the training ground with Slack, replicating with the aid of pieces of string the various angles that balls could come from.

In May 1959 both Anderson and Rodney were pushed down the pecking order by the signing of Gordon Banks from Chesterfield. Although still very green, it was obvious that Banks had talent and was going to prove impossible to displace from the team. Rodney enjoyed a laugh with Banks though and even did some babysitting for him (hopefully never letting Baby Banks slip through his hands).

Rodney was desperate for first-team experience, so he moved to Third Division QPR in March 1961. Again he found himself stuck behind an immovable green-shirted object, this time Ray Drinkwater. Rodney's one moment of glory came in May 1962 at a Third Division game at Halifax, where he made his only League appearance in a 1-1 draw. Aware that he was never going to become a first-team fixture he became disillusioned, and his unhappiness at living in the London area made him turn down a move to nearby Watford.

His escape materialised when he was playing in a reserve game at Bournemouth, when he conceded a sackful of goals. Watching that day were Cambridge United manager Alan Moore and Vice-Chairman Jack Woolley, who were looking for a keeper to replace the injured Andy Smith. Moore told Woolley that he wanted to sign Slack, and Woolley said incredulously 'but he's let in all those goals!' 'Yes,' replied Moore, 'but his shot-stopping before the first one went in was incredible.'

Slack was called a 'line keeper', but in reality he wasn't, it was just that he was so agile, though it must be said that he wasn't at his best when dealing with crosses. He was short for a keeper at only 5ft 9½in, but made up for it by seemingly being fitted with elastic arms with shovel-like hands on the end. Many clubs would not sign a keeper under six feet, and it was to Alan Moore's eternal credit that he was not swayed by standard managerial beliefs. Photographs of the time certainly show that Rodney's arms were out of proportion to his body. He was fearless and brave and would play on seemingly regardless of what injuries befell him in those tough days when bashing the keeper was a legitimate occupation for forwards. He once played with eleven stitches in a chin injury, only to have them burst open three days later. He lost several teeth in a collision with Brian Boggis's knee, and even played half a game with a broken leg.

Slack was a firm favourite with the fans standing behind his goal, who were astonished by his athleticism, charmed by his outgoing jokey character, and finally won over by his apparent willingness to die for the United cause. He won the Supporters Club Player of the Year a record four times in five seasons between 1962 and 1966. He said he could easily go out with half a crown in his pocket, get drunk and still come back with the half a crown, because of the number of drinks plied by U's fans. He remained the first-choice keeper at United for eight years until 1970, refusing offers to join Northampton and Fulham because he was happy where he was.

Rodney's speciality was saving penalties. He never moved before the kick was taken, instead watching to see which way it was going before leaping towards it with the speed and dexterity of a giant chimpanzee. In one season he saved seven out of nine spot-kicks, including a thunderbolt against Hereford that he somehow managed to push away from the top corner.

Rodney was naturally overjoyed at United's accession into the Football League in 1970 and felt he was good enough for a couple of League seasons, but one day somebody showed him a copy of the local paper which stated that Rodney was being released. Slack was heartbroken, but Leivers didn't think he was up to League standard and replaced him with Trevor Roberts. Although Leivers admits Rodney was a good shot-stopper, he feels he didn't hold on to as many balls as he should have done.

Rodney joined Bury Town and wound up his football career by becoming President of the Cambs League. He passed the fire service examination, though he admits he was hopeless at the maths questions. He is convinced that these were rigged so they could have a decent keeper for the England Fire Service team. He is now retired, but still lives within goal-kicking distance of the Abbey Stadium. He remains keen on football and local Under-11 teams now take part in the Rodney Slack League Cup competition. He is currently awaiting a liver transplant.

Magic Moment: *In 1964 'The Charles Buchan Monthly Magazine' voted Rodney Slack as the best non-League goalkeeper in the country.*

Worst Nightmare: *Slack saved a penalty in an FA Cup-tie with Cambridge City to keep the score 1-1. At the end a lad ran onto the pitch. Rodney assumed he was going to be congratulated, but instead the boy punched him in the eye, giving him a shiner.*

CAMBRIDGE RECORD	Appearances	Goals
Southern League	217	–
FA Cup	unknown	–

No 27. **JIM SHARKEY**
Debut: v Clacton, 18 August 1962
Farewell: v Hapoel Tel Aviv, 5 September 1963

Although he was only at Cambridge United for a little over a season, one of the classiest players ever to appear for United was the master of the deep-lying centre-forward position, Jim Sharkey.

Born in Glasgow on 12 February 1934, Jim's first taste of club football was for Haverhill Rovers in Suffolk, because he was stationed at nearby RAF Stradishall during his National Service days. When he returned to Glasgow he played for a juvenile team called League Hearts. One day an old man with white hair and glasses asked him if he would like to play for Celtic. Jim thought he was joking, as did his dad when he relayed the story. But the old man wasn't joking. Sharkey was taken up the road to Celtic Park to meet the manager – the legendary figure of Jimmy McGrory. He signed on amateur terms in 1954, but received £10 for his troubles.

Celtic loaned him to Glencairn Juniors for six months, a virtual prison sentence for Jimmy because he got special attention from the roughest players once they knew he was a Celtic player. He returned to Celtic in December 1954 (signing professional terms) and spent four years there as a centre-forward and outside-right, though he preferred playing in a deeper striking role. On his debut he set up a fine goal for Matt McVittie, who was also to play alongside him at Cambridge United. In 1957 Jim played in a charity match against Manchester United's 'Busby Babes' – six months before the Munich Air Crash that killed so many of them. His fondest memory of that day is selling Duncan Edwards a dummy during the 2-2 draw. He made 23 League appearances for Celtic, scoring seven goals. His greatest game for Celtic came in the Glasgow Cup in Boxing Day 1955 when according to a contemporary report 'he dribbled George Young into bewilderment, scoring two beautiful goals in the 5-3 defeat of Rangers. He caressed the ball with his foot before crashing the ball high into the net behind George Niven.'

In March 1956 Sharkey scored against Clyde in the Scottish Cup semi-final, but was reported to the chairman for an alleged misdemeanour and was dropped for the Cup final, when a poor Celtic side were sunk 1-3 by Hearts. His last game for Celtic was in September 1957 when they beat Rangers at Ibrox for the first time in 22 years.

In November 1957 he moved to Airdrie for £3,000, receiving enough money as a signing-on fee to enable him to buy a house. He became a legendary figure at Airdrie, winning a Player of the Year trophy and becoming known as 'The Tully of Broomfield' in memory of another famous player. He helped a good side challenge for the Scottish title early in 1958-59 (largely down to him), but left under a cloud when he was accused of not trying in a Cup semi-final against Celtic in 1961 which was lost 0-4.

Jim signed for Raith Rovers in May 1961 and played until April 1962, hampered by suffering the agonies of a broken ankle in January 1962 when he twisted his leg awkwardly. In May 1962 he had a trial for Portadown in Northern Ireland, but it was an English club that was the next beneficiary of his talent.

In 1962 United manager Alan Moore spotted that he was available by scouring the Scottish PFA lists. He went up to Scotland and persuaded him to come back down to England (with a £500 signing on fee). He was known as 'Gentleman Jim', being immaculately attired in a smart suit or black raincoat and sporting a bowler hat on top of his smartly trimmed hair. This led to several confusing episodes when he would be mistaken for a director or even an undertaker, but it led to a job delivering the football pools to the local pubs where he cut quite a dash.

Sharkey was the most eagerly anticipated signing since Wilf Mannion, and United gained an expert ball player rather than a goalscorer. Jim's forte was searching out an empty space for the regular strikers, and Jimmy Gibson, Matt McVittie and Norman Bleanch regularly boosted their goalscoring tally with the aid of a Gentleman Jim special. He loved to entertain the Abbey crowd with scissor kicks and double shuffles and almost helped his side to the Southern League championship as well, though rivals City infuriatingly pipped them.

Sharkey left United in 1963 to join Wisbech Town (another £500 fee, thank you very much), and then continued his tour of East Anglian non-League outfits by appearing for Corby Town, Bury Town and Newmarket Town.

He loved to play golf and cannily got a job as a milkman. The 8.30am finishes enabled him to indulge his passion six days a week and helped him to a handicap of five. He followed that routine for a number of years, and then became a porter at Pembroke College in Cambridge until he retired to live on the Arbury estate in Cambridge. If you want to find him now, the golf course is still the best place to look.

Magic Moment: *Against Dartford in December 1962, with United winning 3-0, Sharkey received the ball from keeper Slack, trapped it under his jersey and ran up the pitch with it, to the consternation of the referee who was unsure what to do.*

Worst Nightmare: *In a match against Morton, the opposition goalkeeper cleared the heavy leather ball straight into Sharkey's face, knocking his teeth out.*

CAMBRIDGE RECORD	Appearances	Goals
Southern League	30	5
FA Cup	unknown	1

No 28. JACKIE SCURR

Debut: v Poole Town, 23 February 1963
Farewell: v Hillingdon Borough, 1 March 1969

One of the few players able to rival Sharkey and Slack in the fans' affections at the time was wing-half Jackie Scurr. Indeed it was he who prevented Slack from winning his third successive Player of the Year trophy in 1963-64 by capturing it for himself.

John Thomas Scurr (born 30 September 1940) was playing for his hometown boy's club of North Shields when an Arsenal scout offered him a trial. Though the Gunners didn't offer him a contract immediately, they extracted a promise from Jackie that he wouldn't sign for anyone else until they had reached a decision about him. Newcastle United then weighed in with an offer that owed everything to bad timing and Jackie was forced to rebuff them to keep his pledge to the Londoners. Thankfully he was invited back down to Highbury after all the shenanigans and signed on amateur terms in April 1959.

He did well enough to earn professional status in September 1959. The Gunners were going through the doldrums at the time and though they finished in the top three that season it was a one-off and in reality they were just another mid-table side during that period – a fact that was even harder to take as their neighbours Tottenham were in the ascendant and poised to become the country's top dogs with their double success of 1960-61. Jackie was some way off a first-team place and was mostly to be seen playing for their third team in the Metropolitan League. In 1960-61 he helped Arsenal to the Metropolitan League championship and to the final of the London Challenge Cup. He did briefly break into the reserve team, which competed in the Football Combination, but after eighteen months he hankered to go back up north, so in January 1961 he joined Fourth Division strugglers Carlisle United on a free transfer.

He remained in Cumbria for another eighteen months but made fifteen League appearances, scoring once in the process (at Chester in September 1961), and helping Carlisle to gain promotion in 1961-62, before another move to the other end of the country.

Originally the plan was for him to join Frank O'Farrell (the future Manchester United manager) at Weymouth, but King's Lynn also weighed in with an offer and it seemed the better deal at the time. It didn't turn out that way. The Linnets manager wanted him to sit back and defend, which was the complete antithesis to his game. Jackie was an attacking player, with speed and stamina. He could certainly defend, but was at his best charging out of defence and creating an attack. He was wasted as a pure defender and it inevitably led to an unhappy player who wasn't giving his best to the team – a state of affairs that led to a vicious circle.

That circle was ended when Scurr was transferred to Cambridge for £500. Alan Moore signed him and Jackie regards him as one of United's greatest ever managers, certainly an under-rated one. Moore gave him back his freedom and allowed Jackie's full range of skills to blossom once more. He was a key element in United's rapid rise to Southern League success as a wing-half with many facets to his game. He was Mr Perpetual Motion and given half a chance would never stop running up and down the pitch for 90 minutes. In fact he was the sort of player who would probably cope with playing two games back to back. He was a bite-your-legs tackler who could dispossess a forward and then race away to turn defence into attack, looking to open up the opposition with a well-placed pass. He struck a deal with Moore. In return for a certain degree of freedom on the pitch, he was occasionally required to man-to-man mark a creative opposition player and take him out of the game – a job he would relish. Jackie's 'rottweiler' style even manifested itself in training, and his colleagues wouldn't escape his crunching tackles.

By 1969 Scurr was coming up to the end of his time, his age starting to slow him down a bit. He joined Bedford Town, and helped them to promotion to the Southern League Premier Division in 1969-70. Bedford were managed by an ebullient Barry Fry who was only in his early twenties. Fry was exactly the same then as he is now and the two men got on well together. So well, that Barry made him assistant-manager – the perfect foil. Whereas Fry would shout, swear, threaten and slam doors during half-time team talks, Jackie would be the calming influence who would back up his boss, but put his views forward in a less forceful manner.

The two of them left Bedford in July 1974 to join Dunstable and they once more tasted promotion success. After Fry's unorthodox sacking (see below) Jackie was offered his job, but stayed loyal to his manager and refused it.

By this time Jackie described himself as too old and lazy, so he contented himself with the odd kickabout as a sweeper with Hertfordshire club Stotfold of the South Midlands League. Outside of football he had a variety of jobs. He worked in a garage, then a machine shop, before a long-running post in a finance house, which ended with redundancy in the savage recession of the 1980s. He went on to become a postman and woe betide any dog that dared take him on. He now lives in Baldock.

Magic Moment: *Scurr used to gang up with Gerry Baker to take out dangerous opponents with the ruthlessness of mafia hitmen. They particularly relished taking on players who didn't wear shinpads. Roy Keane wouldn't have lasted five minutes.*

Worst Nightmare: *Scurr's time at Dunstable with Barry Fry ended spectacularly, when Fry threw a glass of scotch into his chairman's face. Fry would have many rows with chairmen, notably at Barnet where he was forever being sacked and reinstated.*

CAMBRIDGE RECORD	Appearances	Goals
Southern League	229 (+1)	17
FA Cup	unknown	1

No 29. **JOHNNY HAASZ**
Debut: v Wellington, 31 August 1963
Farewell: v Corby, 30 August 1965

Scurr's work-rate was tested to the limit to indulge the talents of United's own Magic Magyar – Johnny Haasz. Whereas most inside-forwards were expected to track back with their opposing wing-halves, Johnny would resolutely hang around the goal area awaiting his next opportunity to strike, like a crocodile near a riverbank. Scurr was happy to 'run his nuts off' (as he so delicately phrased it), as he tried to mark two men at the same time. It demonstrates ably what his colleague thought of Johnny, as he wouldn't have done it for anybody else.

Johnny Haasz was born in Budapest, Hungary, on 7 July 1934 and his early footballing career was greatly aided by the fact that his father owned a football club in the city – a working man's club that played in the Second Division. Johnny was expected to work for his place though, tending the pitch, cleaning numerous boots, sweeping the stadium etc. He also played for the Air Force football team, playing in the First Division against the incomparable destroyer of English football – Ferenc Puskas.

Life changed dramatically for Hungary in 1956. The brief Hungarian uprising, challenging the oppressive Soviet rule, was brutally crushed by Russian tanks on the streets of Budapest. Johnny's group of 'bad boys' (as he called them) indulged in guerrilla warfare against them and Johnny hid in a coffin in the cemetery when things got too dangerous. The end came when Johnny (armed only with a pistol), and a group of lads bravely took on the tanks. The Russians opened fire and, of the 200 lads with Johnny, only nine escaped with their lives. Johnny and his friends escaped to Austria to live with his old youth-team manager. He suggested they all went to England to his brother who ran a hotel in Doncaster, so Johnny and company ended up in Yorkshire.

Due to the bureaucratic problems involved in transferring Johnny's registration from Hungary to England, FIFA wouldn't allow him to sign professionally, so he was forced to play amateur football with Bentley Colliery and Gainsborough Trinity. Eventually, in September 1960, he joined Swansea Town and played one game for them – against Bill Shankly's Liverpool – who were trying to escape from the Second Division. At the end of the season he moved as a wing-half to Fourth Division Workington then managed by the ex-Newcastle star Joe Harvey. Haasz played 50 games for them, scoring seventeen goals, including a 50-yard screamer from an opposition goalkeeper's clearance. His time at Workington ended when he had a 'clash of personalities' with new manager Ken Furphy – the old footballing story. He joined Alan Moore's Cambridge as an inside-right and, though dropping out of the League, he actually saw his wages rise from £17 a week to £22.

United gained a footballer unlike any other in their side in the 1960s. Johnny had spent countless hours practising with those unforgiving leather balls on training grounds in Hungary and England and had learned to make it as obedient as the most faithful dog. Although only 5ft 8in tall, with tiny legs, he somehow managed to hide a set of formidable muscles in those dainty pins. When taking a free-kick he would take a small run-up of only two steps, use only a short backlift and then release his leg like the hammer on a pistol. It seemed impossible that somebody could hit a ball so hard anyway; to do it without the aid of a lengthy run-up and extended backlift seemed to defy the laws of nature and physics. He could also bend the ball around defensive walls, a continental skill that also defied belief in those days. It was certain that nobody in the Southern League had a more powerful or accurate shot and any ball within a 40-yard range was likely to test the strength of the goal-nets to the utmost. He once scored with an overhead kick at Bath that even earned a round of applause from the beaten goalkeeper.

Haasz much preferred to stay near to the goal area, though, and poach in the style of Jimmy Greaves. He was a fast and tricky dribbler and also was more than useful in the air. In 1963-64 he chalked up 42 league and cup goals, a figure that nobody has seriously threatened to overtake in later years, and one that has only been bettered by Russell Crane (43 in 1948-49) and Brian Moore (68 in 1957-58).

He fitted in with his colleagues splendidly, despite struggling with his English sometimes. One player recalls him saying that he didn't like 'visky', but he did like 'wodka'. Mind you, the mind boggles at the thought of his colleagues trying to wrap their tongues round some of those impenetrable Hungarian words. He also had an old-fashioned swept-back hairstyle in those Beatle-dominated days, though a perusal of his colleague's barnets confirms that footballers in his era weren't dedicated followers of fashion.

After falling out with one of the trainers at Cambridge United, he left in 1965 to join Corby Town for ten months. He then moved back up north and played for Scarborough until 1967. He had learnt the tyre-fitting trade at Cambridge and carried on doing that in Doncaster till he retired. Having mastered leather so well, he didn't have any problems with the more flexible rubber.

Magic Moment: *In the Cambs Professional Cup final, first leg, at the Abbey in September 1963, Haasz became the first United player to score a hat-trick against their more illustrious rivals City, as United won 5-0 in front of 6,402 people. It was his second hat-trick in three days and the joyous home fans prevented him leaving the pitch.*

Worst Nightmare: *Haasz's Swansea debut v Liverpool ended in a 0-4 thrashing. He had one scoring chance, but slipped on the icy surface in his borrowed boots.*

CAMBRIDGE RECORD	Appearances	Goals
Southern League	53	33
FA Cup	unknown	–

No 49. Bobby Shinton

No 50. Steve Fallon

No 51. Alan Biley goes over a Southport player's knee. Willie Watson is on the right

No 52. Steve Spriggs

No 54. Malcolm Webster

No 55. Tom Finney   No 56. Dave Stringer

Chapter Four

The Escape Committee

No 30. **GERRY BAKER**
Debut: v Cambridge City, 21 August 1965
Farewell: v Kettering Town, 3 May 1969

If Johnny Haasz was a typical Hungarian (whatever that might be), then Gerard Baker was an archetypal Yorkshireman, who 'could give it and could take it'.

Gerry hails from South Hiendley in West Yorkshire, and was born just before war broke out in 1939. His career began on the groundstaff at Sheffield Wednesday, mainly spent polishing boots. His chances proving to be limited there, he moved across to Third Division (North) Bradford Park Avenue in 1955, signing professional terms two years later.

Gerry made his debut at right-back in October 1957. It was a hard slog to keep his place in the team, because ahead of him was Jeff Suddards, who had a ten-year head start on Gerry. Eventually age caught up with Suddards, but Gerry still was only able to make the occasional first-team appearance, though he did play a part in Bradford's first ever promotion season from what was then the Fourth Division. This was an occasion made doubly delightful, as Bradford City were heading in the opposite direction. Sadly, he was sidelined by a serious knee injury for nearly five months, but that coincided with his national service, so he was able to take advantage of the Army's rehabilitation unit, which was equipped with weight-training facilities to rebuild his strength.

Not that everything was sweetness and light at Park Avenue. Gerry was told he was the youngest ever player to serve under six different managers. He once looked poised to make a move to First Division football, but because of another managerial upheaval they were unable to sort it out. He did have the chance to join less glamorous York City, but instead chose to go to King's Lynn in the summer of 1961, then a professional Southern League side.

He remained at The Walks for over four years, this time as a centre-half, but in 1965 finally made the move to Cambridge United, a transfer that United had been keen to make for several years. He was a good old-fashioned stopper, being quite tall and solidly built. He was goalkeeper Rodney Slack's best pal on the pitch, dealing with crosses with ease, aided by the fact that he was once a junior high-jump champion. Baker also protected Slack from onrushing centre-forwards. It was said that a forward might get past him once, sometimes twice, but never a third time. In an emergency he was versatile enough to fill in as a left or right-back.

Baker became the backbone of the United team that claimed their first Southern League championship, in 1968-69, but at the age of 30 he was starting to slow up a bit. Bill Leivers signed a much younger Terry Eades to replace him. Poor Gerry was also badly afflicted by piles, which caused much amusement, and often some alarm, especially when he applied the Vaseline to a delicate part of his anatomy in the dressing room.

He joined Cambridge City, and once again a team of which he was a part hit a successful run. Spurred on by United's success, City gained promotion from the Southern League's First Division in 1969-70 and finished runners-up to Yeovil Town the following season. Gerry was captain, which meant a lot of shouting to keep everyone on their toes. He certainly enjoyed helping to beat United (now a Football League side) in the Cambs Professional Cup final of 1970-71.

Gerry went on to play for Stevenage Athletic, but became a bit cheesed off with working full-time in the building trade, then having to go to train. He moved to the village of Great Shelford, where he allowed himself to be talked into helping to run the local village team.

Magic Moment: *As a manager, Baker took village side Great Shelford to the greatest prize in their history, when they defeated local giants Cambridge City and Chatteris en route to winning the Cambs Invitation Cup final.*

Worst Nightmare: *Leivers used to hold light-hearted dressing room quizzes with oddball questions to help build team spirit. The two losers would have to clean the boots, and invariably Baker would end up as shoeshine boy.*

CAMBRIDGE RECORD	Appearances	Goals
Southern League	161 (+1)	8
FA Cup	unknown	–

No 31. **ALAN O'NEILL**
Debut: v Margate, 26 March 1966
Farewell: v Cambridge City, 15 May 1968

Another colourful accent to be heard in the United dressing rooms in the 1960s was provided by Alan O'Neill, though Alan's was Wearside in origin.

In fact he wasn't christened Alan O'Neill at all, but was known as Alan Hope when he was born in Sunderland on 13 November 1937. He later adopted his stepfather's name. With a double whammy of pleurisy and Hitler's bombs being dropped all around him it was a miracle that Alan survived at all. His grandmother's care and plenty of cod liver oil took care of the first problem, whilst several million heroes dealt with the latter. Alan recovered to join the youth team at Sunderland and played in the Northern Intermediate League against such worthy opponents as Denis Law and Bobby Charlton. He worked his way through the ranks at Sunderland, signing professional terms in February 1955 and making his debut at Ninian Park in a match against Cardiff. Sunderland were one of the biggest clubs at the time, with virtually every player an international. With players like Len Shackleton and Billy Bingham, they should have been championship challengers every season, but the achievements never matched the potential. They were known as the 'Millionaires Club', because they could go out and sign a top player anytime they liked and gained a reputation for slipping players backhanders which almost dropped them in big trouble (though there can't have been many clubs that didn't try to circumvent the maximum wage which was then in existence). Alan O'Neill and Stan Anderson were almost the only local boys at the club. Alan eventually achieved 27 League goals in 74 games, spread over five seasons, before moving on in October 1960.

He went to Aston Villa, then managed by Joe Mercer, but only managed six League goals and 23 League appearances in his two seasons there. He made history by playing in the inaugural League Cup final in 1961, which was a two-legged affair against Rotherham United. Alan scored the first goal in the second leg that helped Villa to overcome a 0-2 first-leg deficit and sneak a 3-2 aggregate win in extra-time. He nearly didn't make it though. He was stuck in the traffic on Chester Road, having underestimated the level of interest for the match, and had to obtain a police escort to reach Villa Park for the kick-off. By this time the maximum wage had ended and Alan's wages had gone up from the £17 10s a week he received at Sunderland, and the £27 10s he had first earned at Villa, to a whopping £60 a week. The end of his Villa career came when Joe Mercer fell ill and was replaced by a man that Alan couldn't get on with.

In November 1962 O'Neill went to Plymouth, where he regained his scoring touch with fourteen League goals in 40 games. He couldn't stand the town though, finding the locals to be hostile to any 'grockles' from anywhere but Devon. He recalls seeing the same bloke getting into his car every morning and not responding to Alan's 'Good Morning' until the chap read in his paper that Alan was leaving, when he finally deigned to answer.

In February 1964 O'Neill moved along the coast to Bournemouth, but in three seasons he could only manage 37 League games and eight goals, mostly due to a serious ankle injury that crippled him for months. A Harley Street specialist couldn't do much for him and it took a visit to the Sunderland physio — the father of Likely Lad actor James Bolam — before a cure was effected. Even then it only proved to be a temporary fix and Alan is still troubled by his ankle to this day.

Near the end of the 1965-66 season O'Neill moved to Cambridge United, who were then managed by Roy Kirk. Alan was an inside-left, quick over ten yards, but still handicapped by that dodgy ankle which prevented him from reaching some balls which he would otherwise have reached with ease. In one friendly match he had to be replaced before the kick-off when his ankle gave way during the warm-up. He wasn't tall for a No 10 and consequently wasn't good in the air (that pesky ankle not helping again), but was more than useful on the ground with his compact frame, topped with a mop of black hair, being forever involved in the action. His good control and vision created numerous chances for the forwards and his accurate left foot was also much in favour for corner-kicks, helped by a series of codes to warn his colleagues what type of ball was coming over.

In October 1966, following a poor start to the season, Roy Kirk resigned as manager and, though nominally he was replaced temporarily by director Matt Wynn, in actual fact it was Alan who took charge of team affairs, aided by Jackie Scurr. This led to a clash of personalities with Bill Leivers when the latter took charge in February 1967 as the new man sought to stamp his authority. Bill felt Alan was too domineering, whilst Alan, for his part, felt Leivers messed about with the side too much when they were nicely placed for a championship push. By March 1967 United were on a run of twelve unbeaten League games before a disastrous week in the West Country led to three successive away defeats and an end to their title aspirations. Having said that, Alan feels that Leivers was an excellent judge of players, whilst the manager set aside his personal feelings for Alan because he recognised he was the focus for the positive team spirit that was evident within the club.

O'Neill left Cambridge at end of the 1967-68 season to go to South Africa, taking Billy Wall, Roy Poole and Dave Barrett with him. Alan coached a side in Johannesburg called Southern Suburbs, but left after twenty months; disillusioned by the way the apartheid system treated the black majority. He moved to Dublin and coached Drumcondra alongside Dave Barrett, before moving to Toronto at the behest of Len Shackleton and coaching a Greek side there.

Eighteen months later Alan was crossing frontiers once more as he joined New York Cosmos, but after a while he moved back to Canada and joined Vancouver in the North Pacific League. It took an illness to his mother-in-law to persuade him to move back to Blighty and he was offered the chance of the manager's job at Darlington in 1972. He flew back to

England and caught the train up to his dad's home in Newcastle, only to find the job had already been given to someone else. He became the manager of South Shields and then Blyth Spartans, where he won a couple of Northern League titles and took the side to the FA Cup fifth round.

Alan still had wanderlust and coached a team in Tobruk, Libya, for a while until the interference of Colonel Gaddafi made the job impossible. Apparently Gaddafi felt that everyone should be encouraged to play football even if it meant teams taking to the pitch with 30 players. Alan moved back to England and is now enjoying his retirement in Boscombe, near Bournemouth.

Magic Moment: *Whilst at Vancouver, O'Neill played in a friendly against Brazilian side Santos, who featured the legendary Pele. The match was due to kick off at 8pm, but was delayed an hour until Pele was paid his $25,000 fee for playing.*

Worst Nightmare: *When O'Neill left New York Cosmos for Vancouver he was advised to stay by the coach, who couldn't reveal the reason. Three months after leaving, Cosmos signed Pele, Franz Beckenbauer and Carlos Alberto.*

Cambridge record	Appearances	Goals
Southern League	78 (+2)	22
FA Cup	unknown	2

No 32. **BUD HOUGHTON**
Debut: v Cambridge City, 19 August 1967
Farewell: v Bedford, 5 February 1968

A prime outlet for O'Neill's through balls was Bud Houghton, who looked as though he was destined to become a truly great striker at United, but who nevertheless showed enough ability and goalscoring talent in his six months to endear himself to the fans and warrant inclusion in this book.

Harry Brian Houghton was born in India on 1 September 1936 to a half-Indian father and retained a dark complexion and a jet-black Asian hairstyle because of it. Bud (as he was always known) moved back to the motherland when he was young and he was playing for St Wreford's Youth Club when Bradford Park Avenue expressed an interest in him. He signed for them in October 1955 and made 28 League appearances in two years, scoring seven times, as they struggled near the foot of the Third Division (North).

In October 1957 Bud transferred to Arthur Turner's Birmingham City, then enjoying a spell in the First Division. He only clocked up four League games in twelve months, scoring just the once. It wasn't until he moved to

Third Division Southend United at the behest of manager Eddie Perry that his goalscoring talent was finally unearthed. It wasn't instant success by any means as it took him three seasons to amass 68 League games, but a total of 32 goals in this total is not to be sniffed at.

In March 1961 he joined Oxford United of the Southern League and formed a lethal striking triumvirate with Alan Willey and future U Graham Atkinson (Ron's brother). The three of them cracked in 81 league goals between them as Oxford won the Southern League Premier title and were consequently voted into the Football League. As with Cambridge later, Oxford found it a daunting step up from the Southern League and generally struggled during their first season. Bud scored seventeen Football League goals in 53 games, which included one in Oxford's first League game at Barrow, before a sideways move to Lincoln City beckoned in October 1963. This time he stayed for a couple of seasons, adding 22 goals to his tally, before moving to Southern League Chelmsford City.

Chelmsford were one of Cambridge United's greatest Southern League rivals, and it was disconcerting to City fans how often Cambridge swooped to pinch their best players. Chelmsford couldn't match the financial muscle of United, and Bill Leivers seemed able to sweet talk the most sceptical pro into putting pen to paper. Bud was captured in time for the start of the 1967-68 season and instantly made a name for himself with a succession of tasty performances in the amber and black. He had everything going for him as a striker. He was tall and athletic, excellent in the air, and the possessor of a hard shot using either foot. He was a tough tackler, but wasn't as robust as he had been in his early playing days, when his challenges sometimes bordered on the violent. All in all he was almost the complete striker – but the key word is 'almost'. Bud's problem was a laid-back attitude that, whilst being very much in the spirit of the late 1960s, when hippydom was at the fore, wasn't as much use on the pitch. Without this degree of laziness, then who knows? Either way, it appears he may have had a falling out with his manager, because that is the only explanation for his shock departure in February 1968. By then he had garnered 28 league and cup goals, a total that nobody else could approach that season. After his departure, United were unable to maintain the pace and they lost the crunch match at home to Chelmsford 0-1 in front of 7,813 to effectively surrender the title to their rivals. Ironically, United replaced Bud with another Chelmsford striker, Tony Butcher, who had scored more Southern League goals than anyone and still holds City's all-time scoring record. Butcher never turned it on in quite the same way as Bud at the Abbey, though, and was a comparative failure.

Houghton was sold to Wellington Town (now Telford United), also of the Southern League for £600. Soon afterwards he moved to Cheltenham

Town, then to Morris Motors of the Hellenic League. He worked for the car company in Oxford for a while, but sadly passed away in 1994.

Magic Moment: *Whilst at Oxford United, Houghton and Ron Atkinson had a window cleaning round together. Not quite early doors, but certainly early windows.*

Worst Nightmare: *Houghton incurred the wrath of Leivers after scoring a 35-yard volley. His manager raged that he should have been in the penalty area at the time.*

CAMBRIDGE RECORD	Appearances	Goals
Southern League	24	15
FA Cup	unknown	4

No 33. **BRIAN GRANT**

Debut: v Kettering, 6 September 1967
Farewell: v Barrow, 30 January 1971

Another roving player making his debut around the same time as Bud Houghton was Brian Grant, though he stayed around a lot longer than his colleague.

Brian Patrick Grant was born in Coatbridge, Scotland on 10 May 1943 and played for a local team – Kirkshaws Amateurs – as a full-back. At the tender age of 15½ he was independently spotted by two scouts – one from Nottingham Forest and one from Manchester United. The United scout was Matt Busby's brother-in-law, but he urged Brian to accept Forest's offer as they were offering terms, as opposed to United's proposal of a mere trial. Brian heeded this sound advice and headed south, but not before taking out an additional insurance policy. He signed with a junior (i.e. leading amateur club) called Bellshill Athletic. Although he never played for them, this document ensured he could return to Scottish amateur football if the English adventure should turn sour. Ironically, Bellshill was a former club of the aforementioned Matt Busby.

A friend travelled down with Brian on the train and saw him safely to his first solo abode – a Nottingham hotel. Brian was able to train with the first team in the morning, then practise with the youth team in the afternoon, so his days weren't lonely. He did feel isolated at night, but his parents visited often, and before long the club provided him with some digs to make him feel more comfortable.

Professional terms were signed in May 1960 (his seventeenth birthday) and before the new season had finished he had replaced Scottish international Joe McDonald in Forest's left-back berth. Interestingly, Brian was predominantly right-footed, which is unusual for a left-sided defender, but it did make life easier when the winger chose to cut inside, as he could be dispossessed with Brian's stronger foot. Not that it mattered much anyway, as his left peg was plenty good enough to cope with top division football. This was proved in his fourth match, against Manchester City, when the *Sunday People* noted how easily he contained Gerry Baker – brother of England international Joe Baker.

Grant remained with Forest until January 1966, but by this time he was treading water in the reserves, having made just eighteen League appearances in the first team. Once again, two teams showed interest, but Hartlepools United were preferred to Brighton, because the manager's sidekick – Peter Taylor – was a well-known Nottingham figure. The manager in question was none other than Brian Clough, just a few months into his first management role, at the tender age of 30. Clough remembers this particular piece of business well, because in trying to chip a £100 off the £2,000 asking price, he was involved in a skirmish with Forest manager John Carey, who broke off negotiations for lunch, then completely ignored Clough when he walked past his car soon afterwards. Anyway, the deal was eventually resurrected (a fortune for impoverished Pool) and Grant was now a Hartlepools player (Pool didn't lose the 's' in their name until 1968).

Clough's appointment was a last-ditch gamble for Pool, as they had finished in the re-election zone for five consecutive seasons, only surviving because Gateshead and Accrington Stanley were even worse. It paid off handsomely. Clough was extremely disciplined, almost tyrannical, but still a fair man. With men like Grant to help him, Clough was able to steer the team out of trouble and eventually on to their first promotion. By this time Clough had unloaded our man to Bradford City on a free transfer, but terms were never signed in his six months there and at the start of the 1967-68 season Grant was captured by Bill Leivers for Cambridge.

Brian was a strong, tenacious left-back, an expert at the sliding tackle, and this fitted in perfectly with the mood of the club at the time. He certainly earned his nickname of 'Tiger'. Football directors are much maligned, but Brian remembers that United's were the hardest-working ones he'd ever seen, forever canvassing the League chairman (who were the men with the power to vote United into the League). With Brian in defence, this determination was evident on the pitch as well as off it, which was essential, given the strength of the Southern League at the time. It's a cliché, but there really weren't any easy games and United's two championships were ground out. That feat was made easier with men like Brian about. He was not a player who would belt the ball out of defence, or try too much trickery, but one who would look for the simple ball (nearly always the best option). He was described by Leivers as a manager's dream. The sort of player who would have wanted to play on even if his leg had been broken. Off the pitch Grant was a joker, who wouldn't take anything seriously.

Things got tougher for Brian after United's elevation into the League. The signing of Colin Meldrum squeezed him out and, although he was versatile enough to be able to play at right-back as well, he was becoming little more than a squad player. The final straw came in an indoor five-a-side match when he was able to vent his frustration on Leivers, who was on the opposing team. After a series of crunching tackles on his boss, Grant went further by resorting to fisticuffs. Managers don't tolerate that and in February 1971 Grant was sold to Kettering, then in the Southern League First Division. He stayed there for three seasons, mostly under another legendary boss – Ron Atkinson – before moving to Stevenage for a couple of years. He became Histon Town's player-manager, then Bishop Stortford's boss, then went back to Histon and finally onto Cambridge City where he was assistant-manager to Roy Johnson, who went on to become Cambridge United's physio. Brian also ran the county side for three years, before taking up painting and decorating (a trade he studied at technical College in Nottingham as a teenager). He still lives in the Cambridge area.

Magic Moment: *In February 1970 winger Roly Horrey bet Grant £1 per goal scored, whilst Brian only had to find a penny for a Horrey goal. Roly felt his money was safe, as Grant had never scored for United. Grant scored in his next match – an 8-0 thrashing of Crawley. The ball just trickled over the line to tease Horrey further.*

Worst Nightmare: *United were favourites to win the new FA Trophy in 1970 to consolidate their bid for League status. Grant ruined things in the second round at Bromsgrove, when he gave away a penalty and 'scored' an own-goal in the 1-2 defeat.*

CAMBRIDGE RECORD	Appearances		Goals
Southern League	97	(+2)	1
Football League	14		–
FA Cup	unknown		–
League Cup	–	(+1)	–

No 34. **ROBIN HARDY**
Debut: v Lowestoft, 1 November 1967
Farewell: v Notts County, 10 April 1971

The unforgettable figure of wing-half Robin Hardy almost mirrored the length of time that Grant stayed at United.

Robin was born in Worksop on 18 January 1941 and began his career as a 15-year-old at Sheffield Wednesday in 1956, signing professional terms on the same day as the Munich Air Crash in February 1958. It took three more years before he was good enough for the first team and in that 1961-62 season he featured in Wednesday's Fairs Cup campaign. Most fans still believe he scored the winner in the 3-2 win over Barcelona in the quarter-final at Hillsborough. He didn't, and Barca won 2-0 in the second leg to end Yorkshire dreams.

Robin made 30 League appearances for the Owls over three seasons, scoring once. Wednesday were a decent side then, finishing in the top eight every season during that spell, but Robin was continually in and out the side. After another lengthy spell in the reserves, he walked out and joined Rotherham in February 1965 and was a regular wing-half until May 1966.

He had eighteen months out of the game and was running a pub in Worksop when Cambridge signed him, beating off interest from rivals Hereford United. Leivers had built up Hardy as the salvation for United, but the other players couldn't believe their eyes when this pot-bellied vision first appeared on the scene. Once he stayed off the beer and chips long enough to get himself fit, the other players could see what Leivers was on about. Hardy became the perfect foil for Gerry Baker, then Terry Eades. He was a good all-rounder, which meant he was sometimes used as a sweeper, though he hated the position, preferring to play in the middle of a back four. He read the game well and passed well. He had an unusual character though. He somehow managed to combine a strong will with a laid-back air of somebody who seemed unperturbed about anything. Not surprisingly 'Knocker' (his schoolboy nickname) was made captain of United at the end of the 1960s, his steadying influence setting a good example to his colleagues.

When he left Cambridge, Hardy moved back to Worksop and has worked as a press operator in a factory for 30 years.

Magic Moment: *Hardy astounded the culinary tastes of his Cambridge colleagues with a range of 'exotic' northern dishes, such as 'mince on chips' and 'blue stalks' (apparently a mushroom-like delicacy). These were washed down with pints of beer.*

Worst Nightmare: *In an ill-tempered match against Lincoln, Hardy raced out to clear ahead of City's Gordon Hughes. Hughes jumped onto Hardy's back like a jockey on a horse, which led to a free-for-all. An FA disciplinary hearing had to sort it out.*

CAMBRIDGE RECORD	Appearances		Goals
Southern League	105	(+1)	4
Football League	15	(+1)	1
FA Cup	unknown		1
League Cup	1		–

No 35. **DAI WARD**
Debut: v Hereford, 11 February 1967
Farewell: v Cambridge City, 15 May 1968

League appearance totals can be deceptive when you try to calculate the importance of a player to the club. Many workaday players can accumulate well over 100 games without doing anything special, whilst sometimes the men who are only at the club briefly can have a marked and lasting effect on the team. Dai's contribution to Cambridge amounts to much more than just playing in 54 league games

Dai was born David Ward in Barry, South Wales on 16 July 1934. After he completed his national service, his ex-schoolmaster recommended Dai to Bristol Rovers and they signed him as an inside-forward from Barry Town in November 1954. Dai was a fierce competitor and that aggression was tempered with a considerable degree of skill. A square-jawed, frightening apparition, he terrorised Second Division defences in his six years at Eastville. His devastating runs through the opposition's rearguard led to an impressive record of 90 goals in 175 League games, but that only tells half the story because he created countless goals for others too. It was no coincidence that his spell with the club is looked upon by fans as the most successful period in Rovers' history, with the side finishing in their highest ever Second Division placing of sixth in 1956 and again in 1959. In 1957-58 they marched to the FA Cup quarter-finals, turning over their Bristol rivals City 4-3 in the fifth round. On a personal level, Ward also set a number of club records – the quickest Rovers hat-trick (three goals in four minutes against Doncaster); the fastest goal (in seven seconds, against Bristol City in the 1959 Gloucestershire Cup final); and the longest spell of scoring in consecutive League games (eight – a record now equalled by Marcus Stewart).

It was during this time that Ward first turned out for Wales, in a 2-2 draw against England in Cardiff in November 1958, acting as 'an intelligent foil' for the incomparable John Charles, and setting up the second goal. Sadly, he had to wait three more years to gain his second (and last cap), also against England, in a 1-1 draw in front of 61,000 at Ninian Park. He was too well shackled by Peter Swan to damage England, apart from when he cleverly sneaked up behind him, separated him from his boot with a crafty tackle which the referee didn't spot, thus allowing Graham Williams to open the scoring.

In February 1961 Ward moved to Cardiff City for £11,000 in a player-exchange with Johnny Watkins, having already had a spell with them as an amateur in his pre-Bristol days. The Bluebirds were then enjoying their last spell in top-flight football. Despite scoring eighteen goals in 35 League games, he left Cardiff in June 1962 as they dropped down into the Second Division. His time at Ninian Park was marred by some bad advice about an injury he was suffering from.

June 1962 saw Ward playing for Watford after a £7,000 move and his goalscoring once more captured the imagination of the fans. That he did so at Vicarage Road was remarkable, as Hornets supporters were still grieving at the sale of the legendary Cliff Holton to Northampton at the beginning of that season. Although Dai's 31 goals in 59 League games could not match Holton's contribution, it was good enough to make him a fondly remembered player.

Ward moved to Brentford in October 1963 for £8,000, and on his debut against Wrexham he nabbed a couple of goals as the Bees romped to a record 9-0 win. His time at Griffin Park was marred by the non-appearance of a club house he'd been promised, and Dai made a dramatic protest by sleeping in his car on Hampstead Heath.

In August 1965 he dropped into the Southern League with Worcester City (£2,000) and then sideways to Bath City a year later. He wasn't there long before Cambridge United came in for him in late 1966.

United gained a fiery player who was never afraid to speak his mind. He was always niggling and badgering the opposition to try to gain an advantage. He was the prime mover in the infamous Cambs Professional Cup final second-leg tie against Cambridge City, which degenerated into a mass brawl after a disallowed goal. Dai had only come on as a substitute five minutes earlier, and his boss had warned him not to get booked. He got his marching orders instead, in what was to be his last game for United. To summarise, he probably didn't receive any Christmas cards from referees.

This is too negative. Let's mention some of Ward's plus points. Yes, he did talk nineteen to the dozen, but he knew what he was talking about, and Leivers trusted him as a coach and as a scout – an ideal lieutenant in fact. As a player Ward was underestimated at United, being sharp around the box. Dai used to say that if there was a picture of the opposition goalkeeper collecting the ball and he wasn't on the photograph, then he'd want to know what had gone wrong.

He was appointed United's youth team manager at the end of the 1967-68 season, but didn't stay long. He went to Kettering Town and Cambridge City, also as a coach, finally putting away his coaching manual in April 1974. He passed away in January 1996.

Magic Moment: *Ward's manager at Watford was Bill McGarry, who was strict with the press. After the* Watford Observer *ran an interview with Ward, McGarry rang the sports editor, demanding to know why he'd done so without his permission. The editor said: 'Bill, he was no longer your player when I spoke to him. You had sold him!'*

Worst Nightmare: *In one of Ward's disciplinary hearings at Lancaster Gate, he made excuses for his lapses. His accuser pulled out Dai's record, listing 47 bookings on two pages and started reading from it. When he reached the part where he had been booked at Warwick, Dai snapped: 'Warwick! I've never played at bloody Warwick!"*

CAMBRIDGE RECORD	Appearances	Goals
Southern League	36 (+8)	19
FA Cup	unknown	3

No 36. **IAN HUTCHINSON**

Debut: v Wellington, 10 February 1968
Farewell: v Cambridge City, 15 May 1968

It was Dai Ward who was sent to Burton Albion to cast his eye over Ian Hutchinson. If Ward's Cambridge career had been brief, then Ian's was by far the shortest of anyone else's in this book. He can't be ignored though. Discerning fans knew they were watching somebody special and he went on to become the first ex-United player to turn himself into a household name.

Ian Hutchinson was born in Derby on 4 August 1948, but he first made a breakthrough playing for Burton Albion, just over ten miles up the road. His performances for the Brewers tickled the antennae of Bill Leivers and the Cambridge manager sent his trusted general Dai Ward off to check him out.

The problem for Ward was that lowly Burton were playing Chelmsford City, who were gunning for the championship. In a bid to try to pin down the Essex side's prolific attack, Burton played with a decidedly defensive strategy that meant Ian was all on his own up front. Almost inevitably he barely had a kick the whole game and all Ward could say to Leivers was that the teenage lad had never stopped searching for the elusive ball the whole game. Ward still reckoned Ian could 'do the business' for United, and his recommendation was good enough for Leivers, who had himself only seen Ian play half a game.

Although impoverished Burton wanted to sell him, Ian's parents were dubious that he would be any better off at Cambridge. He had just started out as an apprentice gas fitter and they didn't want him to end up unemployed if he didn't make it as a professional at Cambridge. In order to convince them, Bill fixed him up with a job at the gasworks in Newmarket Road and paid him £25 per week – five times what hard-up Burton could afford. The only condition that Burton put upon the deal was that Hutchinson wasn't allowed to play against them – they knew what damage he could do.

After the deal was done, Bill bumped into Stan Matthews in the urinals at Burton. Matthews was keen on signing Ian for his Port Vale side and asked Leivers for his opinion on the player, unaware that the ink was now dry on Ian's contract. Leivers rather wickedly kept Matthews in the dark about this new development and his wasted journey. Another interested party was Frank Blunstone – Chelsea's youth coach. He went to see Ian play at Corby and witnessed Ian selling a defender such an outrageous dummy that the poor guy ended up breaking a leg as he fell in a confused heap. To add insult to his painful injury, Ian scored.

Ian was a lovely lad, though the other players couldn't help but pull his leg. Goalkeeper Rodney Slack decided to aid his gas fitting career by offering him some valuable tools, but only if he promised to take special care of the precious objects. Joker Slack barely managed to keep a straight face as Ian looked bemusedly through the bag of tools, which consisted of the rustiest set of implements Slack could find.

Hutchinson was a gangly youth, running with his elbows sticking out at right-angles and it always appeared that the ball wasn't under control and he was in imminent danger of losing possession, though he invariably managed to keep hold of it. Despite his appearance, he was in fact exceptionally strong, with skill and control to match, combined with a deadly finish. Word soon got around about his ability and soon every United game was swelled with a large contingent of visiting scouts.

Ian signed for Chelsea in July 1968 for £14,500 – a seven-fold increase in his value in just five months. Though excited about his new move, he was upset about leaving the Abbey and not long afterwards even considered going back to Cambridge. Leivers watched Chelsea play Coventry City, where Peter Osgood was hogging the ball and not passing to the better-placed Hutch. Leivers told Ian to give Osgood a rollicking the next time it happened, but Ian said 'I can't do that'.

He made an immediate impact at Stamford Bridge and in 1969-70 scored 22 goals in only 36 appearances, a record only bettered by his partner Osgood. The highlight of that season was the FA Cup final of 1970, which was played on a pitch that had been ploughed up by the Horse of the Year Show. Ian headed the vital equaliser that led to a replay at Old Trafford. Watched by a record TV audience of 32 million, the match degenerated into the dirtiest final ever, with fighting breaking out all over the pitch, uncontrolled by the ineffectual referee. When top official David Elleray watched a video replay, he stated that three from each side should have been sent off, which didn't include Ian. In actual fact, the original ref sent no one off and only booked one player, and that was Ian who had got into a fist-fight with Norman Hunter. After a typically violent Leeds first half, Chelsea had emerged into the second with the intention of kicking everything above the grass, according to one observer. Ian made a peaceful contribution by sending over one of his long throws that resulted in David Webb bundling in the winner.

Ian never fulfilled his true potential at Chelsea, hampered by a string of injuries. Leivers had warned him that he was too brave for his own good and he needed to guard himself against the hatchet men that seemed to be liberally sprinkled round every First Division side in those days. In his eight seasons at the Bridge, Ian only managed 119 League games (but scored 44 goals). The damage done by these injuries was compounded by the ignorant use of painkillers, which masked his discomfort and allowed Ian to play on and cripple himself even more. In 2002 the PFA paid for a hip replacement for him, but he was also badly hampered by diabetes. On a personal level, some feel that he fell into the wrong crowd at Chelsea and got dragged into a wilder lifestyle than was sensible – he was still only in his early twenties. His paltry England career consisted of just two Under-23 caps.

The famous long throw was first noticed in training with Cambridge on Coldham's Common, but it came to national prominence on Match of the Day in October 1968, when Ipswich's Billy Baxter headed a Hutchinson special into his own net. A Watford professor was intrigued enough to want to take X-rays of a naked Ian throwing the ball in an aircraft hanger. An embarrassed Ian only agreed to this when the professor got rid of his six watching female assistants. It turned out that Ian had an extended spine and double-jointed shoulders, which explained the 'Windmill Action' when taking throws – i.e. the arms kept revolving instead of going outwards. In the 1970 Cup final an incredulous Kenneth Wolstenholme commentated: 'It's not a throw, it's a free-kick.'

Leivers unsuccessfully tried to bring Hutchinson back to the Abbey on loan in March 1974, but soon afterwards Ian had to quit playing (long before his 30th birthday). He ran a pub in Windsor with Peter Osgood for a while, but although it must have been a lively hostelry, it proved to be unsuccessful. Ian helped out in Chelsea's marketing office, but sadly passed away in September 2002, aged 54.

Magic Moment: *As part of the deal that took Hutchinson to Chelsea, United inserted a clause which stated the Blues would play a friendly at the Abbey. They did so immediately after winning the Cup, enticing the Abbey's highest ever gate of 14,000.*

Worst Nightmare: *In the second leg of the Cambs Professional Cup final in May 1968 against Cambridge City, Hutchinson seemed to have scored the the deciding goal, but the referee ruled it offside. United players protested vehemently and fights broke out between United and City players, which spread to the crowd. The game was abandoned.*

CAMBRIDGE RECORD	Appearances	Goals
Southern League	16	6
FA Cup	—	—

No 37. **DENNIS WALKER**

Debut: v Poole Town, 10 August 1968
Farewell: v Mansfield, 30 August 1972

Hutchinson's United career had been so brief that our next subject never got to play alongside him. Dennis Walker hung around longer and was one of the myriad of players that earned two Southern League championship medals with United, and steered them safely into Football League stability.

Dennis Alan Walker was born in Northwich on 26 October 1944 and will go down in the record books as the first coloured player to appear for just about every one of the clubs that he played for. He was a precocious youngster, captaining Cheshire schoolboys and playing in two international trials, and this brought him to the attention of Manchester United in March 1960. The Red Devils were still rebuilding their side after the horrors of the Munich air crash just two years previously and once more Matt Busby put faith in their excellent youth system that had provided so many riches previously. Dennis progressed well and signed professional terms in November 1961.

Eighteen months of youth and reserve teams later, and Dennis was ready to make his first-team debut. He appeared in the final League game of the 1962-63 season, in place of Bobby Charlton, who was being rested for the FA Cup final five days later. With most players' minds wandering elsewhere, the League game was lost 2-3 to Nottingham Forest.

The end of the season is the worst time to make your debut, as by the time the new season rolls around, your performance has probably been forgotten about. Also, of course, having a wealth of talent ahead of him compounded Walker's problems at Manchester United. I mean, just how do you displace a fit Bobby Charlton from the side? Dennis took the only course of action open to him and dropped down three divisions to join York City in April 1964.

This time his end of season appearances weren't overlooked and he created a sensation at Bootham Crescent by scoring twelve goals in the first fourteen League games of the following season in an attacking role. Unsurprisingly, with that kind of start York were able to win promotion out of the Fourth. In the following years, that momentum was lost and Dennis was switched to left-half as York tumbled down from the Third Division and into the ignominious position of having to apply to the other clubs' chairman to maintain their League status via the re-election system.

York's problems provided opportunities for Bill Leivers to recruit another experienced League player into his Southern League escape committee. Walker joined in July 1968 and became the first coloured player to play for Cambridge, though that didn't seem to cause him any undue problems in those less-enlightened times. He was originally signed as a wing-half, but his adaptability led to him ending up as a utility player.

His Old Trafford pedigree had made him a classy player and he reminded some of his old Manchester United colleague, Pat Crerand. He was highly valued for his ability to find any available space on the pitch with a probing pass and was obviously highly skilled, although somewhat slow and lethargic. This manifested itself in a reluctance to tackle, but these were minor criticisms compared to his many virtues. Although not tall, Walker was a good header of the ball and a great reader of the game. Quite possibly he found it hard to start at the top and then work his way down, which is the opposite of the way in which a footballing career should develop.

Walker left Fourth Division Cambridge in October 1972 to rejoin the Southern League with Poole Town for £1,600, but Poole were relegated that season. He went on to become their player-manager until July 1975, when he moved to South Africa. He later returned to England and was a manager at the Arndale Centre in Manchester.

Magic Moment: *For Walker, what could be more magical in 1963 than playing for Manchester United, even in a dull end of season game ahead of the Cup final?*

Worst Nightmare: *Walker was manager of Manchester's Arndale Centre when the IRA bombed it – a worse horror than anything that can take place on a football pitch.*

CAMBRIDGE RECORD	Appearances	Goals
Southern League	70 (+1)	6
Football League	48 (+8)	4
FA Cup	unknown	2
League Cup	3	–

No 38. **BILL CASSIDY**
Debut: v Yeovil, 26 October 1968
Farewell: v Hartlepool, 1 May 1971

Bill Cassidy was another player who had a varied footballing career.

William Pitt Cassidy was born in Hamilton, Scotland on 4 October 1940 and was on the books of Rangers, though he never appeared for their first team. Rotherham United signed him in August 1961 and he played for

them for fifteen months, scoring just once. He moved to Brighton in
November 1962 for £6,000 and in five seasons racked up a century of
League games with 25 goals to go with them. He was initially a left-half,
but because of his big frame and hard-running characteristics, he was used
in a variety of positions at the Goldstone Ground. His goals helped
Brighton to the Fourth Division championship in 1964-65, but in July 1967
he moved to Chelmsford, where he helped them to the Southern League
title at the end of the season.

Cassidy then became one of the pioneers of American soccer when he
joined the Detroit Cougars during the summer of 1968. He came back to
Blighty during the autumn of 1968 with the intention of rejoining Chelmsford City, and he was actually living in a house belonging to one of their
directors when Leivers paid him a visit. Leivers said: 'Get in your car and
follow me.' Bill replied: 'but I'm signing for . . .' Leivers interjected: 'No
you're not, you're signing for me.' At the United manager's insistence, Bill
meekly followed Leivers and signed a contract.

Bill's incredible versatility had meant he was originally a right-back at
Chelmsford, before being switched to inside-forward, then to centre-forward. It was as a striker that Leivers signed him, and it proved to be a wise
decision. Bill always had this innate belief that he was going to score and
his supreme confidence spread throughout the team. Despite only being of
average height, he was a good header of the ball, being able to place it
accurately as well as using power. He was a good, clean hitter of the ball
when using his feet as well, though he had no pace whatsoever. He was
also a tough man, and goalkeeper Rodney Slack remembers getting a good
kicking from him when Bill was at Chelmsford. Cassidy was top scorer in
United's first championship season, with 26 in league and cup, and he bettered that total in the last Southern League campaign in 1969-70, helped
by a devastating four-goal haul against Wellingborough Town in an FA
Cup qualifier, each one celebrated wildly.

Bill was the life and soul of the dressing room, always joking and laugh-
ing, a trait that was not always appreciated on the pitch, where he tended
to be very cheeky to referees. The supporters adored him, but unfortunately he had a weakness for alcohol. Most of the players were merely
social drinkers, but Bill was liable to take it too far sometimes, such as the
occasion when he was found drunk in the local cemetery after telling
everybody he was nipping out to buy a bottle of Lucozade.

Cassidy's lack of pace was more cruelly exposed in the League and he
returned to the Southern League at the start of the 1971-72 season, when
he joined Ron Atkinson's Kettering Town. With his astonishing track
record for collecting championship medals wherever he went, it was no
surprise that he added another one (Division One North) to the collection.

Cassidy later joined Ramsgate, and then had a spell as Ross County's player-manager. When that ended, Bill was left without the excitement and camaraderie of football to fill his life and he found it harder than most to cope with the outside world. In 1982 he became seriously ill and fell upon hard times, which included a spell in prison. He died in 1995. A tragic end to someone who spread so much joy throughout so many clubs.

Magic Moment: *On a trip to Germany, Cassidy got hold of a novelty laughing-bag. He hid it in a train compartment where it puzzled the travelling German public, who couldn't understand this strange noise or why the crazy Englishmen found it funny.*

Worst Nightmare: *Cassidy spent too long in the pub once and returned home to find his dinner on the front doorstep, with knife and fork neatly laid out alongside it.*

CAMBRIDGE RECORD	Appearances		Goals
Southern League	69	(+1)	33
Football League	27	(+5)	6
FA Cup	unknown		8

No 39. **JIMMY THOMPSON**
Debut: v Margate, 18 January 1969
Farewell: v Mansfield, 28 April 1973

All of the players that Bill Leivers recruited for the final assault on Football League membership seemed to be clapped out by the time Cambridge United had reached the Third Division in 1973. That was basically because Leivers went for experience – men who already knew what League football was all about.

Born in Felling (just outside Newcastle) on 7 January 1943, Thompson was christened with the delightful names of James Butters. He went to school with Howard Kendall, Colin Todd and Colin Suggett, so his footballing pedigree began at an early age. Grimsby Town signed him from St Mary's Boys Club, Newcastle, in September 1961, Jimmy being in the fortunate position of his parents knowing the scout and having a relation – Clarrie Williams – already at the club.

Thompson took over from the Irish international right-back Don Donovan, who taught Jimmy all the tricks of the trade, including how to bodycheck opponents using your arm. Indeed, they used to say of Donovan, that if he broke his arm he'd be finished. Jimmy's first three games came against Sunderland, Newcastle and Chelsea – a baptism of fire indeed. He also played with Graham Taylor. The highlight of his time at Grimsby was playing in a League Cup quarter-final tie with West Ham in

1965-66. Grimsby got a 2-2 draw at Blundell Park and were 0-0 in the final minute at Upton Park when the linesman signalled handball. Everybody stopped except for Geoff Hurst, who put the ball into the net. The referee gave the goal. Jimmy played over 150 League games for the Mariners, spread over five seasons. Leivers tried to sign him whilst he was there, but Jimmy decided to go over to South Africa instead, near to where his father was.

Jimmy played for Port Elizabeth alongside the future QPR legend Terry Mancini, working in a motor factory when the club went part-time. They won the championship and Jimmy recalls how they deliberately went to the Black section of the ground to parade the trophy before they went to the Whites. Jimmy hated the apartheid system and it was his major reservation about playing there.

Leivers did eventually get his man and Jimmy made his debut in January 1969, midway through United's first Southern League championship season. 'The sort of player who would die for you,' says Leivers. If you ran through him, he'd barely notice: if you kicked the ball in his face he wouldn't bat an eyelid. Jimmy was brought up to wear cuts and bruises like medals and he was regarded as the hit man in the team if anyone needed sorting out. Not that Thompson was just a clogger. He had boundless energy and was a fast right-back who liked to pass the ball to his winger, rather than hoof it. Indeed, his whole game was based on the belief that if the right-winger had a good game, then so had he. He was a serious player and was dedicated to keeping the ball from going in the net. If his team lost he would be morose. He was regarded as the sort of person you could know for years and yet never really know. He was very strung-up and couldn't relax for thinking about any mistakes he may have made. Not surprisingly, this attitude was storing up problems, coupled with the fact that he was burnt out from playing almost every game in every season. One day he came up to Leivers and said: 'Boss, I've forgotten how to kick the ball.' Leivers told him not to be so daft and put a ball in front of him and told him to kick it into the empty net, which he did. The manager recognised the symptoms of a nervous breakdown, though, and Jimmy was rested from the team, whilst the problem of getting him to relax was addressed. In the end, he went with the team on a tour of Cyprus as a non-playing addition, but it still took the combined efforts of the team to get him to take it easy.

Jimmy's last game for Cambridge came in the promotion decider against Mansfield that took them into the Third Division in April 1973. Jimmy had been plagued with injuries, made worse by the (stupid) old football philosophy that 'lions and tigers never go to the doctors with broken legs – they just run it off.' This time Jimmy couldn't do it, so he retired.

He didn't fancy coaching, so he ran the 'Spot The Ball' promotion in the United office for a while, before moving back up to Grimsby. He worked in a variety of jobs in the area and is now happily retired.

Magic Moment: *Even in training runs alongside the River Cam, Thompson was determined to win. Anybody ahead of him was liable to be pushed into the water.*

Worst Nightmare: *Whilst in South Africa, Thompson's club called in a witch doctor, who advised them to bury a cow in the goalmouth to stop the opposition scoring. He failed to realise that it would only stop them till half-time, when the teams switched ends.*

CAMBRIDGE RECORD	Appearances		Goals
Southern League	55	(+2)	–
Football League	117	(+1)	–
FA Cup	5+		–
League Cup	2		–

No 58. Jim Hall (far right)

No 57. Jamie Murray

No 59. Floyd Streete

No 60. Sammy Morgan

No 61. Lindsay Smith

No 62. Derrick Christie

No 63. Chris Turner, with his arm up

Chapter Five

Leivers' Leaguers

No 40. **TERRY EADES**
Debut: v Bedford Town, 31 March 1969
Farewell: v Stockport, 6 May 1977

Although Jimmy Thompson fitted into Leivers' philosophy of being an experienced ex-League pro who was finished in the early 1970s, there had to be an exception to the rule, and that was Terry Eades. He hadn't played a League game prior to joining United and was young enough to be the only player in United's first League game in August 1970 to still be around when Ron Atkinson's side won the Fourth Division title in 1976-77.

Terence Gerald Eades was born in Bambridge, Northern Ireland on 5 March 1944, but his family left in 1948 to move to Chelmsford. Like Jimmy Thompson, Eades also had a few famous future pupils at his school, namely Geoff Hurst of West Ham and England (Terry once did an action replay of Hurst's controversial World Cup goal at Cambridge that wasn't given), and Tony Butcher of Chelmsford and Cambridge (the record Southern League goalscorer of all time).

Terry joined Chelmsford City in 1962 as a central defender, becoming one of the Essex side's first young professionals. City were one of the top sides in the Southern League throughout the 1960s and therefore great rivals to the U's. City finished in the top half every season whilst Terry was there, finishing as runners-up twice, and champions in 1967-68. Like Cambridge, they harboured ambitions of joining the League, but they upset one or two League chairman by poaching players, and the bosses exacted revenge by not voting for them when the annual re-election meetings came around. Chelmsford decided to revert to becoming part-timers and Cambridge took advantage by signing three of their best players – Tony Butcher, Bill Cassidy, and Terry Eades.

Terry arrived in March 1969 and became one of the final links in the chain that took United into the League. He was a solid player, as strong a man as you could ever see. Once on the ball, there was no one who could shove him aside. He was also one of the most skilful central defenders to have appeared for the U's. A fine header and tackler, Terry also showed skill on the ball after he had won it. He wasn't a dirty player either, which ties in with his quiet, placid character. Eades had a slight weakness in dealing with balls from the flanks, but anything coming straight towards him was easy meat. He was consistent, and was United's record appearance maker in the League until his successor, Steve Fallon, overtook his total in the early 1980s. When the teenage Fallon joined Cambridge at the end of 1974, Terry's natural Mr Nice Guy persona shone through. He made the youngster feel welcome and helped him with his game, even though his place was now under threat. Terry's pleasant personality was reflected in his looks, which weren't fearsome like those of many central defenders. He was tall, athletic, with a mass of dark hair that clashed with the unfashionable short haircuts worn by his Southern League colleagues, but blended in nicely with the longer hairstyles of the mid-1970s.

In September 1976 Eades had a brief loan spell with Watford after having been effectively replaced by Dave Stringer. He also had the chance to move to Huddersfield or Scunthorpe, but didn't want to uproot his young family. Eades played part-time in United's reserves for a season, then returned to Chelmsford for a while, which only confirmed the old adage that you should never go back. He then moved to Histon Town, eventually becoming player-manager.

Terry had prepared for his retirement from football by retaking his 'O' and 'A' levels, and winning a place at teacher training college, but the level of grant was insufficient to support his family. Instead he became a salesman for a Mercedes-Benz dealership. Like so many footballers, he is a keen golfer, but unlike most he was good enough to represent his county (his handicap being five at one stage). In April 1980 a crowd of 3,660 turned up for his Cambridge testimonial with Ron Atkinson's West Bromwich.

Magic Moment: *In May 1970 Eades won his third consecutive Southern League championship medal. His first was at Chelmsford and the last two at Cambridge.*

Worst Nightmare: *Eades' gentle image took a turn for the worse in September 1975 when he had a punch-up with Exeter's Lammie Robertson. Both were sent off.*

CAMBRIDGE RECORD	Appearances		Goals
Southern League	38	(+5)	2
Football League	248		5
FA Cup	15+		1
League Cup	9		—

No 41. **GEORGE HARRIS**
Debut v Nuneaton Borough, 25 October 1969
Farewell: v Exeter City, 22 January 1972

The last player in this list to have debuted at Cambridge in the Southern League was George Alfred Harris, born in Lambeth on 10 June 1940.

George played for South London schoolboys and twice for the combined London schoolboys team. He had spells as an amateur with Spurs, Chelsea and Woking, and was on Woking's books when he signed for Newport County in July 1961. Though scoring a hat-trick against Bristol City in October 1961, he was unable to prevent them finishing twelve points adrift at the foot of the Third Division at season's end. Harris was acquired by Watford in April 1962 for £2,000 and in five seasons with the Hornets he cracked in an impressive 55 goals from 163 League games from the outside-left position. His astonishing heading ability really came to prominence with Watford, and this was a major factor in his remarkable goals tally for a non-striker.

Incredibly, Harris did even better at Reading, where he moved in July 1966 and where he managed one more goal from 27 fewer games. In 1966-67 he was Reading's Player of the Year, but by the end of the 1960s he was seemingly coming to the end of his League career.

He signed for Cambridge in October 1969 for £3,000. It took a lot of persuading to get George to drop into non-League football once more, but Leivers is glad he did because he rates him as one of his very best signings. Even so, George refused to uproot from Reading and commuted the 87 miles to Cambridge each day. Even in those pre-M11 and M25 times (or perhaps because of it) George never missed a day, nor was he late. He came to Cambridge with his pal Colin Meldrum (the scorer of United's first ever League goal). The two of them had played together at both Watford and Reading before carrying on the tradition at the Abbey.

Even though he missed the first eleven games of that final Southern League season, Harris created a sensation by cracking in an incredible 35 league and cup goals that season. The tally was particularly remarkable because by this time George was playing on the left wing. He immediately won over the fans by the useful ploy of scoring a hat-trick on his debut, and from that moment it was more a question of 'how many' had he scored, rather than 'if' he had. His secret to success was blinding pace, to skin the fastest of right-backs, combined with clinical finishing to ensure that he didn't need to cross the ball to provide the U's with a goal. His other gift, to which I have already alluded, was in the air. Although George was only 5ft 9in, his dynamic physique and textbook technique meant he ranks in Leivers' eyes as 'the best aerial player I've seen at any level'. As Leivers was a regular with top division Manchester City in the 1950s, that is high praise indeed. Harris is far and away the most proficient master of this art amongst wingers, as it is not a gift you expect touchline-huggers to possess. This skill in the air meant that his opposite number on the right could hit deep crosses with confidence, knowing that if the regular strikers missed the ball, George would be stealing in at the far post to bury it.

Leivers had an arrangement with his players that, when the time came for them to call it a day, he would have a quiet word in their ear to avoid animosity. George was in his early 30s and had started to lose pace and finishing ability due to numerous injuries when Leivers whispered in George's ear that perhaps it was time he left. George went without a murmur – he agreed with the boss.

He moved to Colin Meldrum's Hillingdon Borough in July 1972, and helped them to the Southern League Cup final the following season. He went to Wokingham Town as player-coach in June 1974, later becoming player-manager. He was also manager with Maidenhead United for two years until June 1977.

George became a painter and decorator in Reading. Presumably his finishing was just as good as it always was.

Magic Moment: *Boring trips to away games were considerably enlivened by Harris's guitar. Though perhaps not of the same calibre as his Beatle namesake (almost), it must be with some regret that the team never got round to making a record together (I think).*

Worst Nightmare: *Harris's last game at the Abbey was marked by him letting rip with a scorching volley, only to have a linesman rule it offside. It would have been his 131st League goal – an outstanding total for a non-striker.*

CAMBRIDGE RECORD	Appearances		Goals
Southern League	27	(+1)	23
Football League	33	(+2)	11
FA Cup	+		1
League Cup	1		–

No 42. **TREVOR ROBERTS**
Debut: v Lincoln, 15 August 1970
Farewell: v Southport, 8 January 1972

The only player Leivers brought in at the start of United's League odyssey was Trevor Roberts, whose story is the saddest one in this book.

Trevor Edwin Roberts was born in Bangor, North Wales on 25 February 1942. He was definitely smarter than the average footballer. He qualified as a teacher and taught geography. Clever Trevor certainly had no difficulty in finding his way around penalty areas, because he progressed from playing in goal for Liverpool University, winning a Welsh amateur cap, and then signing for Liverpool Football Club in June 1963.

Trevor's arrival coincided with Liverpool's return as a First Division force. Bill Shankly had rescued them from seven years of Second Division obscurity and in Roberts' first season at Anfield they won their first League championship for seventeen years. Not that Trevor was seriously in contention for a first-team place, because his way was barred by the formidable presence of Scottish international Tommy Lawrence. Trevor did well enough to make the reserve side, but it was obvious he was going to have to drop down the divisions to play big boys football.

Alvan Williams was manager of Southend United in January 1966 and he brought his fellow Welshman to Roots Hall. Trevor's presence wasn't enough to keep Southend in the Third Division, and in just under five seasons in Essex he was part of a side that were then frustrated in their quest for a first-ever promotion (Southend had only qualified for Division Three by finishing in the top half of the Southern section in 1957-58). Roberts' final season was a poor one though, as he lost his place to Brian Lloyd, who was another Welshman.

Bill Leivers didn't think that Cambridge United keeper Rodney Slack was good enough for League football, so he signed Trevor as his replacement. Unlike Slack, Trevor was a big lad, blessed with a fantastic physique for a keeper. He was superb at taking crosses and brave enough to go boldly into any situation. On one occasion he challenged two Gillingham players for a cross and got a broken nose and two black eyes for his trouble. Another time, at Workington, he put on a fantastic display, but the only accolade he received was being attacked by the Cumbrian crowd near the tunnel at the end of the game. Whereas Slack had been unconventional in just about every department, Trevor was every fan's identikit image of a good all-round keeper.

In September 1970, just eight games into his United career; he got permission to teach at a school in the afternoons. They gave him a routine medical, but found something amiss in one of his lungs. He had two operations to remove a suspicious growth, which resulted in him losing an eighth of one of his lungs. He seemed as right as rain afterwards and was able to make a comeback to training the day after he was discharged from hospital. He amazed everybody by his uncomplaining attitude and insisted that there was to be no special favours for him. He wasn't mollycoddled in any way and took part in all the training, and the hope was that he would make a full recovery. He returned to the first team in April 1971 and made 31 further appearances before, in January 1972, his performances started to suffer. It was the first signs of the return of the disease, which turned out be lung cancer.

The cancer came back with a vengeance, spread to his brain and his condition deteriorated rapidly. Whereas before he had been a huge, solid physical specimen, he became gaunt and it was a desperately sad sight to see him waste away so quickly. He had tried to keep the cancer secret from his parents, but when the *News of the World* ran a feature on it, he was forced to tell them. Leivers signed him a new contract to keep his spirits up, but there was no hope that he could ever fulfil it. Roberts' tale sent shock-waves round a footballing world that was used to hearing mere broken limbs as a tragedy. He went on Welsh television with his story and a testimonial was quickly arranged against Ron Greenwood's West Ham, who were keen to help. A combined Cambridge and Southend side beat the Hammers 3-2 on 8 May 1972 in front of a crowd of 6,309. Trevor turned up, though he was too ill to play, but a photograph of him in the dressing room still shows him breaking out into a cheeky smile, despite his pitiful state. Trevor passed away in Cambridge less than a month later on 2 June 1972. He was only 30 years old.

Magic Moment: *Roberts' return to the Abbey after surgery came in a massive game against Notts County, who needed a win to clinch promotion. Though beaten by a scorching Tony Hateley header in the first half, Roberts helped United win 2-1.*

Worst Nightmare: *What else could it be, but the realisation that Roberts' cancer was terminal? His brave handling of the situation won him huge respect and guaranteed more tears amongst Cambridge United fans than any other event before or since.*

CAMBRIDGE RECORD	Appearances	Goals
Football League	36	–
FA Cup	2	–
League Cup	2	–

No. 43 **PETER VASPER**

Debut: v Hartlepool, 26 September 1970
Farewell: v Plymouth, 1 May 1974

The keeper who was brought to the Abbey to replace Trevor Roberts after he first took ill was Peter John Vasper.

Peter hailed from Bromley and was born on 3 September 1945, in the immediate aftermath of World War Two. He was on Orient's books in 1963, but he never got a game. After dropping down to Southern League Guildford, one of United's great rivals at the time, he joined Norwich City in February 1968. There can be few more frustrating things in football than a goalkeeper who is understudy to a consistent and injury-free keeper. Peter was stuck behind the fixed presence of Kevin Keelan and did well to play 31 League games in his three seasons. In September 1970 Peter was brought to Cambridge when Trevor Roberts was laid low with the mystery chest complaint that tragically turned out to be lung cancer. Vasper played whenever Roberts was unable to, and after his death took over the goal-keeping jersey full-time, the worst possible way to regain your place.

At six feet, Vasper was almost as tall as Roberts, but his blond hair topped a slimmer frame, and there was a passing resemblance to Bob Wilson. Vasper didn't have the gung-ho attitude of Roberts, but was more cautious and calculating, relying on his expert positional sense to rescue the day. Although generally consistent, it must be said that when he did make a mistake it tended to be an absolute howler, usually as a result of misjudging the flight or bounce of the ball. Unusually for a goalie (at least in those days), he was a neat header of the ball and he occasionally abandoned his natural caution to try his luck in attack for the last corner of a struggling game, though he regrettably never managed to score a goal.

Vasper kept the No 1 shirt in the promotion side of 1972-73, despite competition from Graham Smith, and was ever present in Cambridge's first foray into the Third Division. Although that campaign ended unhappily for the U's, with relegation and 81 League goals conceded, the fans recognised that Peter hadn't let them down and graciously voted him their Player of the Year. He was then released by Leivers, with Smith finally easing him out, and he dropped into non-League football with Dartford.

Peter later moved back into the Cambridge area and had spells with St Ives, Saffron Walden and St Ives again. He moved to Birmingham and worked for an insurance company alongside another Abbey favourite at the time – Dave Simmons.

Magic Moment: *In October 1973 Cambridge featured on Match of the Day against fellow new boys Hereford United. Though the outfield players did little to keep the viewers awake, Vasper kept a clean sheet in front of his biggest audience.*

Worst Nightmare: *In November 1973 Vasper conceded an early goal against fellow strugglers Aldershot. Dazzled by the sun, he let Jack Howarth's cross float in.*

CAMBRIDGE RECORD	Appearances	Goals
Football League	136	–
FA Cup	8	–
League Cup	4	–

No 44. **VIC AKERS**
Debut: v Chester, 14 August 1971
Farewell: v Newport, 15 November 1974

If goalkeeper Peter Vasper looked to his left, he would usually spot the medium frame of Victor David Akers (born in Islington on 24 August

1946), whose head was surmounted with a snazzy shoulder-length hairstyle that was prevalent amongst the younger players in the early 1970s.

Bill Leivers had been seeking a left-back to strengthen his squad, when Luton's Harry Haslam tipped him the wink that there was a useful chap at Bexley United. Leivers went along to see them playing at Cheltenham and was impressed with the high degree of ball control and passing ability that Akers displayed, despite the rock-hard, bumpy pitch. In July 1971 Leivers bought him to Cambridge for the gratifyingly low sum of £500.

United effectively gained two 25-year-old players. On the one hand they had a steady, solid player, who made sure that a minimum number of mistakes would be made on his corner of the pitch, but they also acquired a frustrated striker. Akers demonstrated this on his debut against Chester, by delicately chipping in a last-minute equaliser, and later that month by cracking in a 35-yard screamer against Southport. With this keenness to get forward and supply the attack, whilst keeping a sharp guard at the back, it's no wonder that United only lost nine League games in 1972-73 to secure promotion. Leivers did permit Akers to play as a striker in the last game of the 1973-74 season, and he demonstrated his usefulness in that position by knocking in a couple of goals. He really was a clean striker of the ball.

Vic went to Tooting and Mitcham United in 1974-75, but with only nineteen appearances and six goals he never featured in any of their famous giantkillings. He jumped back into the League with Mike Keen's Watford in July 1975, but only played half a season as they dropped into the Fourth Division.

Akers went to Arsenal, originally as Community Liaison Officer, but then took over duties as the team's kit man and Ladies Team manager. When he started coaching the Ladies in 1987, it was something of a joke to most Gunners' fans, but over time they have been given a far greater prominence at Arsenal and they are now a source of much pride at Highbury. Vic became the first salaried manager in women's football (at one stage he was in charge of four teams), and they are now the most powerful Ladies team in the country. Vic is a regular recipient of awards and is the Sir Alex Ferguson of Ladies football (or should I say the Arsene Wenger?).

Magic Moment: *In the 1992-93 season, Akers led his Arsenal ladies to the treble of Premier League, League Cup and WFA Cup.*

Worst Nightmare: *Akers was virtually frozen out in his final season at United, with Ray Seary relegating his more experienced colleague to the reserves, with the odd game on the bench to relieve the frustration. Akers' last appearance came wearing the No 10 shirt, but he gave a disappointing display.*

CAMBRIDGE RECORD	Appearances		Goals
Football League	122	(+7)	5
FA Cup	8		–
League Cup	5		–

No 45. **BRIAN GREENHALGH**

Debut: v Chester, 14 August 1971
Farewell: v Rochdale, 5 February 1974

Akers' striking ambitions were thwarted by the presence of Brian Arthur Greenhalgh, who was United's first goalscoring superstar as far as the Football League is concerned. With his long, flowing light-brown hair, he had the appearance of one, too, though at Huddersfield he looked more like a Beatle.

Brian was born in Chesterfield on 20 February 1947, but was brought up on the Lancashire coast at Southport. He joined Preston as an apprentice, signing full terms in February 1965. He made his first-team debut ten months later and went on to score nine goals in nineteen League games. In September 1967 he moved to Aston Villa, along with Brian Godfrey, for a combined fee of £35,000. He scored twelve times in 40 games for a crumbling Villa side, but couldn't get on with the abrasive and unhelpful Tommy Docherty and moved to Leicester in February 1969 for £15,000 as cover for Allan Clarke.

Greenhalgh's time with Leicester was an unmitigated disaster. The Foxes were struggling to hold onto their First Division status and his debut for them sums up his time there. He came on as substitute in a tight game against bitter rivals Coventry and was upended in the box for a penalty. The referee then reversed his decision, awarded Coventry a free-kick, from which they proceeded to race up the pitch and score the only goal. Brian's time at Leicester totalled four months, during which he played four games.

He then joined Huddersfield, also for £15,000. He played a bit part in the side that won the Second Division title in 1969-70, but fell out with manager Ian Greaves over his lack of opportunities and was on his way again. A move to his childhood favourites Bolton fell through due to a dodgy medical, but he passed the Cambridge one with no problems and arrived in July 1971 on a free transfer.

Manager Leivers was convinced that there was a fine player underneath, but nobody had managed to discover the secret of how to get him to play. Brian was a thoroughbred and thought that all other players were inferior – not in a boastful way – he just thought he was better. Leivers had a plan. He let the other players in on the secret, then, when Brian was present, he told the rest of them that they had to start playing quality balls, because you couldn't expect a thoroughbred like Brian to chase all over the park after bad balls. Brian then realised that everybody thought he was a good player, which reassured him. He also realised that he was going to have to do a bit more to get on the end of these balls. He expected perfection and wasn't prepared to work for it if it didn't happen. Against his old club, Huddersfield, everyone was amazed at how well Brian played, but Leivers replied that it was his worst game for the club. When he was on song, Brian was a racehorse amongst carthorses (no disrespect intended to his team-mates). He was a silky smooth mover and in practice he could send half a dozen players the wrong way, including the goalie. He was a wonderful fin-isher at the near post and had more ability than anyone: it was getting him to perform that was the tricky part. He hated training, telling everyone he would still do the business on Saturday.

And boy, did he perform. Brian scored four goals against Darlington in September 1971 on the way to a 19-goal haul for the season that stood as United's League record for six years. He was United's top scorer in each of his three seasons, but that underlines the problem they had – they relied on him too much. Brian's last game for Cambridge came in front of 450 spectators at Rochdale, but at least he scored. He left in February 1974. Leivers needed the cash for other buys, and Brian joined Bournemouth to replace Phil Boyer for a club record fee received of £35,000. His time there only lasted a year, including a loan spell with Torquay.

Greenhalgh wound up his League career with Watford in March 1975, but failed to score in his eleven outings for the cash-strapped club. Obviously, no other manager had learned the Leivers lesson. Brian quit professional football aged 29 to spend more time with his family, which he regretted when the club prospered with Elton John's money.

He joined Southern League Dartford (alongside Vic Akers) and then went on a lengthy journey via Bedford Town, Hillingdon Borough, Staines Town, Wealdstone, Cambridge City, Carshalton Athletic (player-coach and manager), Maidenhead United and Chesham United. He became a part-time scout for Everton and in 1990 took the job on a full-time basis and became chief scout, a position he later filled at Watford and Aston Villa. With the influx of foreigners into the game, this now necessitates lots of foreign travel – more glamorous than Staines and Wealdstone certainly.

Magic Moment: *Greenhalgh scored twice on his Division One debut for Hudders-field at Burnley. In his next away game he also found the net against a Lancashire side, a wise move when playing for a Yorkshire side. This time it was Manchester United.*

Worst Nightmare: *When United toured Portugal, Greenhalgh was asked if he had his passport. He said he had, but neglected to mention that is was packed in his case.*

CAMBRIDGE RECORD	Appearances	Goals
Football League	116	47
FA Cup	7	–
League Cup	5	1

No 46. **DAVID LILL**

Debut: v Chester, 14 August 1971
Farewell: v Barnsley, 20 December 1975

The runner-up to Greenhalgh in United's goalscoring charts in their promotion season was David Arthur Lill.

Lill was born in the seaside village of Aldbrough (near Bridlington) on
17 February 1947 and began his career with Hull City as a 14-year-old
apprentice. He graduated to full terms in March 1965 and made his debut
the following season, but only appeared in the first team occasionally as he
was stuck behind the prolific striking duo of Chris Chilton and Ken
Wagstaffe. It's hard now to imagine Hull as a big side, but when they won
the Third Division title in 1965-66 their average crowd was 35,000. Even
the reserve side, where David was usually playing, attracted gates of
around 5,000.

He moved to Rotherham in October 1969 and made 39 League appearances over two seasons, more than double what he managed with the
Tigers. David had a bust-up with manager Jimmy McAnearney and was
put on the transfer list, where he attracted the interest of McAnearney's
brother Tom at Bury. Bill Leivers also came calling, urging him not to sign
anything until he'd visited the Abbey Stadium. David agreed, more out of
politeness than expectation, but was bowled over by the smart appearance
of the newly painted ground and the friendliness of the people. He signed
for them in July 1971.

Although he was originally Greenhalgh's strike partner, Lill preferred to
think of himself as a playmaker rather than a striker. He was an enthusiastic player who was always in search of the ball, and invariably found it.
If you wanted to find David on the pitch it was no good looking at his
nominal position; instead you looked for the ball and you invariably found
him. He covered huge swathes of the pitch, running down either flank or
chasing near the penalty areas, seeking to create opportunities for others.
He had a wicked shot and was capable of giving goalkeepers nightmares
from 40 yards, but he very rarely let fly. He also seemed to have a phobia
about heading the ball, and this reluctance to grab the limelight for himself
explains his low strike-rate. Leivers believes he was capable of grabbing up
to 30 goals a season with a more selfish attitude, but his highest seasonal
tally was twelve.

After Ron Atkinson took over, David was used as a squad player, filling in at left-back for example. Not that he bears a grudge against Big Ron: indeed he counts him as a friend. Ron was diplomatic in telling David it was time to go and offered to help him find a new club. Lill left in February 1976 and ran a sports shop in Cambridge for a while, with goalkeeper Graham Smith. He joined King's Lynn, scoring one goal in 39 Southern League appearances for them, before becoming a coach at Cambridge City. He has managed local sides Somersham Town and Over with great success and still lives in the area.

Magic Moment: *Rotherham took mighty Leeds to an FA Cup replay at Elland Road in 1971. Lill's side stormed into a 2-0 lead, but Leeds roared back in ill-tempered fashion (surprise surprise) to win 3-2. Colchester sorted them out in round five.*

Worst Nightmare: *David earned the nickname of 'Lay-by Lill', because of the number of times he wanted to stop the coach to relieve himself.*

CAMBRIDGE RECORD	Appearances		Goals
Football League	166	(+6)	22
FA Cup	9		–
League Cup	6		–

No. 47. **WILLIE WATSON**
Debut: v Newport, 16 September 1972
Final Farewell: v Notts Co, 8 April 1980

The team-mate who Lill believes was blessed with a first touch as great as Kenny Dalglish's was Graham Sidney Watson (born Doncaster, 3 August 1949), but who was better known as Willie.

Bill Leivers had just been appointed to his first managerial post at Doncaster Rovers when he and his assistant Jackie Bestall were asked to cast their eyes over some Doncaster schoolboy trialists. The Rovers men stood one each side of the pitch, but they both picked out the same lad as being the most promising. Although Willie was the smallest kid on the park, he stood out for his talent and enthusiasm, which was evident because when he was substituted he left the field in tears – so desperate was he to play for Rovers. He achieved his wish and signed on schoolboy terms on his fifteenth birthday. He made his debut as a 17-year-old against Swindon and scored after only four minutes. He played around 50 games for Rovers, before moving to Rotherham in February 1968 in one of those complicated player-exchange deals. The new boss at Millmoor was Tommy Docherty who had promised his chairman he would get them out of the

Third. He did – into the Fourth! Willie rejoined Rovers in January 1969 at the behest of the youthful Lawrie McMenemy and added another century of appearances to his total, bringing his goals tally to 34 for the club. Doncaster had got off to a dreadful start in 1972-73, but once again Bill Leivers rode to the rescue and signed Willie for his poorly performing Cambridge side for the princely sum of £4,500.

Willie's signing acted as a catalyst and United immediately embarked on a club record fourteen-match unbeaten League run that took them from the re-election zone into a promotion place. United won promotion to the Third Division with a dramatic 3-2 win over Mansfield and that game gave Willie the thrill of seeing the Abbey Stadium jam-packed full, 45 minutes before kick-off. Unfortunately, the team wasn't strengthened in the 1973-74 season and Willie often found himself as the youngest player in the team at the age of 24.

Watson was slightly built at first, but gradually filled out over the years. His hair grew long and distinctive with a centre parting and a slightly receding hairline, and he occasionally frightened people with a small moustache. He was a talented midfield player with good vision and control. He wasn't a firm tackler, because he wasn't strong enough or vicious enough, but he had an ability to steal the ball off opponent's toes without them realising it. Instead, he was a creative force and the brains of the team. It was said of him that his thinking was five minutes ahead of everyone else on the pitch. This often made him look like a fool, because he tended to pass the ball to where a player should be, not where he actually was. Unthinking fans would give him stick for sloppy passing, when in fact it was the recipient's fault for not being alert to the possibility that Willie had spotted.

Although only of average height, Willie had a long stride, which is usually a bad sign in a footballer. He was a little bit lazy, which may have hampered his career, but was a player who could inspire those around him. He was also blessed with a tremendous shot – if he made up his mind that the ball was going in the net, then it would invariably end up there. He was a two-footed player and was a great crosser of the ball. He brought out the best in Alan Biley and the two formed an understanding that bordered on the telepathic. Watson believes that if Atkinson had stayed at Cambridge they may have reached the First Division, but he wasn't used much by his successor, John Docherty.

In September 1978 he joined Lincoln for £15,000, after having made just a solitary substitute's appearance in United's debut Second Division season. He played about a season's worth of games for the Imps before rejoining Cambridge in March 1980 as cover for injured players. He was glimpsed only briefly at the Abbey – as a substitute against Notts County in April 1980 – but he was a permanent fixture in reserve games for three years. It's unusual for a long-established player to enjoy playing for the 'stiffs', but Willie was proud to have helped the careers of talented young-sters like Andy Sinton and seemed happy enough.

Watson ran the Vice-President's Club and scouted for York. He ran pubs in Wilburton and Comberton and played for local sides Soham Town Rangers and Histon Town. He now works for Cambridge Glasshouses.

Magic Moment: *At the start of 1974-75, Watson was disillusioned at the Abbey. Whilst drinking with his buddy Graham Rathbone, in came Rathbone's manager at Kettering, Ron Atkinson, who asked Watson to sign for the Poppies. Willie agreed, but when he reported to the Abbey on the Monday Big Ron had been installed as manager.*

Worst Nightmare: *In his first day of training as a raw 15-year-old at Doncaster, Watson had his front tooth accidentally kicked out by his fearsome boss Bill Leivers.*

CAMBRIDGE RECORD	Appearances		Goals
Football League	206	(+4)	24
FA Cup	11		3
League Cup	12		1

No 48. **BRENDON BATSON M.B.E.**
Debut: v Chesterfield, 2 February 1974
Farewell: v Tranmere, 3 February 1978

Another player to successfully make the transition from Bill Leivers' team to Ron Atkinson's was Brendon Batson.

Brendon Martin Batson was born in Grenada in the West Indies on 6 February 1953 and his family emigrated to England when he was nine. He grew up in Walthamstow and played for Waltham Forest Schoolboys and Essex Schoolboys. His mature performances were picked up on Arsenal's antennae and he signed schoolboy forms at fourteen. Being a part of prob-ably the best youth set-up in the country at that time enabled him to make rapid progress and, after signing his apprenticeship forms at sixteen, he assisted the reserves as they won the Football Combination Cup in 1970. Batson turned professional in June 1971 at the same time as the first team were basking in the glory of just having completed the League and FA Cup double.

He made his first-team debut for the Gunners in March 1972, coming on as substitute for Charlie George in a 0-2 defeat at Newcastle. It was a momentous occasion. Every one of his colleagues that day was a house-hold name and the fact that he was the first black player to appear for Arsenal naturally attracted a plenty of attention. He made his first start for the Gunners eleven months later and was used as a squad player during injury crises. His versatility was remarkable and he started games in place of defender Peter Storey and even striker John Radford. He made a total of ten appearances, spread over three seasons, but was unable to seriously challenge for a permanent place in the first team. In order to play regular League football, he would have to drop down the divisions.

Bill Leivers had been after him for twelve months, but Arsenal had been holding out for £50,000 – too much money for careful Cambridge. A knee injury to Brendon enabled Bill to reduce the fee to a manageable £5,000 and in January 1974 Batson moved to the Abbey, bringing with him his classic mid-1970s Afro hairstyle and subtle moustache.

For a couple of years he continued in his play-anywhere role, usually wearing the No 6 shirt, but popping up all over the park, often in midfield or defence. Although a couple of inches under six feet, he could even fill in as a central defender. It wasn't until the autumn of 1976 that Ron Atkinson converted him to a right-back. At first, his frequent forays into enemy territory were inclined to leave his side exposed at the back on occasions, but once he had learned to time his forward excursions, he became probably the finest attacking right-back in United's history.

The other problem Brendon had to learn to control was his temper. He was an easy player to wind up on the pitch, which certain opponents took advantage of. He frequently got into fights and episodes of violent retaliation. In the first month of the 1974-75 season alone he had racked up three bookings. He gradually calmed down, helped no doubt by the responsibility of being made skipper in August 1976 at the age of 23.

In February 1978 Batson followed Atkinson to West Brom for £30,000 and was an integral part of the club's best ever spell. They finished in sixth place in the First Division that season, which was good enough to get them into the following season's UEFA Cup. West Brom defied expectations by marching to the quarter-finals, knocking out a Valencia side featuring two players who had come to prominence in the World Cup – Rainer Bonhof and Mario Kempes. In the League, West Brom had challenged for the title, only to finish third behind Liverpool and Nottingham Forest. Their points total of 59 was the highest ever for a team finishing third under the two-points-for-a-win system. At the Hawthorns, Brendon, Cyrille Regis and Laurie Cunningham became known as the 'Three Degrees'. More than anyone else, they probably helped to break down prejudice and racism that was much in evidence in Britain at the time.

Brendon was capped three times at England 'B' level in 1980-81 and the next season helped his club to semi-final appearances in the FA and League Cups. A knee injury against Ipswich ended his career in October 1982 after a West Brom career of 172 League games and one goal.

Brendon had been the Professional Footballers' Association (PFA) delegate at both Cambridge and West Brom, and just before his playing career came to an end had been elected onto the Management Committee. The PFA is the players' trade union and is affiliated to the Trades Union Congress. It represents the interest of the players and it has become a complex organisation with many roles. The PFA knows that three-quarters of 16-year-old footballers are out of the game by the age of 21, sometimes with little or no qualifications for jobs outside football. They provide grants and funds for training courses, not just in football coaching, but such offbeat activities as chiropody and fish farming. The Benevolent Fund provides assistance to members who have fallen on hard times and the Accident Insurance Fund aids players who have received injuries during their playing careers, for example by paying for medical treatment.

The Association has also provided wages to players with impoverished clubs. The PFA is funded by an annual subscription of £50 and were canny enough in the early 1950s to have negotiated a percentage of the television money with the Football League. It was a pittance then, but it is now a substantial sum as the recent controversy with the Premier League over the money from these rights can testify. The PFA represents the millionaire Beckhams and Owens of the Premier League and also the squad players of struggling Third Division clubs, and has to reconcile the clash of interests between the top sides and those at the bottom. Brendon was the Deputy Chief Executive of the organisation, but has since returned to West Brom as Chief Executive.

Magic Moment: *In the New Year's Honours in 2001 Batson was awarded the M.B.E. for services to football, the only ex-United player to receive such an award.*

Worst Nightmare: *Against Stockport in December 1974, Batson was sent off for punching Tony Coleman. The next season he was off again, fouling the same player.*

CAMBRIDGE RECORD	Appearances		Goals
Football League	162	(+1)	6
FA Cup	9		–
League Cup	8		–

No 49. **BOBBY SHINTON**
Debut: v Blackburn, 16 March 1974
Farewell: v Bradford C, 24 April 1976

Unlike Batson, who hit the heights, Bobby Shinton frustratingly never hit the superstardom he seemed destined for, either at United or elsewhere.

Robert Thomas Shinton entered the world on 6 January 1952 in West Bromwich. By his late teens he was working as a glazier by day, whilst playing for Lye Town in the West Midlands League in his spare time. His window of opportunity into the Football league came at the relatively advanced age of twenty when he joined Walsall, scoring on his debut against Swansea in March 1972. He partnered Chris Jones in the Saddlers' attack and was a member of the team that forced Manchester City to play two replays in the League Cup in the autumn of 1973.

Walsall were in the Third Division alongside Cambridge in 1973-74 and Shinton scored against the U's on Boxing Day 1973. That goal helped to attract the attention of Bill Leivers. He was an emergency buy in March 1974 as United desperately tried to cling onto their Third Division status. United splashed out a club record fee of £30,000, as well as a partner for him – Nigel Cassidy (£25,000 from Oxford) – some of the money coming from the sale of Brian Greenhalgh a month earlier. One disgruntled Walsall fan called it 'a rubbish piece of business [for the Saddlers].'

Shinton was virtually unique for a Leivers signing, in that he was still a youngster at 22. He certainly got himself noticed on the pitch because of his shoulder-length hair (similar to the style adopted by Alan Biley in later years) and beard, though it must be said that sprouting facial hair was a feature of several of his colleagues (e.g. Nigel Cassidy and Ray Seary). At least the players all looked different in those days and commentators' lives were much easier. It was also an improvement on Shinton's earlier Walsall days, when a frightening Kevin Keegan perm was on display.

Unfortunately, Bobby's arrival was all too late to save United that season, despite him using four Plymouth players as slalom poles before tucking the ball away in the final game of the season. Indeed, the reassembled team never had time to gel before Leivers was sacked the following season. Shinton didn't link with Nigel Cassidy at all well, but Leivers thinks they might have got it together if it wasn't for an injury to Cassidy. Just before Leivers was sacked, Shinton typified his style by bagging two great goals against Chester, whilst missing some easy ones. He comfortably finished as United's top scorer that season with sixteen goals.

Perhaps the reason for letting the easy opportunities go begging was a slightly bow-legged stance, which gave him problems shooting straight, a fact that led Leivers into calling him 'banana-foot.' It didn't hinder Bobby's close control, because defenders had a hard job to dispossess him, though he wasn't noticeably quick. He was a fierce competitor and very supple, as he had to be, for most of his goals would be celebrated with a double-somersault. Although just under six feet tall, most goals came from his feet.

Apparently Shinton didn't get on with Ron Atkinson. This prompted him to slap in a transfer request and at the end of the 1975-76 season he was sold to Wrexham for £12,000, which some U's supporters thought was a rubbish piece of business. In 1977-78 he helped Wrexham to the Third Division championship (just pipping Cambridge), and to the quarter-finals of both the League Cup and FA Cup. They also won the Welsh Cup for good measure.

After a competent, if unspectacular Second Division season, Bobby was signed to Manchester City for £300,000 in July 1979. City were managed by Malcolm Allison who, in the spirit of the times, was convinced he could buy his way to success (remember the million pound signings of Steve Daley and Kevin Reeves?). It didn't work out for Allison, or for Bobby. He only played six times for City that season, firing blanks in all of them. He did show what he was capable of in a loan spell at Millwall, when he scored three times in five games.

In March 1980 Shinton was sold to Second Division Newcastle United for £175,000 and featured in one of their worst ever sides too. In 1980-81 they only scored 30 League goals, and Bobby was top scorer with seven. In three seasons he scored ten goals in 42 League games. He moved to Millwall in March 1982 for a couple of seasons, before dropping into the lower leagues with Worcester City (manager till February 1985), Weymouth and Malvern Town. In 1987 he appeared in the FA Sunday Cup final in Birmingham and scored the winning goal for Lodge Cottrill. He now runs his own double-glazing business in Worcestershire.

Magic Moment: *In September 1997 Shinton was named player-coach of Newmarket Town. He made his debut as a sub and laid on the winner at the tender age of 45.*

Worst Nightmare: *In his last game for Manchester City, Shinton's multi-million pound team were dumped out of the FA Cup by Halifax's multi-pence side.*

CAMBRIDGE RECORD	Appearances	Goals
Football League	99	25
FA Cup	5	1
League Cup	3	–

No 64. George Reilly

No 65. Dave Donaldson

No 66. Andy Sinton

No 69. David Crown

No 68. Mark Cooper

Chapter Six

Atkinson's Atoms

No 50. **STEVE FALLON**
Debut: v Swansea, 4 March 1975
Farewell: v Wolves, 23 August 1986

Stephen Paul Fallon (born in Whittlesey on 3 August 1956) never had the opportunity to shine on the First Division stage, but he was undoubtedly good enough to do so. He did enough with Cambridge to cement his place as United's greatest central defender of all time.

Steve started out in Kettering Town's youth team, but nearly quit due to the difficulties of getting to the place, because he had yet to pass his driving test. His career was saved by the intervention of the manager, who whisked him into the first team and kept him keen. That man was Ron Atkinson.

When Atkinson was appointed Cambridge boss in December 1974 he told Steve not to sign a new contact for the Poppies, as he intended coming back for him. True to his word, Big Ron did come back for him later that month and Steve became a Cambridge player, snatched from under the noses of Peterborough, for whom he had turned out a couple of times in their reserve side.

Terry Eades was the established central defender at Cambridge and though he must have been aware that Fallon was being groomed to replace him, he magnanimously coached and helped the callow youngster. Indeed, during the 1975-76 season there was a period when the two players were tussling over that No 5 shirt, but after Steve was dropped, following a run in the team, Big Ron assured the disappointed youngster that he was very much part of his future plans.

In 1976-77 Atkinson signed Dave Stringer to effectively replace Eades and once more Steve had a mentor to guide him. They made the perfect pair. Steve was tall and elegant, and not a stopper in the old-fashioned sense, but a player who relied on acute positional sense and perfect timing when it came to tackling. Opposition strikers bursting past him would look down at their feet having done so and wonder where the ball had gone. By then it was probably halfway up the field as Steve gracefully strode away looking for a midfield player to pass to. Had Fagin got hold of him, Fallon would have made a perfect pickpocket.

Steve had other strings to his bow. He was a good ball-player and passer and was thus adept in a sweeping role as well. Stringer would stay resolutely in his own half, scanning the horizon for the distant figure of Steve somewhere near the opposition's goal. Fallon was much in demand at set pieces, because he scored an awful lot of goals with his head, but he also had a strong shot, which he demonstrated against Gillingham in January 1978 when he scored with an astonishing 40-yard drive. He became the first recipient of the Cambridge *Evening News'* Player of the Year award in 1976-77 and retained it the following year, when he also grabbed the supporters' award. The newspaper gave him a record third award in the 1981-82 season. Fallon even appeared as a midfield player when the occasion demanded and his colleague Alan Biley compared him to Paul Madeley – that wonderful play-anywhere man of the formidable late 1960s and early 70s Leeds side.

Steve coped with the ascent from Fourth Division to Second Division football with ease. He was so self-assured, even though he was still in his early twenties, that opposition fans probably thought he'd played at that level all his life. Steve himself states that playing in front of 36,000 at West Ham was far less daunting than a 1,000 crowd at Southport, where the dead atmosphere would affect him much more. Playing in the Second Division for six years, there were many occasions when rumours surfaced of a move to the top division, such as a transfer to Spurs, but nothing ever came of them. A quiet, thoughtful person who was happy to take each day as it came, he was never bitter or disappointed that he stayed at Cambridge. To underline this, his biggest regret is for his club and not himself – namely that Cambridge fell back into Fourth Division football, a fact that was certainly not due in any way to Steve, whose consistency was legendary. In May 1981 he (temporarily) became the club's record appearance maker in the League, celebrating the occasion by smashing in another long-distance volley as Grimsby were routed 5-1.

Steve hung around long enough to witness the start of the rebirth under Chris Turner and the quality of his defensive partners – which had been dire in the Ryan-Shellitto era – began to improve. Unfortunately, Steve suffered badly with a knee injury and despite a cartilage operation in March 1985 things just got worse. He played his final game at the start of the 1986-87 season, enabling Spriggs to overtake his superb total of 410 League games for United. The two players had been awarded a joint testimonial against Atkinson's Manchester United in July 1985, and Steve also earned one in his own right against Wimbledon in August 1987.

Fallon worked briefly in Cambridge's commercial department before becoming player-coach with Histon Town. He went on to play for and manage Cambridge City, leading them into an FA Cup first round tussle with Hereford, but after being out of football for three years he rejoined Histon as boss in 1999. They look as though they might soon be challenging Cambridge City as the area's top non-League outfit, proving that nice guys can make good managers.

Magic Moment: *In April 1978 Fallon rose majestically at an 85th-minute corner-kick against Exeter to head United into the Second Division for the first time.*

Worst Nightmare: *Fallon was injured when Ken Shellitto was appointed U's boss in March 1985. Shellito ignored Steve until he regained his fitness in November.*

CAMBRIDGE RECORD	Appearances		Goals
Football League	405	(+5)	27
FA Cup	16		1
League Cup	21		2

No 51. **ALAN BILEY**
Debut: v Doncaster, 16 August 1975
Final Farewell: v Cardiff, 29 November 1986

If Fallon gave the exciting new United solidity, then it was Alan Biley who provided the flair.

Alan Paul Biley was born in Leighton Buzzard on 26 February 1957 and was an apprentice at his local club, Luton Town. He played on the left wing, but didn't impress manager Harry Haslam enough to give him a try in the first team. When Luton disbanded their youth team for financial reasons, Alan was surplus to requirements.

He had impressed Luton's coach, Paddy Sowden, at Kenilworth Road and when Sowden moved to Cambridge to assist Ron Atkinson he alerted his new boss. Atkinson signed Biley for nothing and put him on the substitutes bench for the opening game of the 1975-76 season. He replaced Batson on 53 minutes, moments later he had created the equaliser, and then near the end he headed in the second. Although playing on the left wing, his style was more like that of a classic inside-forward. Biley's promising start was curtailed in his fourth game, when he broke his leg in a 50-50 accidental collision with Mark Penfold of Charlton.

Most players deteriorate after breaking a leg, but when Alan returned to full fitness at the start of the next season he was actually a better player. Unable to use his natural right foot, he practised hard with his left and this enabled him to take instant scoring opportunities without wasting time transferring the ball onto his right peg. Towards the end of his rehabilitation he also dedicated many hours to his heading. Although only 5ft 8in, he was spring-heeled and he scored countless goals with his noddle. Alan was always a dedicated trainer, and another one of his favourite routines was to practise sticking away crosses. Even on the training pitch he got a big buzz from scoring.

With Alan now as a striker, he and United took off together during the next few seasons. With a glorious combination of searing pace, jack-in-the-box heading ability, the bravery to dive in among defenders' boots, and the confidence to try the spectacular (which always seemed to come off), Biley was the spark that ignited United's charge up to the Second Division. He created League history between 1976-77 and 1978-79 by becoming the first player to be leading scorer for his club for three consecutive seasons in three different divisions.

Alan's appearance also attracted a lot of attention. He graduated from a typical mid-1970s perm to an outrageous Rod Stewart cut. It was very blond, very big and was very noticeable amongst his more conservative team-mates. Biley also had a habit of clutching the inside of his shirt-cuffs in cold weather, which tended to rip the stitching from the shoulder. He was issued with short-sleeved shirts to cut down on costs.

As time advanced and Second Division defences got better, he altered his style away from the spectacular and towards a less exciting, but more prolific, poaching type of game. He also scored plenty of goals from the penalty spot, converting twelve of his thirteen spot-kicks for United.

When you score 75 League goals in your first four and a bit league seasons, it's inevitable that you are going to attract a lot of interest from the top clubs. Rumours abounded that Spurs had made an offer of £280,000 for him, a figure that was contemptuously rejected by ambitious United. He was instead sold to Derby for a fee of £350,000 in January 1980, which was United's most expensive sale at the time.

Derby were deep in the First Division doggy-doo at the time, and though Alan scored nine goals in his eighteen games to finish as top scorer, it wasn't enough to save his team. Both player and club had a mediocre 1980-81, typified by 0-3 reverses at the hands of Cambridge in the League.

Howard Kendall bought Biley for Everton in July 1981 for £350,000, one of a series of signings that were known as the 'Magnificent Seven'. Unfortunately, the script at Goodison read more like 'Carry On Cowboy' for Alan – even with a pair of dashing white boots to match the bleached hair. After just three goals in nineteen games he was loaned to Stoke in March 1982.

Portsmouth put everybody out of their misery in August 1982 by paying Everton £125,000 for Alan's services. He scored on his home debut against Sheffield Wednesday and formed a great partnership with Billy Rafferty that led to an upturn in fortunes for Pompey in the early 1980s. Biley's eye-catching goals, bubbly personality and outrageous haircut made him an instant favourite at Fratton Park. His 23 goals were a major factor in Pompey's Division Three championship season of 1982-83, and he performed just as well with Mark Hateley the following season, but fell out with new manager Alan Ball, who was appointed at the end of the campaign. In March 1985 Biley was sold to near-neighbours Brighton for a knockdown £60,000 after scoring 51 Pompey goals in 105 League games. The move caused uproar amongst Fratton Park fans.

His stuttering form at the Goldstone Ground signalled that the end was near, and Alan had a brief spell playing in New York in the summer of 1986. He returned to Cambridge United in November 1986 on a non-contract basis, but although he rekindled happy memories by scoring a trademark volley in the FA Cup against Exeter, he was disappointed that he was only used as a substitute in the League.

He has managed Ely City, Barton Rovers and Diss Town, and has run a fitness centre in Biggleswade, as well as spells as a council worker, a landscape gardener and a nanny.

Magic Moment: *In 1983-84, the* Roy of the Rovers *comic sponsored Biley. Though he bore a likeness to Roy Race, more importantly the editor was a Pompey fan.*

Worst Nightmare: *The* Observer *newspaper voted Biley's 'peroxide mullet' as the eighth dodgiest haircut in the history of football.*

CAMBRIDGE RECORD	Appearances		Goals
Football League	160	(+8)	75
FA Cup	6	(+1)	4
League Cup	12	(+1)	3

No 52. STEVE SPRIGGS
Debut: v Doncaster, 16 August 1975
Farewell: v Aldershot, 17 March 1987

Rivalling Biley in his love of scoring spectacular goals was Steve Spriggs – United's record appearance maker of all time.

Stephen Spriggs was born in Armthorpe, near Doncaster on 16 February 1956. He joined Huddersfield Town as a 15-year-old apprentice at a time when the Terriers were still a top division side. Steve was then fractionally under 5ft tall and, in true size-obsessed footballing fashion, they put him on a diet containing plenty of bodybuilding protein. It may have beefed him up, because he looked frail at that age, but it didn't make him grow upwards. It didn't matter. Huddersfield were a grand old club in decline and by the time Steve got to make his first-team debut against Peterborough in August 1974 they were a Third Division outfit. By the end

of the season, Steve had only played four times and they were relegated
once more. The club were desperate to save money and half the youngsters, including Steve, were jettisoned.

It was Cambridge's assistant manager, Paddy Sowden, who invited
Steve down on a week's trial, where he impressed the big boss himself –
Ron Atkinson. He made his debut at the start of the season (ironically in
Doncaster), and for the next twelve years he was an integral part of the
team. He found Atkinson to be a great motivator and very aware tactical-
ly, but also a manager who wouldn't snow his players under with a welter
of instructions, but would allow them to play their natural game. And what
a game Steve had. Naturally enough it was his 5ft 2in frame (he grew a little bit) that drew everybody's attention, but any thoughts that the mascot
had slipped unnoticed onto the pitch were soon dispelled when the game
started. It was apt that he began his career as a Terrier, because he was a
tenacious battler with a seemingly inexhaustible supply of energy. Many
footballers are described as having an engine, but Steve's was turbo-
charged. Atkinson believes that it was only his lack of height that stopped
him playing for England. He also described him as 'having a seven-foot
heart'.

Spriggs was a ball-winner, steaming in to dispossess any midfielder
foolish enough to dally on the ball and then surging forward to find the
best attacking opportunities. He created 65 League goals for other United
players, more than anyone else in the League era, thrusting his way through
the first part of the defensive fortifications and setting up the clinical fin-
ishers like Biley, Finney and Reilly. He was also a keen sharpshooter himself (his League total of 58 is a record for a United midfielder since 1970,
and only three strikers can better it).

Never mind the quantity though, feel the quality. Very few of Spriggs'
goals were tap-ins. A large proportion of them were fearsome cracks from
outside the area. Anything from about 35 yards out was within range and
the Abbey crowd would lean forward if he received the ball in his opponents' half. As time wore on he became chunkier (though never fat) and
this pocket-battleship physique no doubt increased the power output from
that right peg. The face also became less angelic and the permed hair was
restrained enough not to draw ridicule. Incidentally, Spriggs is not the
shortest player to have played League football: Fred Le May (a 1930s outside-right) never grew above five feet.

It may be wondered how it was that a bigger club never came in for
Steve. Nobody knows the answer, but he lost count of the number of
deals that were proposed and then fell through for one reason or another.
Like Fallon, he just shrugs it off as one of those things. It did mean that
the two longest-serving United players missed out on lucrative signing-on

deals, but their loyalty was rewarded with a joint benefit game against Atkinson's Manchester United in July 1985.

Steve's last game in March 1987 was his 416th League game for the U's, a club record and one that is beginning to look unsurpassable. That month he also played three times on loan for Third Division Middlesbrough, but any permanent move to Boro, or to the other interested party, Notts County, were scotched because of the poor terms on offer. Spriggs did try his luck in Cypriot football for a time, but came back to Cambridgeshire and is now a sub-contractor in the roofing industry.

Magic Moment: *A typical 30-yard screamer from Spriggs decided a League Cup-tie in September 1980 against that season's eventual League champions – Aston Villa.*

Worst Nightmare: *Seeking a £20 a week wage rise from Big Ron, but only offered a fiver, Spriggs was horrified later that night at a beauty contest. Ron was a judge, and handed him a fiver. Instead of his wage rise, the money was to buy a round of drinks.*

CAMBRIDGE RECORD	Appearances		Goals
Football League	411	(+5)	58
FA Cup	17		1
League Cup	30		1

No 53. **TREVOR HOWARD**
Debut: v Oxford, 14 August 1976
Farewell: v Leicester, 18 November 1978

One of the most underrated players in the squad that jumped from the Fourth Division to the Second in consecutive seasons was Trevor Edward Howard.

Trevor attended Gaywood Park Secondary Modern School in his home town of King's Lynn (born 2 June 1949) and represented Norfolk County at football. It was whilst playing in a county trial that he was spotted by Norwich City boss Ron Ashman – not surprisingly, perhaps, as Trevor had just scored a hat-trick.

Howard signed professional terms for Norwich in July 1967 and made his debut for them at home to Rotherham in the Second Division seven months later. He featured prominently in Norwich's 1971-72 championship season under Ron Saunders and became a pioneering Canary as they strode in the top division for the first time. In 1973 he was a League Cup finalist.

Ex-Bournemouth boss John Bond took over in 1973 and the following season organised a swap which involved Trevor going to Dean Court and

Tony Powell coming the other way. Howard was Bournemouth's leading scorer in 1974-75 but, without Bond's magic at the helm, Bournemouth were a spent force and were relegated into the Fourth Division. Trevor still managed to impress in central midfield, but by July 1976 things had got so bad on the south coast that the Cherries were forced to make savings and offloaded Trevor to Cambridge. It was Trevor's ex-colleague at Carrow Road, Dave Stringer, who had advised Ron Atkinson to buy him.

Howard was one of those players who went about his business quietly and efficiently, without drawing attention to himself (which may explain why he felt the need for permed hair). He eschewed the flash and played a nice, simple steady game most of the time (see his Magic Moment below). He was five inches taller than Spriggs. That still meant United had the shortest midfield in the League, but it rarely mattered as they complemented one another perfectly. Whereas Spriggs was attack-minded, Trevor would tend to drop back and deal resolutely with any breakaways from the opposition. His defensive capabilities led him to be a useful stopgap at right-back, though he was needed much more in midfield.

Trevor was an ever present in Cambridge's glorious Fourth Division title triumph in 1976-77 and he followed that up by playing a major part in their elevation to the Second Division the next season. One bitter-sweet match against Bury that season featured a goal from Trevor that lifted his spirits after his house had been burgled. He played for the first few months of United's virginal Second Division campaign, but sadly suffered a nasty knee injury against Leicester that ended his career.

He continued to serve the club as a lottery agent and he also billeted many young players in his club house, among them Floyd Streete. He also built a career as a meter inspector for British Gas. He did that for seventeen years, and is now a self-employed taxi driver in Cambridge.

Magic Moment: *In a game at Brentford in the 1976-77 championship season, Howard weaved through three Bees players to score the killer second goal. His manager Ron Atkinson was so impressed he ran onto the pitch to personally congratulate him.*

Worst Nightmare: *In a League Cup-tie against Northampton in August 1978, Howard managed to cut opponent Derrick Christie's head open with his studs. Presumably there was no malice intended, because the two of them were able to joke about it when Christie joined Cambridge soon afterwards.*

CAMBRIDGE RECORD	Appearances	Goals
Football League	105	5
FA Cup	4	–
League Cup	8	–

No 54. **MALCOLM WEBSTER**
Debut: v Oxford, 14 August 1976
Farewell: v Oldham, 4 February 1984

Making his United debut on the same day as Trevor Howard was the goal-keeper who would make more League appearances for Cambridge than any other in that position.

Malcolm Walter Webster is a Yorkshireman, born in Rossington, near Doncaster, on 12 November 1950. Several local clubs expressed an interest in him, but he turned them down for the bright lights of Arsenal in 1966, being impressed by the professionalism of their youth system compared to the ramshackle set-ups at other clubs.

He was an understudy to Bob Wilson, whose concentration on the pitch and high standards off it taught Malcolm a great deal. He found everyone at Highbury helpful, especially Wilson and Bertie Mee – the manager. He worked hard and made his debut appearance as an 18-year-old in the cauldron of a local derby against Tottenham, in front of 55,000 at Highbury in September 1969. Unfortunately Arsenal lost 2-3, but Malcolm played in the next two games – against Manchester United (where he was nutmegged by George Best in a 2-2 draw), and Chelsea (lost 0-3). Sadly, Malcolm was then struck down by the debilitating glandular fever and Geoff Barnett was signed from Everton as Wilson's cover. Webster took a long time to recuperate and, even though he won an England Youth cap, Mee decided he wasn't fit enough and moved him to Fulham in December 1969, initially on loan.

Webster immediately hit it off with the genial manager Alec Stock and made about 100 appearances in four years. The signing of Peter Mellor from Burnley in February 1972 ended his first-team dreams, though, and he was cast adrift in the reserves.

In January 1974 Malcolm moved to Southend and made his debut against Cambridge in January 1974 (Cambridge won 3-2). This was the unhappiest move of his career, despite getting another 100 games under his belt. He felt that manager Arthur Rowley tried unsuccessfully to change his style of play and when the Shrimpers were relegated from the Third Division in 1975-76 he was scapegoated for the failings of the manager and the team.

He moved to Cambridge in August 1976 on the recommendation of his ex-Arsenal colleague Brendon Batson, and the contrast between his old and new manager couldn't have been greater. Ron Atkinson's motivational skills instilled Malcolm with a conviction that he was on the winning side before the match even started. United raced away with the championship and Malcolm was awarded the coveted accolade of Supporters' Player of the Year. Like his 1960s equivalent, Rodney Slack, Malcolm was described as being a line man, and it was true that when the ball came floating in from the wings Malcolm would resolutely hug his goal-line. His defence was that with great big ugly defenders like Turner, Smith and Donaldson ahead of him, he could safely leave them to deal with these balls, whilst he stayed alert to any breaches of the amber wall. The comparisons with Slack didn't end there. Malcolm, too, was short for a keeper at an inch and a half under six feet, but he had a physical bulk to repel advancing forwards and was blessed with an agility that could see him leaping with ease to the far corners of the goal.

Malcolm was first-choice keeper for eight years and his understudy, Richard Key, only rarely threatened to displace him. Webster's career came to an abrupt end at Oldham in February 1984, when he came out for a 50-50 ball with Mick Quinn and the resulting collision tore his knee ligaments.

He had a couple of years as youth-team manager and a short spell as assistant manager under Ken Shellitto (replacing the sacked John Cozens), before becoming disillusioned with football (as everybody seemed to be under Shellitto). He became a representative for a roofing company before Cambridge boss John Beck asked him to coach Jon Sheffield, which led to Chris Turner asking him to help out at Peterborough. This led to him renewing his love of football by running goalkeeping schools. In August 2000 he became a full-time coach at Ipswich and made such an impression that when Richard Wright moved to Arsenal he wanted to take Malcolm with him – unacceptable to Arsenal, who already had Bob Wilson.

Magic Moment: *In the 1-0 victory over Newcastle in April 1983, Webster set a new Football League record by keeping clean sheets in twelve consecutive home games.*

Worst Nightmare: *In the following home match Webster received an award for this achievement at half-time and then promptly let in four goals in eight minutes.*

CAMBRIDGE RECORD	Appearances	Goals
Football League	256	–
FA Cup	11	–
League Cup	19	–

No 55. **TOM FINNEY**

Debut: v Exeter, 28 August 1976
Final Farewell: v Torquay, 3 May 1986

Another long servant of the club was Tom Finney, who wasn't related to the 'Preston plumber' of the 1950s who enthralled England. This was the

Belfast-born (6 November 1952) version, though at the Abbey Stadium he is no less adored.

Tom started his career with Distillery in the (Northern) Irish League, before switching to Crusaders. In the 1972-73 season he was part of the team that gained for Crusaders their first ever League title, but despite the carrot of European Cup football being dangled in front of him, he was desperate to escape the troubled province and begin a new life in England. In August 1973 he joined Luton Town after starring in a pre-season tournament. Sheffield Wednesday were also interested, but could only offer him a trial. Harry Haslam's Luton had £17,000 on the table for Crusaders.

To say he got off to a dream start doesn't do him justice. In his first full League game he scored twice as Luton raced into a 6-0 half-time lead over Carlisle, though they eased off in the second half and it ended 6-1. He also scored in the next three games and was already being compared to the ex-Luton legend Malcolm MacDonald. Finney then hit a barren spell, suffered a knee injury that kept him out for three months, and was released at the end of 1973-74 to Bob Stokoe's Sunderland for £50,000.

Finney's chances were instantly curtailed by the almost simultaneous signing of north-eastern superstar Bryan 'Pop' Robson. Tom was restricted to a handful of substitute appearances, but one of those was in a massive Division Two promotion game against Manchester United in front of 60,000 at Old Trafford. His only start that season was in the return fixture at Roker Park in front of a mere 45,000. Though the Rokerites failed in their promotion bid, they won the championship the following season, with Tom playing a handful of games over the Christmas period and scoring twice. Once he lost his place though, he was unable to regain it and he was offloaded to Cambridge in August 1976 for £15,000.

Although he pulled a hamstring on his debut, Finney was soon back and struck up a scintillating partnership with Alan Biley that ripped apart Fourth Division defences wherever they went. Tom racked up sixteen League goals that season (1976-77), including consecutive home hat-tricks in the run-in to the championship and a hand in eleven consecutive goals. The duo continued to weave their magic spell in the Third Division and by the end of that promotion campaign had totted up 64 goals between them in two seasons. Tom remained at the Abbey throughout the Second Division days, winning the Supporters' Player of the Year trophy in 1979-80 as United finished in eighth place. Carlisle made a £100,000 bid for him at around this time, but he didn't want to drop down a division. It did look as though Tom was on his way out at the start of 1981-82, as he had a falling-out with his manager John Docherty, apparently because Doc wanted to move Tom into midfield to beef it up, whilst Tom was keen to remain as a striker, something that was becoming more difficult as Doc opted for more height up front. Thankfully a compromise was reached and Finney seemed to adapt himself to whatever was required of him.

One of the biggest joys for United fans was seeing the tall but slim dervish racing down the left and wreaking havoc amongst defenders. Able to put himself about anywhere in midfield or up front, opponents found themselves unable to gauge where the next threat was coming from. With ball control that enabled him to mesmerise his opposite number, and then pace to skin him, he created countless goals for his colleagues. He was a clinical finisher too, and his League goals total of 61 is only beaten by John Taylor and Alan Biley, both out-and-out strikers. Whilst Doc and Tom might have had raging rows about where best to play him, the fans could recall a similar disagreement in the press over Kenny Dalglish. Jock Stein ended the debate with the words: 'Och, just let him on the park'. The same holds true for Tom. Let him play, and he did the business.

Tom's natural aggression also manifested itself with a fearful temper on the pitch. He earned himself five sendings-off in his United career – more than any other player. Three of these came after his mid-1980s comeback, but they were worth it. After all, a calmer attitude on the pitch might have made him a toothless, emasculated player. Better to keep the fire burning within him.

One positive Cambridge record Tom holds is the seven Northern Ireland caps he won as a United player, out of a total of fourteen he earned overall. He won his first cap in September 1974, just before making his Sunderland debut, scoring in a 1-2 defeat by Norway. He also scored against Wales, but was then frozen out for four years until his exploits with Second Division high-flyers Cambridge earned him another chance in the green shirt in 1980. His seven United caps all came in that year, the final two earned during a tour of Australia.

Finney moved to Brentford in February 1984 as impoverished United unloaded their prize assets. He went to Griffin Park initially on loan, but he was unhappy there and delighted to return to the Abbey in December 1984 at the behest of John Ryan, who played alongside Tom at Luton. Though United were rock bottom of the Third and playing dreadful football, Tom was the best of a bad bunch and won himself another Player of the Year trophy.

Tom was unique in being the only United player to get on with new boss Ken Shellitto, but he remained as Chris Turner came in to save the club. Colchester wanted to sign him, but a bad back injury put paid to that. Instead he moved to that rest home for ex-U's players called Cambridge City. Unfortunately he only lasted half a season before that dodgy back gave way again. He still managed to slip in a few games for Len Ashurst in the United Arab Emirates.

Finney later managed Ely City, March Town United and Histon Town, before becoming Cambridge City's assistant manager under Steve Fallon. These days he works at Securicor. His son Nick has played for Cambridge City reserves.

Magic Moment: *On his first full League game for Luton against Carlisle, Finney scored twice to put Luton 6-0 up at half-time. A Cumbrian reporter turned up late and missed them all, but was in place to see the Carlisle consolation goal in the second half.*

Worst Nightmare: *Finney's fiery reputation was confirmed against Hartlepool in September 1976 when he was sent off for retaliation after only five minutes.*

CAMBRIDGE RECORD	Appearances		Goals
Football League	323	(+9)	61
FA Cup	13		–
League Cup	18		4

No 56. **DAVE STRINGER**
Debut: v Southend, 2 October 1976
Farewell: v Oldham, 11 October 1980

If Tom Finney was providing will-o'-the-wisp magic in attack, then it was Dave Stringer who was the defence's foundation stone that United's ambitions were built upon.

David Ronald Stringer was born in Great Yarmouth on 15 October 1944 and began his career with nearby Gorleston Minors, before signing for Norwich City in May 1963. He made his debut as a right-back in the 1964-65 season before switching to central defence. His confident, classy performances at Carrow Road elevated him to genuine legend status in Norwich fan's eyes and he was an integral part of their success. He won a Second Division championship medal in 1971-72, putting them in the elite for the first time. No Norfolk-born player has made as many as the 419 League appearances for the Canaries as Dave did. He also was capped at England Youth level whilst at Carrow Road.

He joined Cambridge United in September 1976 in his familiar central defensive role, partnering the inexperienced Steve Fallon. Many ex-stars coming down the divisions tend to look down on their new colleagues and stand aloof, but not Dave. His professional, disciplined attitude rubbed off on everybody and helped raise the standards of the team. His manager Ron Atkinson described him as 'the model pro'. Fallon remembers him fondly as someone who was prepared to help and guide him, aiding him to become almost as good as his mentor. It is a footballing cliché that great sides are built from the back, but there can be little doubt that Cambridge's was. The Stringer-Fallon pairing was almost certainly the greatest in the club's history. They took United to a Fourth Division championship, then to runners-up spot in the Third Division (where the partnership remained unbroken all season) and subsequently as high as eighth in the Second Division. The breakdown of League matches in which the pair played together reads: P 148, W 64, D 49, L 35, F 224, A 167. These figures speak for themselves.

Although Stringer had an unhappy debut, conceding a goal when he allowed himself to be beaten by a header, it was a rare mistake. He wasn't tall for a centre-back at a couple of inches under six feet, and his affable face didn't sit on top of a heavy frame either. Instead he relied on his vast experience to ensure he was perfectly placed to snuff out any opposition raids and to make certain he didn't have to over-extend himself physically (he was well into his 30s at United). He organised his defence with an assuredness that most of his colleagues were unable to equal and he was the consummate defender. He rarely ventured beyond the halfway line and his only United goal was a wind-assisted 50-yard free-kick at Halifax in October 1976.

After leaving Cambridge in 1980 (just before he celebrated his 36th birthday) Stringer went back to Norwich as youth-team manager, leading them to victory in the FA Youth Cup in 1983. In December 1987 he replaced Ken Brown as first-team boss and kept Norwich in the top flight for five seasons. They finished as high as fourth in 1988-89 and also reached two FA Cup semi-finals. He resigned from the hot seat in May 1992 as the Canaries only just avoided relegation and returned to coaching duties. He then became involved with City's Football Academy, along with Sammy Morgan. He retired in 2001.

Magic Moment: *It was Stringer's first-half goal at Watford in April 1972 that helped Norwich to a 1-1 draw, putting them out of reach of championship rivals Birmingham City. He also won the Canaries' Player of the Year award to round off the perfect season.*

Worst Nightmare: *Sammy Morgan insists that Stringer is renowned in Norwich circles for never buying a drink. I wish to go on the record stating I don't believe that allegation, just in case Dave consults his lawyers.*

CAMBRIDGE RECORD	Appearances		Goals
Football League	153	(+4)	1
FA Cup	8		–
League Cup	6		–

No 57. **JAMIE MURRAY**

Debut: v Colchester, 24 November 1976
Final Farewell: v Stockport, 11 December 1987

Whilst Stringer was part of the old guard, it was Jamie Murray who was part of the new wave that swept United to untold heights. His bubbly playing style (combined with a bubbly hairstyle sometimes) made the Scotsman a feature of United's left flank for the best part of a decade.

James Gerald Murray was born in Ayr on 27 December 1958, but as a youngster briefly featured on the books at Ipswich Town. He failed to make an impact at Portman Road and was playing for Rivet Sports alongside Floyd Streete when Ron Atkinson whisked him off to the Abbey to strengthen the squad as part of United's promotion charge. Ironically, Murray made his debut alongside Streete when he came on as a substitute for Willie Watson, but that was the only part he took in the championship season of 1976-77.

He won a place at left-back when Atkinson sold Bill Baldry to Barry Fry's Bedford for a case of champagne, but was usurped by the arrival of Lindsay Smith, who gallingly played out of position in Jamie's No 3 shirt (though Smith was far bigger than the medium-built Jamie to literally use his jersey).

For a couple of seasons Murray continued as a squad player, before winning a spell as a left winger in the 1979-80 team that finished eighth in the Second Division. He still wasn't sure of his place and it took the departure of left-back Ian Buckley and the switching of Smith into central defence to enable Jamie to finally settle at left-back.

Once he grabbed that No 3 shirt this time round there was nobody who was going to take it off him. United effectively gained two players. There was the quick, tenacious-tackling left-back, who made his flank an effective dead-end to opposition right-wingers, and then there was the lightning-fast left-winger who raced forward along with Derrick Christie to frighten the life out of his opposing full-back. Jamie was a superb deliverer of the ball either by means of a pass (short or long) or a cross, and created plenty of goals for the likes of George Reilly and Robbie Cooke. Jamie's consistency and ability to avoid injury (his tackles were well timed) meant that he was able to embark on a run of 148 unbroken first-class games between November 1980 and January 1984 to set a club record.

Murray escaped John Ryan's relegated side when Frank McLintock signed him for Brentford in July 1984. He was ever present at left-back in his first season at Griffin Park, which culminated in a 1-3 defeat against Wigan in the Freight Rover Trophy final at Wembley, and he only missed one match during the next season, playing alongside his former United colleagues Andy Sinton and Richard Key. After 130 League games and three goals he rejoined Chris Turner's Cambridge in September 1987 and displaced Alan Kimble from the left-back spot for fifteen games.

In July 1988 Murray joined Soham Town Rangers of the Jewson League, but now races down the left flank of the road in his job as a Cambridge taxi driver.

Magic Moment: *Against Tommy Docherty's Second Division leaders QPR in December 1979, it was 1-1 when Murray raced 40 yards down the left. Spriggs lobbed the ball into his path. Murray feigned to cross but unleashed a volley past Chris Woods.*

Worst Nightmare: *In his first match after his three-year run of consecutive appearances ended, Murray watched from the stands as United conceded five goals at Charlton. In the match before his run began, they had let in six at Oldham.*

CAMBRIDGE RECORD	Appearances	Goals
Football League	226 (+16)	3
FA Cup	12 (+2)	–
League Cup	11 (+2)	–

No 58. **JIM HALL**
Debut: v Newport, 27 December 1976
Farewell: v Aldershot, 18 May 1977

Unique in this book, because he wasn't ever officially a Cambridge United player, Jim Hall nevertheless earns his inclusion because of his amazing loan spell, which greatly aided United's run to the 1976-77 Fourth Division championship.

James Leonard Hall was a Northampton lad and was born on 21 March 1945, the last war baby to be featured in this book. He began with his local club Northampton Town, signing professional terms in July 1963 and making his debut at Charlton in March 1964. He was part of the Cobblers' finest ever side, starting out just in time to help them to runners-up spot in the Second Division just behind Newcastle United. He played fifteen top division games as Town succumbed to relegation. From there they rapidly slipped back to the Fourth (though not in consecutive seasons as many people think). Jim bailed out in December 1967 to Peterborough United in a player-exchange deal with Johnny Byrne, after 56 League appearances for the Cobblers and seven goals.

Hall became a legend at London Road, earning the affectionate nickname 'Big Jim'. He was selected for the PFA's 'All-Star Fourth Division Team' in Posh's championship-winning season of 1973-74, during which he formed a sparkling partnership with John Cozens (who also went on to play for Cambridge). Hall was described as a 'barnstorming centre-forward', making 302 League appearances for Posh and scoring 122 goals, making him their all-time leading scorer and their fifth-highest appearance-maker.

In January 1975 Hall moved back to Northampton, initially on loan, and scored an additional 28 goals in 69 appearances over four seasons at the County Ground.

In season 1976-77, though Cambridge United were second in the table, they were drawing too many matches and lacked variety in attack. Both Biley and Finney were short, so Atkinson figured a tall target-man was required and Ron persuaded Northampton to bring Jim in on loan for the rest of that season. With a bunch of players adept at creating goals, it was no wonder that with the final piece of the jigsaw in place the team romped away with the championship. United's record that season with and without Hall speaks for itself. Without him: P22, W9, D9, L4, F34, A19, Pts27. With him: P24, W17, D4, L3, F53, A21, Pts38.

Hall's importance was demonstrated most effectively against Workington in March 1977, when he scored with a hat-trick of headers, but he wasn't just a mere 'head boy', as his goalscoring record implies. He scored a fair proportion with his feet and even knocked one in with his knee against Halifax. When he wasn't scoring, his stocky frame was busily creating goals for the likes of Biley, Finney and Spriggs. His United strike rate of a goal every 140 minutes is amongst the best in the club's history, though his lack of games plays a part in this.

Northampton wisely kept hold of him, but Hall stopped playing for the Cobblers in the 1977-78 season and became a teacher. He went on to work for Social Services, but has recently been pensioned off following leg and ankle operations – the curse of the ex-footballer.

Magic Moment: *Posh fans sang a song about Hall to the tune of 'The British Grenadiers.' 'Some talk of Tony Hateley and some of Jimmy Greaves, of Charlton and Wyn Davies and such great names as these. But of all the centre-forwards who ever kicked a ball, there's none so good, there's none so great, as United's Jimmy Hall.'*

Worst Nightmare: *Nick Hornby wasn't impressed by Hall in his best-seller* Fever Pitch, *describing Jim in his United days as 'looking and moving like a 45-year-old.'*

CAMBRIDGE RECORD	Appearances	Goals
Football League	24	15
FA Cup	—	—
League Cup	—	—

No 59. **FLOYD STREETE**
Debut: v Crewe, 19 February 1977
Farewell: v Bolton, 23 April 1983

Coming on as a substitute for Jim Hall on the final day of the 1976-77 season at Aldershot was Floyd Streete, who celebrated the feat by scoring his first United goal within a minute of showing his face. Prior to this he had racked up one full and one substitute appearance for the U's.

Floyd Anthony Streete is a West Indian, having been born on the island of Jamaica on 5 May 1959. His family emigrated to England when Floyd was young, and he was playing for Rivet Sports (alongside Jamie Murray) when Cambridge made a move for him in July 1976. He was a natural central defender, but found it impossible to dislodge players like Fallon and Stringer from that position, which says more about the strength in depth at United at the time, rather than any deficiencies on Floyd's part. In a way this was a pity, because Floyd was forced to play in midfield or up front where he wasn't quite as effective, although such was his versatility that you would never guess he was out of position (most of the time) unless you had been told.

With his huge physical bulk (at just under fourteen stone he is one of the heaviest players to have played for United in the League), he didn't appear to be your typical midfielder, but underneath the Afro there was a player who disguised his bulk with a wonderful first touch. His defensive abilities were highlighted when United achieved a fine 2-0 victory over West Ham in April 1980, largely due to Floyd's stifling man-to-man marking job on danger-man Trevor Brooking. He occasionally put in the occasional guest appearance as a striker and didn't disgrace himself there either, with a useful strike rate for someone who wasn't allowed to settle in any one position. His best goal came against Grimsby in October 1981 when he let rip with a 25-yard volley.

Floyd's biggest failing was his typically Jamaican laid-back approach to playing, which meant that he perhaps lacked the drive and determination to reach the First Division, when his ability undoubtedly deserved to have done so. Having said that, he was often accused of being a 'mood player', one who only performed when he wanted too. But this is unfair, as he never let United down. It was just that his style meant he sometimes looked as though he wasn't trying. Indeed, Ron Atkinson used to call him all the names under the sun to wind him up and get him to play with that killer instinct.

In June 1983 Streete went over to the Netherlands to play for Utrecht. That August he played against Ajax Amsterdam and was given the unenviable task of marking the infamous (to English eyes) Marco Van Basten. He also played for SC Cambur, where he scored three goals, but in October 1984 he joined Derby County for a year on a non-contract basis.

That wasn't a success. Indeed, one disgruntled Rams fan later picked him for an all-time 'Worst XI'. Streete joined Wolves for £5,000 in October 1985, and it was hoped that his arrival could halt their plummet down the divisions, although he was powerless to prevent relegation to the Fourth Division at the end of that season. Playing with a bewildering array of partners he did manage to stabilise the sinking ship and in 1986-87 won himself a Fourth Division championship medal. The following season he played in the Sherpa Van Trophy final, where he helped Wolves to a 2-0 victory over fellow fallen-giants Burnley in front of an improbable crowd of 80,841 at Wembley. He made it a hat-trick of medals in 1988-89 when he added a Third Division championship one to his burgeoning collection, as well as a Supporters' Player of the Year trophy.

He joined Reading in July 1990, playing 38 League games before retiring. He was assistant manager with Aylesbury in 2000, but left in October 2001 after failing to agree personal terms with the club. He is now a PE teacher in Berkshire.

Magic Moment: *One Derby fan's first sighting of Streete came when Floyd made a sliding tackle. The supporter, who was standing on the terraces, was somewhat alarmed as what appeared to be two tree trunks heading straight towards him.*

Worst Nightmare: *Derby's black players were barracked by racist Millwall 'fans' in one game at the Den. Charlie Palmer almost cracked under the pressure but potential disaster was averted when Streete calmed him down with some wise words.*

CAMBRIDGE RECORD	Appearances		Goals
Football League	111	(+14)	19
FA Cup	4	(+2)	–
League Cup	9	(+2)	1

No 60. **SAMMY MORGAN**

Debut: v Bradford C, 20 August 1977
Farewell: v Northampton, 16 August 1978

The old country singer Hank Snow used to sing a song entitled 'The Night I Stole Sammy Morgan's Gin'. Snow wasn't singing about this Sammy Morgan, otherwise the follow-up hit would have been 'Help!' because our Sammy wasn't a person you would want to upset.

Samuel John Morgan was born in Belfast on 3 December 1946 and grew up alongside George Best, who played on his estate and went to his school. Sammy's mother came from Great Yarmouth, and in 1958 the family moved to Norfolk, settling in Gorleston. Sammy played for Gorleston, working his way through the ranks from Gorleston Minors, the reserves, and finally the first team, who were playing in the Anglian Combination. During this time he had trials for Ipswich Town and Arsenal, but was deemed to be too small to make the grade.

In 1968 Sammy went to teacher training college in Nottingham. Roger Carter, manager at Gorleston, was friendly with Gordon Lee who had just taken over from Stan Matthews as manager of Port Vale. Sammy joined Port Vale as a part-time professional in July 1970 and qualified from college the following year in the interesting subject combination of maths and PE (physical education). This enabled him to become a full-time pro with Vale with a back-up career if things didn't work out.

Sammy had originally been an inside-forward, but at the age of eighteen he spurted up in height to over six feet and was converted to a centre-forward. He played in 114 League games between 1970 and 1973, finishing as joint top scorer in his final season as Vale narrowly missed out on promotion to the Second Division.

In August 1973 he signed for Second Division Aston Villa, playing regularly until halted by a bad groin injury in November 1974. This kept him out for the rest of the season, which included the promotion and League Cup double. By the time he was fit again, he effectively became redundant when Ron Saunders signed Andy Gray from Dundee United. Morgan is fondly looked upon by Villa fans for his total commitment and they used to sing: 'Six foot two, eyes of blue, Sammy Morgan's after you.'

Sammy moved to Brighton in 1975, but history repeated itself when the manager who had signed him departed just after he had settled in the team. This time it was Peter Taylor who departed (at Villa it had been Vic Crowe). Alan Mullery was Albion's new boss, and Sammy was perpetual substitute in their promotion season of 1976-77. Brighton's lower-division status had also cost him his international place.

Morgan debuted for Northern Ireland in 1972 against Spain, scoring in the process. Although they failed to qualify for the 1974 World Cup finals, he took part in consecutive victories over Scotland at Hampden Park in the Home International Championships, and also played against Eusebio in a match against Portugal. He won eighteen caps between 1972 and 1976, scoring three goals. But for injuries, he may have doubled that total.

Sammy joined Ron Atkinson's newly promoted Cambridge in August 1977, becoming the battering ram to disintegrate the Third Division defences. Though he had height, he didn't have bulk, but this didn't stop him from going in hard against defenders and generally turning them into nervous wrecks. Though he wasn't a prolific scorer, his style enabled shorter strikers to grab them by the score, notably Brian Little at Villa, Peter Ward at Brighton, and Alan Biley at Cambridge. That gung-ho approach also endeared him to the fans, one old Villa boy reminiscing later, that with Sammy they always had somebody fighting for them. It also gained him a lot of injuries. Morgan was always more than just a clogger, showing deft skill on the ground with his loping gait and reasonable prowess in the air. Off the pitch he was a different character, jovial and relaxed. The fanzine contributor who rather cruelly voted him as one of Cambridge's ugliest players was obviously swayed by his on-field expression. Incidentally, he was one of the first players to wear contact lenses on the pitch.

United won promotion to the Second in that 1977-78 season, but a major bust up with new manager John Docherty led to him walking out. He joined Dutch sides Sparta Rotterdam and Groningen, but a combination of injuries and stricter refereeing finally finished him, though not before a one-match international comeback in 1979.

He went back to school, teaching maths and PE in Gorleston, and rejoined his local side as player and manager. One local described him as 'Gorleston's best-loved manager … and a thoroughly nice bloke.' His work with coaching youngsters led to him helping out at Norwich City in the late 1980s and he is now their Academy Director.

Magic Moment: *In the promotion decider in April 1978, Cambridge were 0-1 down, with Exeter's keeper Richard Key defiant. Morgan came on as sub and hit the keeper so hard that that 'Key could see what was growing in the allotments over the wall'. Key was reduced to a wreck, enabling Cambridge to win the game and thus promotion.*

Worst Nightmare: *In an FA Cup-tie tie at Highbury in 1974, Morgan put Villa in front but was sent off by Clive Thomas for fouling keeper Bob Wilson. Some thought Wilson had made a meal of the challenge to spare himself further pain. Morgan felt he had let everybody down, especially when Arsenal equalised and then won the replay.*

CAMBRIDGE RECORD	Appearances		Goals
Football League	34	(+3)	4
FA Cup	2		–
League Cup	3		1

No 61 **LINDSAY SMITH**
Debut: v Colchester, 22 October 1977
Final Farewell: v Bognor Regis, 10 December 1988

Another player who could never be taunted as a 'pretty boy' was Lindsay Smith, and many a striker must have awoken from a nightmare with

Lindsay's tough face, moustache and curly blond hair indelibly imprinted on his mind.

On 18 September 1954, Lindsay James Smith made his first appearance in the world, in Enfield. He was an apprentice with Colchester, and made such an impact in his youth that he became their youngest ever player in a League game when he took the field from the substitutes bench in a match at Grimsby in April 1971. He was sixteen years and 218 days old at the time. His precocious talent would lead to two call-ups for the England Youth Team trials at Bisham Abbey, though a Youth Team cap was never earned.

Lindsay's timing at Layer Road was impeccable. Dick Graham's 'Grandad's Army' had just reached it's zenith with the legendary 3-2 defeat of the fearsome Leeds just two months before his debut. Now youngsters were being blooded to replace the ageing stars. Lindsay was gradually eased into the team, the only problem being that nobody seemed to know which was his best position. He started out as a striker, then gradually worked his way back through the positions. He had a spell as a right winger, which was unusual because his right foot was an 'unused resource'. The idea, apparently, was that he could cut inside and deliver passes with his left foot. It took the arrival of manager Jim Smith to suss out that the centre of defence was his natural position, and once his partner Ray Harford had taught him the art of stopping, a long and happy relationship ensued. He twice helped lift Colchester out of the Fourth, but at the end of the 1976-77 season, with 211 League games under his belt, problems materialised. Lindsay's contract had expired, but manager Bobby Roberts' new offer was unimpressive to Lindsay, who said he was leaving. Roberts told him he couldn't because he held his registration, but Lindsay just walked out. The negotiations were put on hold for a while as Lindsay went on loan to Charlton, then Millwall, but with no solution in sight he was sold to Cambridge for £12,000

He soon won the nickname 'Wolfie' after Robert Lindsay's character in the TV comedy 'Citizen Smith', and if an opposition player clattered a United player, the crowd would chant 'Wolfie's gonna get ya,' and quite often he would. A combination of fearlessness, passion and a refusal to let any player go past him led to some crunching tackles. One early lesson Lindsay learned was that you don't back out of tackles or you get hurt. He never did back out, but to a certain extent it was the fans who built up this image of Mr Nasty on the pitch, which belied his good heading ability and his effective clearances with his sweet left foot.

In August 1981, in a bizarre experiment, John Docherty put striker George Reilly in defence and loaned Lindsay to Lincoln. The writing was perhaps now on the dressing room wall, and in October 1982 Lindsay left for Plymouth for the measly figure of £20,000, though he insists there was no bust-up with Docherty and that it was merely because first-team opportunities were becoming limited with increased competition from the likes of Chris Turner.

Smith played a big part in Plymouth's march to the FA Cup semi-final in 1984. Although everybody remembers the fact that he allowed his ex-colleague George Reilly to nip in ahead of him for the winner, it is largely forgotten that Lindsay saved his side from embarrassment in the second round by 'heading' the winner against Barking (it actually came off his shoulder).

Lindsay moved to George Graham's Millwall in July 1984 for £17,500, lifting them back in the Second Division, before Chris Turner brought him back to the Abbey in July 1986 to beef up the defence. Lindsay had always kept a house in Cambridge, so the move suited him. He left Cambridge United in 1988 (he was then 34 and fed up with football) and started driving for an electrical company. He turned out for Bury Town and Ely City briefly and now lives in Cherry Hinton.

Magic Moment: *Lindsay Smith once cleared the ball out into touch, and it landed in the trainer's bucket and wedged fast.*

Worst Nightmare: *When Smith was trying desperately to justify his demand for a big wage increase at Colchester in 1977, manager Bobby Roberts said he closed his eyes and thought he must be talking to Pele.*

CAMBRIDGE RECORD	Appearances		Goals
Football League	275	(+1)	23
FA Cup	14	(+1)	–
League Cup	20		–

No 71. John Beck

No 72. Alan Kimble   No 73. Gary Clayton

No 74. Phil Chapple

No 75. Colin Bailie

No 76. Chris Leadbitter

No 77. John Taylor

No 78. John Vaughan

No 79. Liam Daish

Chapter Seven

Something Old, Something New

No 62. **DERRICK CHRISTIE**
Debut: v Orient, 4 November 1978
Farewell: v Manchester C, 12 May 1984

Though he ultimately didn't last as long as Lindsay Smith, Derrick Christie played all of his six United seasons in the Second Division.

Derrick Hugh Michael Christie was born in Hackney on 15 March 1957, but grew up in Northamptonshire. He was a sports-mad youngster, but regarded athletics and football as his two favourites. He represented the county at running and by the age of fifteen was training with Southern League Bletchley Town, even playing half a dozen reserve games with the men, despite only being a small, slightly-built youth.

His manager at Bletchley was Brian Gibbs, who began transfer talks with his old friend Bobby Robson at Ipswich Town. Northampton Town were quicker off the block, however, and after a series of trials he was offered an apprenticeship. It had been Derrick's plan to stay on at school, but he wisely negotiated a clause in his contract to allow him to learn Business Studies at a Further Education College. This is common practice now, but it was unusual in 1973. His foresight paid handsome dividends for him after his playing career ended.

Derrick played in the youth team and was blooded for the reserves, where the left-winger had the good fortune to score a few goals. Even so, he was astonished to be told by manager Bill Dodgin Jnr that in two days time he would make his first-team debut against Reading. It was January 1974 and Christie was still two months shy of his seventeenth birthday. He was even luckier to be playing in front of full-back Phil Neal, later a Liverpool and England regular. Neal continually fed him simple balls forward and helped him to settle in. Despite this, Christie was dropped and endured several months of non-stop youth and reserve games, combined with travelling with the first team and only brief glimpses of the subs bench. It was frustrating, but the medium height, medium build Derrick knew he wasn't ready for the hurly-burly of Fourth Division football.

By the time the wonderful 1975-76 promotion squad had been assembled, he was used more often, though he was still a squad player rather than a guaranteed regular. The Cobblers then went through a rapid change of management. Former Red Devil, Pat Crerand, was a major influence, but soon gave way to John Petts and Mike Keen. By this time, Derrick was busy feeding left-wing crosses onto the head of George Reilly, and the two players wrecked Cambridge United's League Cup ambitions in August 1978. United were newly promoted to the Second Division and took the hint. Less than three months later John Docherty signed him, though apparently Ron Atkinson had showed an earlier interest.

Derrick discovered the step-up to the Second Division exciting. He found more time to spend on the ball and suddenly he was coming face to face almost every game with star players that he had only seen on television. He was used on the left wing, where he could showboat his pace, but he also had an ability to beat his full-back either way because he could cross with both feet. He was an enthusiastic tackler, but not so keen on tracking back when defending. Despite his lack of inches he was useful in the air, but most U's fans will remember his fearsome shooting power. His value can be proved by one statistic. Despite being injury-ridden in his last few seasons, United only won a solitary Second Division away game without Derrick in the side (at Preston in April 1979). He was a major factor in United surviving in the Second Division for six seasons, with a hard-working everything-for-the-team attitude, allied to regular glimpses of outstanding flair, such as when he destroyed Derby at the Baseball Ground in November 1980 by beating two men and chipping the goalie from twenty yards.

Derrick's injury-plagued ending began in 1981 with a bad back. He then seemed to fill up the I-Spy Book of Footballing Injuries in quick succession. No sooner had he recovered from one setback, then he seemed to undergo another mishap. Derrick feels football is about rhythm and when coming back he couldn't perform at his best for three games, so in his final three seasons (when he barely made a season's-worth of appearances) the fans never saw the best he had to offer.

His final game for United was their last in the Second Division in that first spell and though manager John Ryan offered him a new two-year deal, he felt he was becoming jinxed at the Abbey. He moved to Reading, but was only used as a squad player, so in October 1985 he went to Cardiff. Unfortunately the injuries still followed Derrick and he added damaged ligaments and hamstrings to the collection. He moved to Peterborough in August 1986, but only played eight League games before cutting his ankle badly in a Boxing Day game and contacting cellulitis when the wound became infected. A damaged cartilage persuaded him that it was all over soon afterwards and he wasn't even 30.

Derrick had studied at the Institute for Legal Executives and was able to land an administrative job at Boxworth Experimental Husbandry Farm for two years, before being promoted and working in the legal department of the Peterborough District Land Registry – a job he has held since 1989.

Magic Moment: *Christie underlined U's ambitions in their first Division Two season by scoring two super solo goals at Roker to beat Sunderland 2-0 in December 1978.*

Worst Nightmare: *Christie's luck with injuries was illustrated when he pulled a groin against QPR in November 1982. He was out for six weeks and then, in his first training game after recovering, he nicked a cartilage and had another five weeks off.*

CAMBRIDGE RECORD	Appearances		Goals
Football League	132	(+6)	19
FA Cup	3	(+1)	–
League Cup	11	(+1)	1

No 63. **CHRIS TURNER**

Debut: v Sunderland, 8 September 1979
Final Farewell: v Huddersfield, 18 October 1983

Chris Turner played in the same team as Christie, and went on to become one of United's greatest managers.

Christopher James Turner was born in St Neots on 3 April 1951 and he left school at the age of fifteen and got a job in a paper mill. His interest in football waned as he discovered the temptations that life throws at teenagers, but it was the chance of a four-hour skive off work to play in a county youth trial that marked the turning point of his life. That trial led to an £8 a week part-time professional posting at Bedford Town in 1967 (and a brief stint with Eynesbury Rovers) and soon afterwards the offer of a full-time six-month contract at Peterborough.

Turner began his career in his usual centre-half spot, but many would be surprised to learn that he also had a spell as a striker. After all, he appeared to be the archetypal stopper – big and bulky, the immovable object. He scored in Posh's championship decider with Gillingham in May 1974, but it was definitely as a defender that he starred. In 1977-78 he and his partner Ian Ross helped ensure that Posh conceded just 33 goals in 46 Third Division matches, although a lack of goals at the other end cost Peterborough promotion to the Second Division on goal-difference from Preston. His 314 appearances mean that only Tommy Robson and Jack Carmichael have played more League games for Posh.

In January 1978 Turner went to Luton Town for a season, then joined Cambridge United in September 1979. He found it difficult to dislodge the Stringer-Fallon pairing and was forced to fill the problematic right-back berth instead, which effectively gave United three centre-backs as well as a full-back. For a long time he was a reserve-team fixture, but in September 1982 he pushed Lindsay Smith out of his centre-back spot and resolutely held onto it until he was replaced by David Moyes (who would become another acclaimed manager).

In the summer Chris would often jet off to the United States. He had three spells in America with the Connecticut Bicentennials and the New England Teamen, which meant First Division wages for an average Third Division player, as he readily admits. Sandwiched in between his American jaunts and his two Cambridge spells was a short loan spell with Swindon Town.

Chris has an interesting and complex character. Away from the club he was very much a loner, but in the dressing room he was one of the jokers. The biggest laughs he provided were on the training pitch though. He hated training and would devise any excuse to escape from the more physical aspects of it. Inevitably he was the last figure to appear on the ground and the first one off it. In a match situation it was totally different. He was totally committed and would give his all to enable his side to end up as winners. He had no desire to go into management after playing – he felt there weren't so many laughs in football, due to the pressure and the fear factor.

He was working on a building site in December 1985 when he rang up chairman David Ruston about some money he was owed. Ruston assumed he was after the vacant manager's job and offered it to him, which Turner accepted, though it went against his earlier principles. United were in a 'hell of a mess' after two disastrous seasons under John Docherty, John Ryan and Ken Shellito that had earned just eight League wins. Chris took over a side that was plummeting towards oblivion and helped to stabilise it both on the pitch and financially as he ploughed some of his own money into them. Football became fun again for the players, though he was able to spot the training-ground shirkers a mile off due to his own shortcomings in that area. Though he was one of the most unlikely managers, he was a winner who couldn't stand losing and also had a wonderful eye for a player. Though United never achieved promotion under him, it was he who built the wonderful side that Beck took to glory in the early 1990s. Turner had suddenly quit the manager's chair in January 1990, physically and mentally exhausted after a debilitating bout of flu. He wanted to become general manager, but the board refused.

Turner rejoined Peterborough United and replaced Mark Lawrenson as manager in January 1991. He emulated the astonishing success that Beck had achieved with Boro's Cambridgeshire rivals by taking Posh to Fourth Division promotion, then to a play-off final against Stockport which they duly won 2-1 to earn themselves a place in the new First Division for the first time (alongside Cambridge). He stepped down in 1992, to be replaced by his assistant Lil Fuccillo (another ex-Cambridge player), and became chief executive before quitting due to another spell of ill health.

Magic Moment: *In one of his first games as manager of Posh in February 1991 Turner told his players to beat Middlesbrough in a Rumbelows Cup quarter-final, so he could afford to go out and replace them. They lost 0-1 in a replay at Ayresome Park.*

Worst Nightmare: *Whilst at Posh, Turner and five others brought a greyhound for £150. It didn't win a race. He later brought a stake in a greyhound stud company.*

CAMBRIDGE RECORD	Appearances		Goals
Football League	83	(+7)	3
FA Cup	6		2
League Cup	4		–

No 64. **GEORGE REILLY**

Debut: v Birmingham, 10 November 1979
Final Farewell: v Lincoln, 4 February 1989

One player who Turner re-signed for Cambridge United was George Reilly, one of Cambridge's best-loved strikers.

George Gerard Reilly was born in Bellshill on 14 September 1957, but his family headed down from their native Scotland when he was still a toddler. They settled in Corby, and on leaving school George got a job as a bricklayer, turning out for Corby Town in his spare time. Northampton Town were impressed by his playing ability and signed him in June 1976. He became a favourite Cobbler and he went on to bag 45 League goals in 127 games, finishing as the club's top scorer in his last two seasons at the County Ground. In those days he was so tall and lean he was described as being like a 'circus tent's circular pole'. This physical peculiarity meant he often hunched his shoulders to compensate for the gangliness. He was incredibly athletic though, both over short and middle distances, and possessed a good touch for such a big man. When Cambridge United manager John Docherty sought a tall striker to compensate for the relative shortness of Biley and Finney, he had no hesitation in splashing out £140,000 to capture Reilly in November 1979. Not only was this United's record transfer fee paid (taking inflation into account, it still is), but also it was a record for any Fourth Division player at the time.

He effectively replaced Biley and, though not as prolific as him, he still finished top or top-equal in his first three full United seasons. Docherty's desire for big target men was confirmed when Joe Mayo was signed from Orient in September 1981 and the partnership became known as the 'Twin Towers'. Though George obviously dominated in the air with his 6ft 3in frame and giant stature (sometimes he looked like an adult in a kids' kick-about), this takes something away from his ability on the ground, where his surprising mobility could cause defenders problems. He also had a spell as a central defender and acquitted himself well with his quickness to adapt in his new role. He certainly did not let anybody down.

When Reilly rowed with Docherty it led to the player going on strike, determined to better himself and to extricate himself from his contract. He left Cambridge for Watford in August 1983 for £100,000. It was unsurprising that Graham Taylor liked him, as he has a predilection for lanky strikers. Reilly formed a great pairing with Mo Johnston, a partnership that replaced the legendary Ross Jenkins-Luther Blissett one. Reilly played in the 1984 Cup final, but experienced heartache when Everton won 2-0.

In February 1985 he joined Newcastle United and scored ten goals in 21 League games, before joining West Brom in December 1985. He made a season's worth of appearances in his 31 months at the Hawthorns, but had another set-to with a manager that cut short his career there.

Reilly rejoined the U's in July 1988 and scored seven goals in 20 League games alongside Laurie Ryan, John Taylor and Dion Dublin. He left in March 1989 as he had effectively been displaced by the emergence of Dion Dublin, and moved to Barnet which was nearer his London home. He relished the new challenge as Barnet sought to gain League status and scored twice for them on his debut to help them towards their ultimate goal. He also played for Alvechurch and Cambridge City, before injury ended his playing career. He went on to run his own building company in Ely.

Magic Moment: *In the 1984 FA Cup semi-final against Plymouth, Reilly beat his old colleague Lindsay Smith to a header. The battle for supremacy between the two was the most intriguing part of the game, but afterwards they were still able to shake hands.*

Worst Nightmare: *Reilly's row at WBA was with Ron Atkinson, who allegedly called him a cheat for feigning injury, although the player was diagnosed with a stress fracture of the leg. True or otherwise, Ron dropped him into the reserves for ten months.*

CAMBRIDGE RECORD	Appearances	Goals
Football League	156	43
FA Cup	9 (+1)	4
League Cup	9	3

No 65. **DAVE DONALDSON**
Debut: v Bristol R, 2 February 1980
Farewell: v Barnsley, 21 April 1984

Another giant physical presence for the U's was Dave Donaldson at right-back, though he had bulk rather than height, at 5ft 10in and 13st.

David John Donaldson was born in Islington on 12 November 1954 and was on the books of Arsenal until June 1973, but failed to make that vital breakthrough to the first team, though he was an England schoolboy international. He later felt that with more patience he might have made the vital breakthrough at Highbury. The 18-year-old Dave joined Millwall on a free transfer, where he had no such trouble winning a place and he became their first-choice right back for the remainder of the 1970s, notching up 216 League games in the process, but scoring just once.

In February 1980 Donaldson joined United for £50,000, having felt he was getting into a rut at the Den. It was becoming apparent that the defenders that Docherty preferred were out and out stoppers, in the manner of Donaldson and Turner, rather than the more attack-minded players like Fallon. Donaldson had an intimidating presence about him, which made him appear much bigger than he actually was, but had probably already peaked by the time he reached the Abbey. He was a steady player and an excellent striker of the ball, but showed no inclination to do anything in attack whatsoever.

United had found it difficult to fill that No 2 shirt since Batson had departed and had resorted to forcing non-specialist full-backs to occupy that position instead of their regular berths. After he left, the club were faced with a similar problem and a succession of poorer right-backs were tried in his place. Though he can hardly claim to be the greatest of players in that position, it's hard to think of any better than Dave Donaldson in the 1980s.

He left Cambridge in July 1984 to join Royston Town and worked in a dairy at Fenstanton. He then achieved an unusual career double of managing Ramsey Town whilst running a fish and chip shop. No jokes please about battering fish as well as opposition left-wingers. He is now a sales manager for a national food company. His sons Dave and Craig play for Harrogate and Stamford respectively.

Magic Moment: *Donaldson's only goal in a 348-game League career came on the last day of 1974-75 for Millwall against Bristol Rovers. The Lions still got relegated.*

Worst Nightmare: *Donaldson's scoring record at Cambridge was even worse. For many years he was saddled with the statistic of having played most League games in the outfield for United without scoring. Marc Joseph currently holds that dubious honour.*

CAMBRIDGE RECORD	Appearances		Goals
Football League	130	(+2)	–
FA Cup	4		–
League Cup	9		–

No 66. **ANDY SINTON**

Debut: v Wolves, 2 November 1982
Farewell: v Northampton, 30 November 1985

Andy Sinton was barely out of nappies when Donaldson started strutting his stuff and he is the proudest product of Cambridge United's youth system in its history.

Andrew Sinton (born Cramlington, 19 March 1966) came down from the north-east as a 15-year-old and even then it was apparent that he had something special. Luckily it was picked up quickly by United. Andy was originally a striker, but was converted to the left side of midfield.

He made his debut against Wolves in November 1982 and became the youngest ever player to turn out for the U's in the League at the age of sixteen years and 228 days. He wasn't overawed either, showing enough enthusiasm to overcome his nerves. He was a clean striker of the ball and could use both feet to good advantage. He was that rare type of player who was quick in both body and mind. From an early age he was dedicated to training, to eradicate any weak points in his game, and it's no wonder that a big future was predicted for him. That was confirmed when he made his debut as an England Schoolboy against Northern Ireland and scored in the process.

Initially Docherty used him sparingly, but he turned in such a sensational performance against fellow-relegation strugglers Burnley in March 1983 that he was given an extended run in the side. He scored two superb goals – a cheeky chip and a screaming volley – and it was hard to believe he had only just turned seventeen. He was the catalyst that kept United up that season, but in the next United plummeted to unheard-of depths as they set off on a 31-game winless League run. The temptation to use Andy all the time proved too great for Doc, and his successor John Ryan, and the youngster was pushed too hard, once being forced to play on with an ankle injury that caused him to limp badly.

Sinton moved to Brentford for £25,000 in December 1985, surely the biggest bargain in their history, a fact underlined when they sold him in March 1989 to QPR for £350,000. He played wide on the left for Rangers, which is usually something you can only do effectively if you are a natural in that position. Andy wasn't (being happier in a more central midfield role), but such was his ability and hard work, that he quickly mastered his new role. Whilst at Loftus Road he picked up six England caps, including two in the European Championships in Sweden in 1992, eventually reaching twelve England appearances – the most by any ex-United player.

His hard work on the training ground and on the pitch was demonstrated once more in the transfer market when Trevor Francis at Sheffield

Wednesday bought him in August 1993 for £2.75 million. After 60 League games it was felt that Sinton was a declining force and in January 1996 Tottenham Hotspur only had to shell out £1.5 million for him. He was still in his twenties, and fast and enthusiastic enough to turn in a succession of great displays for Spurs. He proved this by scoring probably the best goal of his career in an FA-Cup tie against Wimbledon. Collecting the ball in his own half, he strode down the wing, shimmied his way past the Dons' midfield and then drove a powerful shot into the top corner. He had a spell at left-back to accommodate David Ginola, but came on as a substitute for that player in the 1999 Worthington Cup final triumph over Leicester.

Sinton's age finally caught up with him and he moved to Wolves in July 1999 on a free transfer. When he was fit for Wolves, he could rip defences apart with his accurate crossing (with either foot), but sadly he was largely unfit and his contract with Wolves expired in the summer of 2002. He has now joined Nigel Clough's Burton Albion in the Conference.

Magic Moment: *A radio reporter once boldly stated that 'it could be bad news for Andy Sinton – his knee is locked-up in the dressing room.'*

Worst Nightmare: *Another player who tried to show off his silky skills at United, at the same time as Sinton, didn't meet with quite the same success. He kept falling over on an icy pitch and was promptly rejected. His name was Peter Beardsley.*

CAMBRIDGE RECORD	Appearances		Goals
Football League	90	(+3)	13
FA Cup	3		–
League Cup	6		1

No 67. **KEITH BRANAGAN**
Debut: v Carlisle, 14 January 1984
Farewell: v Tranmere, 19 March 1988

Sinton wasn't the only youngster who looked destined for bigger things. Keeping goal in the mid-1980s was definitely the finest teenage goalkeeper in the club's history.

Keith Graham Branagan was born in Fulham three weeks before England won the World Cup final in July 1966, but was in Norfolk when he was signed up to Cambridge's youth team. He turned in a succession of good displays that earned him a professional contract in August 1983.

In January 1984, United were in the middle of their record-breaking winless run when caretaker-manager John Cozens thrust 17-year-old Keith into the first team, after Malcolm Webster had failed a fitness test. He turned in a confident, mature performance, despite playing in a near gale, and wasn't to blame for either of the two goals he conceded. The appointment of John Ryan for the next game briefly stalled his career, as the barely older Dean Greygoose was preferred as the successor to the retiring Webster.

Keith was given several games at the beginning of the equally disastrous 1984-85 season, but was roughly cast aside by Ken Shellito when the ex-Chelsea man became United's boss in March 1985. Richard Key and Roger Hansbury were the preferred options and our man became *persona non grata*. The exile lasted a year until Shellito's replacement, Chris Turner, sold Hansbury to Birmingham in March 1986. Turner was sufficiently impressed to make Keith goalkeeper for 102 consecutive League and Cup games over the next two years. The attributes that Turner admired were assured shot-stopping, confident handling and bravery. All in all, Keith can lay claim to being the best all-round keeper in the club's history – especially if you choose absence of faults as your criteria.

In December 1987, Sunderland manager Denis Smith tried to lure Keith to Roker Park by offering Turner £50,000 plus a player – a move that was rejected by Turner who valued Keith at £300,000. When Millwall came in with an offer of £100,000, Turner realistically saw it as the best he was going to get, and in March 1988 Keith rejoined John Docherty, the man who had originally signed him for Cambridge.

Docherty took Millwall into the top division for the first time in their history, but for two years Keith was stuck in the reserves behind Brian Horne, finally playing a couple of loan games for Brentford in November 1989. Millwall were in freefall by the time he made his debut in early 1990 and of the 22 games he played that season for the Lions, he was only on the winning side once – in an FA Cup triumph over Manchester City. He had enough self-belief to overcome his *annus horribilis*, but after that he was only able to share goalkeeping duties with others.

Branagan played a game on loan to Gillingham in October 1991, but moved permanently to Bolton at the end of that season on a free transfer. It was a masterstroke by manager Billy Ayre. Keith was the green wall that enabled them to march from the new Second Division into the Premiership. In 1994-95 he played at Wembley twice, in the Coca-Cola Cup final against Liverpool (lost 1-2), and the play-off final (won 4-3). He made 214 League appearances for Bolton and they relied heavily on him to keep them in the Premiership, but towards the end of his time with Wanderers he was frustrated by a shoulder injury, and he fell out of favour as well. He had earlier won his first Republic of Ireland cap, in February 1997, in a goalless draw against Wales, but subsequently dropped down to fourth in the international pecking order.

He moved to Ipswich Town in April 2000 as understudy to Richard Wright, but found himself in the team almost straight away when Wright got injured. He kept a clean sheet in the win over Coventry that booked Town a place in the UEFA Cup, but the 2000-01 season was a frustrating one for Keith and he found himself as third-choice keeper behind Matteo Sereni and Andy Marshall, before a shoulder operation kept him out of contention for several months.

Magic Moment: *Can a keeper ever be happy about conceding three goals? Branagan was after the 4-3 extra-time play-off win over Reading that put Bolton Wanderers into the Premiership in May 1995.*

Worst Nightmare: *Branagan kept goal for Millwall in an FA Cup replay against U's in 1990. Near the end of extra-time, at 0-0, he came out to collect a back-pass from future U's defender Dave Thompson. Thompson kicked the ball past Keith and, as the keeper frantically raced back, a gust of wind blew it beyond him and into the net.*

CAMBRIDGE RECORD	Appearances	Goals
Football League	110	–
FA Cup	6	–
League Cup	12	–

No 68. **MARK COOPER**
Debut: v Barnsley, 21 April 1984
Farewell: v Preston, 21 March 1987

Another player who looked as though he was going to hit the big time was Mark David Cooper, but things didn't come off for the youngster.

He was born in Watford on 5 April 1967 and was yet another successful product of United's revamped youth set-up. Like so many of his contemporaries, manager John Ryan threw him into the first team too early, during that catastrophic winless run of 1983-84. The striker, barely seventeen and playing in a weak three-man attack, hardly saw the ball as Barnsley cruised to a 3-0 victory in front of one of the Second Division's lowest ever crowds of 2,200. If anything, the following Division Three campaign was even worse and Mark's callow 6ft 3in frame was occasionally seen stranded up front alongside a bewildering variety of strike partners, including Robbie Cooke, Steve McDonough and Steve Pyle. Under the equally hapless stewardship of Ken Shellito, Mark was largely frozen out as new signing David Crown took centre-stage. Under Chris Turner the team slowly improved, but Crown was relied on far too much as he dominated the scoring charts with a record 24-goal haul. It took a while for Crown and Cooper to become a double act. When they did, the goals started to flow evenly for them. In fact, Mark pipped his partner to become leading scorer in 1986-87 with thirteen League goals.

Mark complemented Crown perfectly. Whereas Crown was of medium height, curly-haired Mark was five inches taller. Although decidedly gangly in his early days, he filled out a bit towards the end of his teens and became much less weedy on the pitch as a result. Although it's hardly an astonishing revelation that he was always good in the air (he could have been used to illustrate an 'art of heading' textbook), he was a more versatile striker than that. He learnt to use his feet to good effect and probably scored more goals with his shots and chips than his headers. He became braver and more confident too, and this was shown when he scored a hat-trick against Rochdale in December 1986 with a header and two powerful bursts through the defence, topped with strong shots.

He grabbed the attention of Tottenham manager David Pleat by scoring against them in a Littlewoods Cup-tie and generally terrorising defender Graham Roberts. The Rochdale hat-trick a month later helped matters along nicely and even a sending off for elbowing at Northampton didn't deter Pleat. In April 1987 Spurs swooped in one of those fiendishly complicated transfer deals that were starting to become popular. Basically, it involved a little cash up front, then more payments depending on appearances etc. Unhappily, United didn't become rich on the deal.

Spurs were having a great season, finishing third in the old First Division, runners-up in the FA Cup and semi-finalists in the Littlewoods Cup. This was due largely to the prolific marksmanship of Clive Allen, aided and abetted by Nico Claesen. Mark was not in contention for a first-team place and had to bide his time in the reserves. The breakthrough never came and in September 1987 he went on loan to Shrewsbury and the following month signed for Gillingham for a club record £100,000, the money coming from the sale of fans' favourite Tony Cascarino to Millwall. Unfortunately, having to follow in his footsteps proved difficult. The supporters got on his back and it seemed to visibly put him off his game. He scored eleven League goals in 49 games before joining Orient in February 1989.

Cooper rattled in 45 goals in five years at Brisbane Road and moved to Barnet in July 1994 (nineteen goals in 67 games). From there he moved up to Northampton Town in August 1996, where his ten League goals took them to the Third Division play-offs, though he was frustratingly dropped for the Wembley victory over Swansea City. He went to Welling United in June 1997 before going on loan to Bishop Stortford in January 1999, and thence to Gravesend & Northfleet in March 1999. He retired at the end of the season.

Magic Moment: *Some players plug away for hundreds of games before they are noticed: some just do something special in one. Cooper chose the latter route, turning it on in a Littlewoods Cup-tie against Spurs in November 1986. Trailing to a Clive Allen goal after five minutes, Mark sent a corking 15-yard header past Ray Clemence.*

Worst Nightmare: *Not only was Cooper's time at Gillingham an unrewarding one for him personally, it was also catastrophic for his manager Keith Peacock, who some believed got the sack because of Mark's signing not working out.*

CAMBRIDGE RECORD	Appearances		Goals
Football League	62	(+9)	17
FA Cup	4		–
League Cup	7		3

No 69. **DAVID CROWN**

Debut: v Hartlepool, 17 August 1985
Farewell: v Hereford, 3 November 1987

Cooper's partner at Cambridge was David Crown, who was even more prolific when it came to sticking the ball in the onion bag.

David Ian Crown was also from the London area, having been born in Enfield on 16 February 1958. He kicked off with Barking reserves and then Grays Athletic, for whom he made his first-team debut whilst still at school. He then moved onto Walthamstow Avenue. Their pitch was so boggy in the middle that the manager thoughtfully shunted David onto the left wing to give his ball-playing skills a chance.

Crown signed for Brentford in July 1980 for £26,000. Grays had cleverly added a sell-on clause to the contract when they sold him, so they received half the money, which made him their record transfer fee received at the time – unusual for an indirect transfer. He played 46 games in Division Three, still on the left wing, scoring eight goals, before joining Portsmouth in October 1981. He initially won his place in Pompey's side, but was then dropped and spent an unhappy 1982-83 in the reserves, before being loaned out to Exeter (where he scored three goals in seven games, one more than in 28 League games at Fratton Park).

In August 1983 he joined Reading, still as a left-winger, but whilst there an injury to Trevor Senior forced them into trying David as an attacker. In April 1985 he scored two goals against a hapless Cambridge and impressed United boss Ken Shellitto in the process. Although Shellito is the most-maligned Cambridge manager in history, he deserves credit for signing such a talent for peanuts. David also had an offer from Northampton, but wasn't impressed by their manager Graham Carr, though most people would be surprised to hear that Shellito was perceived to be a more charismatic person.

Shellito's instincts about David were correct, even though the player had never had a chance to prove what he could do with an extended run as a striker. David was only just above average height, but he was strongly built and cut quite a handsome dash in his old No 11 shirt (the same number that Biley used to wear as a striker most of the time). At first, Crown was just another player in the weary eyes of the 1,500 regular U's fans still mad enough to watch a side that had dropped into the Fourth Division as quickly as an elephant jumping out of an aeroplane. David went eight games without scoring and everyone was distinctly unimpressed. The famine ended with a consolation goal at Colchester and suddenly the confidence and goals started to flow. Eight goals were added in nine games and United rose from second-bottom of the League to the edge of the re-election zone.

It wasn't enough to keep the disillusioned Shellito in his job and he resigned to be replaced by Chris Turner. He kept faith with Crown, but with seven games remaining the player had only managed fifteen goals – a pretty good strike rate, but a long way short of Biley's record of 21 League goals in a season set in 1977-78. It was then that David moved into overdrive with a superb run of nine goals in seven games, including a hat-trick against Halifax. It wasn't until that game that he took over penalty-taking duties from Steve Massey in order to nab his third goal, and he added a further couple of penalties in his last two games to take his total to 24 for the season, a record which still stands today. Most of Crown's goals were classic poaches, waiting for the right time to pounce on balls forward and sloppy back-passes. He was quick and instinctive and able to beat defenders to slot the ball home. He could score with his head, but it was mostly with his feet.

United still had to apply for re-election, but they played Mark Cooper alongside Crown from then on and the whole team started scoring more goals. David's total was halved in consequence, but more importantly the defence conceded fewer. It was inevitable that David was going to be sold, not only because the U's were impoverished, but also because his contract was coming to an end and United knew they would get even less for him at a transfer tribunal. He signed for Southend in November 1987, partly because he had family in the area. In 1988-89 he bagged 25 League goals for the Shrimpers, despite their relegation. To say he was popular at Roots Hall is an understatement, as he bagged 61 goals in 113 League games, and was recently voted their fifth best player of all time. Southend fans were upset when he left to join Gillingham in 1990, but he couldn't match his incredible goalscoring rate and after three more years he dropped into non-League football with Dagenham & Redbridge. His overall League goalscoring total had reached 171 by this time.

David also had spells at Billericay Town and then Purfleet, where he became their coach and assistant manager. He now runs his own accountancy business in Leigh-on-Sea, but in November 2001 returned to Roots Hall as assistant manager, alongside Steve Tilson.

Magic Moment: *Crown overtook Alan Biley's total of 21 League goals in a season with a mis-hit shot early in the second half at Northampton. The Cobblers' manager was Graham Carr who had wanted to sign him at the start of the season.*

Worst Nightmare: *Southend were drawing 3-3 with Spurs on aggregate in a Littlewoods Cup-tie when Crown hit the post. Spurs went through on away goals.*

CAMBRIDGE RECORD	Appearances	Goals
Football League	106	45
FA Cup	3	2
League Cup	12	6

No 80. Dion Dublin

No 81. Danny O'Shea

No 82. Lee Philpott

No 83. Michael Cheetham

No 84. Steve Claridge

No 85. Richard Wilkins

No 86. Gary Rowett

No 87. Mick Heathcote

No 88. Steve Butler

Chapter Eight

Turner's Fresh Faces

No 70. **IAN MEASHAM**
Debut: v Scunthorpe, 23 August 1986
Farewell: v Hereford, 9 May 1987

Although he didn't hang around very long, right-back Ian Measham quickly won the hearts of most fans with his ability in his one and only U's season of 1986-87.

Measham was a Barnsley boy, making his world debut on 14 December 1964. He was an apprentice at Huddersfield Town and signed full terms for them in December 1982. It took him a couple of years to break into the first team and he made just seventeen League starts for them as a right-back. He had loan spells at Lincoln City and Rochdale in the 1985-86 season, but was sold to Cambridge United in July 1986.

He was a steady, honest workmanlike player, which made him something of a revelation in the right-back role that had always been a problem for Chris Turner. He replaced Steve Clark and immediately the number of goals conceded down the opposition's left flank was considerably reduced. Overall, United only conceded 62 goals in the season that Ian played, not exactly a low figure, but far better than the 80 they had let in the season before. It was enough to lift the team into mid-table, which was outrageous success in the long-suffering fans' eyes. By early 1987 the U's defence had settled, with Ian and Alan Kimble as full-backs and Lindsay Smith and Mark Crowe in the centre in front of goalie Keith Branagan. There is nothing like having a set of established defenders to give the whole team confidence and now Chris Turner had something to build on as he turned his attention towards thoughts of promotion. Ian played in every game of that season and the fans voted him as their Player of the Year.

Everything seemed set fair for a long and happy relationship, but then came disaster. Ian picked up what was thought to be a serious pelvic injury, but which turned out to be a simple hernia. By the time this was diagnosed, Turner had signed Gary Poole and then Colin Bailie to replace him. When eventually Ian did regain fitness after eighteen months, he found that he was no longer part of the manager's plans – a shame because he was certainly a better right-back than either of his two replacements. At the time, it created much upset amongst the normally placid Cambridge fans.

In November 1988 Measham moved to Burnley and performed a similar role in their defence, staunching a rapid flow of goals conceded and lifting the team. He helped the Clarets to the Fourth Division title in 1991-92 (the last winners of that Division before it became known as the Third Division in the reorganisation of the League's structure). In five years at Turf Moor he made 182 League appearances, scoring twice.

In September 1993 he joined Doncaster, but played only 32 games in three seasons because of injury, which eventually forced his retirement.

Magic Moment: *Measham's Burnley needed a point for promotion at York in 1992 and three for the title. They went a goal down, equalised in the second half and then grabbed a dramatic winner four minutes into injury-time.*

Worst Nightmare: *At Doncaster Rovers, Measham broke his neck and there were fears (thankfully allayed) that he may have been paralysed.*

CAMBRIDGE RECORD	Appearances	Goals
Football League	46	—
FA Cup	3	—
League Cup	6	—

No 71. **JOHN BECK**
Debut: v Halifax, 30 August 1986
Farewell: v Hereford, 26 August 1989

Although infamous for his controversial management style, in which the midfield tended to get bypassed, strangely it was as a pass-master in the middle that earns John Beck a place in this book.

John Alexander Beck was born in Edmonton on 25 May 1954 and spent the Saturdays of his youth on the terraces at White Hart Lane admiring the skills of Jimmy Greaves and Jimmy Robertson. He joined QPR as an apprentice in 1970 and made his debut on Boxing Day 1972, coming on as a substitute for Terry Clement. Rangers won promotion to the First Division that season, but John only appeared sporadically, being under the shadow of Terry Venables and Gerry Francis. His best season was 1974-75 when he played the bulk of his 40 League games for them. The following season manager Dave Sexton strengthened his squad by signing Don Masson, and John only played bit parts in the squad that very nearly snatched the League championship from Liverpool's grasp.

In June 1976 he moved to Coventry City for £40,000. This time he found it easier keeping his place and in a little over two seasons he made 69 appearances, scoring six times from midfield.

Beck transferred to Fulham in October 1978 for double his previous fee, experiencing relegation to the Third and promotion back to the

Second whilst he was there. Overall it was an unhappy time for John, as manager Bobby Campbell refused him permission to sign for Ipswich for £150,000, or Chelsea for £200,000.

He did leave in September 1982 for the less-glamorous Bournemouth, initially on loan. In 1984 they won the new Associate Members Cup final against Hull. Sadly, it was played at Boothferry Park – not Wembley. Fans at Bournemouth remember John for his ghastly Kevin-Keegan perm and his high-pitched shouting (he was captain by then).

Beck joined Cambridge in July 1986 at the age of 32 and became one of the most influential midfielders ever to grace the Abbey. To start with, he would often be seen hanging around on the right wing, but once he moved inside to the middle of the park he found his true position. Happy to let the younger players (like 30-year-old Steve Spriggs) do the chasing and winning of the ball, he stayed around the centre-circle and sprayed out passes to the best-positioned player on the pitch, his experience and authority earning him the nickname of 'General'.

It was a rare luxury to have a player of that ability in a Fourth Division side and it definitely led to the creation of more goals within the team. Defenders would be less inclined to lump the ball out of defence in time-honoured lower-division fashion, but instead would search out the man in the No 6 shirt (defender Lindsay Smith having bagged the No 4). From there, the wingers and strikers would place themselves into attacking positions, knowing that an inch-perfect pass would probably be on the cards. Obviously John lacked speed (though he was still very fit), but with ability like that he didn't need to run. He did attract criticism for his lack of tackling and poor heading ability, and wasn't one of the 'get stuck in' players so beloved of the fans.

His other great strength was his striking of a dead ball. It is astonishing that so many players seem to find it impossible to direct a free-kick or corner into a precise area of the pitch, but it appears to be a rarer commodity for a lower division player to possess. Corners would almost invariably find their way onto the desired head, and free-kicks anywhere inside the opposition half were likely to result in a United goal. He first demonstrated this attribute on his debut. A stale 0-0 draw with Halifax looked inevitable until United won a free-kick 25 yards out. The Halifax wall looked good enough. Paddy Roche (the ex-Manchester United keeper) seemed to have all the angles covered, but John was still able to bend the ball round the wall and into the top corner. He would score many similar goals in his time with United, working with the players on set-piece ploys that gave the opposition headaches and the fans high expectations.

John wasn't just signed for his playing ability. Such an experienced top-class player was a godsend on the training pitch and he became a very good coach. He also became assistant-manager and to start with he and Turner had to drive all over the country scouting for players, which meant neglecting the first team, so John helped set up a scouting network with the help of chief scout Neville Proctor. A large number of players featured in this book are included thanks to the sharp instincts of Mr Beck's nose for a good player.

When Turner felt he had taken United as far as they could go, he handed the reins to John, who made one of the greatest starts to management in footballing history. He led United to victory in the Fourth Division play-offs at Wembley in 1990, the Third Division championship in 1991 and the play-offs to the Premier League the following season, not forgetting the two incredible runs to the FA Cup quarter-finals.

Of course, Beck is famous for his long-ball style, but that was something that evolved over the course of the first year and only really came to be applied rigidly in the Third Division. The idea came to him by studying the statistics of Charles Hughes at the FA. Most goals were scored from crosses, following three passes or fewer, and suchlike. He worked out a rigid system of getting the ball to the wings quickly and demanding that the wingers whip in crosses to the forwards. It worked spectacularly well for the first two years but because it was such a simple system it was easy for other managers to frustrate. United missed out on promotion to the Premier League and then struggled badly in the 1992-93 season. By then he had subtly altered his game plan to make the players advance as far forward up the pitch as was possible to pressurise the opponents. He was also accused of gamesmanship (undrinkably sweet tea, overheated dressing rooms, and extra-light training balls for the opposition, for example). Some referred to him as Dracula because he was sucking the life out of football. Whatever the merits of the style, the fact is that he was sacked in October 1992.

John went to Second Division strugglers Preston in December 1992, but relegation followed. He took them to the play-off final the following season, but they lost 2-4 to Wycombe. They started the 1994-95 season badly and he was sacked in December 1994.

Third Division Lincoln were willing to give him another go and in 1997-98 he steered them to automatic promotion. He took over at Barrow before coming back to Cambridge in February 2001 after a spell as a van driver. Though playing a more conventional style of football and managing to pull United out of the relegation zone, the recruits he signed on high wages and long contracts proved to be of poor quality. He resigned in November 2001 with the U's heading back towards Division Three. He is now able to spend more time on the golf course where long balls are much more appreciated.

Magic Moment: *On 9 November 1991, Beck's United side beat Ipswich 2-1 to sit on top of the old Second Division. When John had taken over, 22 months beforehand, United were fourteenth in the Fourth Division.*

Worst Nightmare: *With his side just two wins away from joining the Premier League, Beck's side succumbed to a crippling 0-5 defeat in the play-off semi-final, second leg, at Leicester, in May 1992.*

CAMBRIDGE RECORD	Appearances		Goals
Football League	105	(+7)	11
FA Cup	6		–
League Cup	8		2

No 72. **ALAN KIMBLE**
Debut: v Aldershot, 21 October 1986
Farewell: v West Ham, 8 May 1993

United's most successful left-back in the League era, both alongside and under Beck, was Alan Kimble.

Alan's mother and father lived in Dagenham, but whilst on a family holiday in Poole, Dorset, on 6 August 1966, his mother gave birth to twin sons – Alan Frank and Garry Leslie.

The twins' father was a semi-pro player with Dagenham, Grays Athletic and Ford's, but failed to make the professional grade after a trial with Orient. His dad buying them a Chelsea kit for their third birthday heavily influenced the kids' future career. The Kimbles both won schoolboy honours with Dagenham Priory Schools and moved to the junior team of Charlton Athletic. Alan played in Athletic's reserve team as centre-forward and notched up 23 League goals but it was in his familiar left-back role that he made his debut against Sheffield United in 1983-84, helping Charlton to avoid relegation from the Second. Despite impressing with his left foot at a succession of wonderful crosses, free-kicks and corners, he was effectively replaced the following season by Mark Reed – signed from Celtic. Both Kimbles were loaned out to Exeter, but after three games failed to impress manager Colin Appleton and returned back to Charlton, where they were retained for the next season.

The twins joined Cambridge in August 1986 (like two little ferrets, according to boss Chris Turner). They found the atmosphere much friendlier at the Abbey, compared to Charlton. Alan was originally second-choice left-back behind Brian Mundee, but eventually forced his way into the first team, playing well on his debut at Aldershot, despite the team losing 1-4. He played behind Garry, who was on the left wing, but Alan was dropped in September 1987 when Jamie Murray rejoined Cambridge and a spell in the reserves followed. The following month, the twins separated for the first time when Garry joined Doncaster. He later joined Peterborough United and grabbed national headlines when he scored the goal that dumped Liverpool from the Rumbelows Cup in December 1991. Incidentally, the twins were easy to tell apart because one of them, Garry, had a skin blemish on his face.

Alan got back in the side when Murray was injured, and then won the Supporters' Player of the Year trophy two seasons running. He was nearly always the first name down on the team-sheet, his sheer consistency setting him apart from nearly all the other lower division players. He just didn't seem to have any bad games. Mostly, his contribution was just taken for granted. Opposition winger races down pitch, Kimble tackles him and comes away with ball. It happened week after week. His strengths were basically a combination of factors. He was very fast – only the lightning-quick would beat him. He was a clean, efficient tackler and he was adept at forcing players to go the long way round. His running action was distinctive: he kept his head down in a sort of crouched way, with an occasional glance up to see what was ahead of him. His body language when defending was also similar. He would crouch down, spread his arms out wide and burn his eyes into the winger. It reminded one of a lion preparing to pounce on an unsuspecting gazelle. He was an introverted player on the pitch, totally professional, an attitude that was also apparent off it. When defending deep he would guard the near post. He had a sweet left foot that earned its own nickname of 'the wand' because it could magically transport a ball to wherever Alan wanted it to go. He had a powerful shot, but the trait that really stood out was his penalty taking.

Kimble used to take penalties in Charlton's reserve team, so when Cambridge needed someone to replace Lindsay Smith, he volunteered. Supremely confident, he ran quickly up to the ball, struck it sweet and low and as wide of the keeper as possible. His haul of twenty penalties scored puts him well ahead of anyone else at Cambridge and nineteen of them were directed into the bottom right corner as he saw it. The goalies never seemed to twig, not that they could have reached the ball if they had. He only missed five penalties, inevitably when the ball would roll wide of the post.

He was transferred to Wimbledon in July 1993 for £175,000. He helped the Dons reach the FA Cup semi-final in 1997, but was dropped for a while when Ben Thatcher briefly replaced him. A knee injury kept him out for most of the 2001-02 season

Kimble joined Derby County, knowing that it would be his last season. It was a disaster: Alan never got a game and when he announced his intention to retire at the end of the season he was informed that he wasn't entitled to any severance pay. In March 2002 he joined Peterborough on loan, Barry Fry having been impressed by how fit the 35-year-old player was. A keen greyhound owner, Kimble joined Luton in August 2002.

Magic Moment: *The only time Kimble kicked a penalty to the goalie's left was at Carlisle in April 1990. Gary Johnson had tipped him that keeeper Kevin Rose had checked his technique, so Alan coolly bamboozled Rose by sending him the wrong way.*

Worst Nightmare: *When Derby told Kimble that he wasn't entitled to any severance pay he expressed his feelings memorably by stating: 'I feel violated.'*

CAMBRIDGE RECORD	Appearances		Goals
Football League	295	(+4)	24
FA Cup	29		1
League Cup	23		–
Play-Offs	4		–

No 73. **GARY CLAYTON**
Debut: v Exeter, 15 August 1987
Farewell: v York, 12 February 1994

Another of United's longest-serving players in the early 1990s was Gary Clayton – the joker in the pack.

Gary was born on 2 February 1963 in Sheffield, but began his career at Rotherham. This proved to be a short-lived affair when Ian Porterfield took charge in 1979 and promptly sacked all the apprentices. Gary became a roofer and played for Spalding United, before switching to a bigger Lincolnshire club, Gainsborough Trinity in the Northern Premier League.

In 1986 he continued with his tour of non-League clubs by joining Burton Albion for £1,000. He only stayed there for eight months, but did well enough to play a couple of games for England's semi-professional side against the Republic of Ireland. This led to a trial at Sheffield Wednesday, but manager Howard Wilkinson wasn't impressed enough to offer him a contract, though he did help to improve Gary as a player.

In August 1986 Clayton signed for Doncaster for £8,000 and became an important member of their midfield. Rovers had a good side that season, but any dreams of promotion were snuffed out as the best players were sold on. Gary felt it was time for a move at the end of the season and Cambridge paid £8,000 for him in June 1987.

He became an integral part of Chris Turner's side that put the pride back at the Abbey. In his first two seasons he only missed one game, playing in midfield for the first season and switching to right back in 1988-89 when United struggled to find a specialist in that position. He was very enthusiastic and was the joker in the dressing room. He was a fine long-passer and not many people got past him.

Season 1989-90 was a personal disaster for Gary. A serious ankle injury kept him out of the team, and when he had recovered he found it almost impossible to win his place back, due to the strengthening of the team that had taken place. He didn't make the team for the Wembley play-off final, the second time he had missed out on playing under the twin towers. The first occasion had been for Burton in the FA Trophy, as Gary had turned professional. New manager John Beck froze him out. Gary's typically Yorkshire no-nonsense attitude didn't lend itself to bowing to Beck's rigid system because Gary was so set in his ways. All credit too him, though, for sticking valiantly in the squad waiting for better times, when most would have said goodbye. He had a loan spell with Peterborough United in January 1991 and later flourished under Gary Johnson, who valued his ability in holding his inexperienced side together. Sadly, he then tore his ankle ligaments, which necessitated surgery, but then amazed the surgeon, who had never seen anybody return to top-quality football after such an operation. Clayton came back in triumph in the 4-5 defeat by Huddersfield in April 1994.

In July 1994 Clayton joined Huddersfield (who must have been might-ily impressed in that match) for £20,000, and helped them to promotion to the First Division via the play-offs, but of course he wasn't selected for the Wembley final. He then moved to Plymouth (August 1995) and again helped his side to a victorious play-off final (and yes, of course he never got to play in it). Then he went to Torquay (free in August 1997) where he was admired for his passing ability and leadership qualities. In March 1999 he suffered what was at first believed to be a minor knee injury, but the prognosis turned out to be career-ending.

Magic Moment: *Clayton finally got to play at Wembley at the fifth time of asking when Torquay reached the Third Division play-off final in May 1998. Did he finish up on the winning side? Of course not. This isn't a fairy story, you know.*

Worst Nightmare: *In a friendly against Cambridge City to benefit Addenbrookes Hospital in 1989, Clayton dislocated his elbow and ended up there as a patient.*

CAMBRIDGE RECORD	Appearances		Goals
Football League	166	(+13)	14
FA Cup	9		–
League Cup	17	(+1)	3

No 74. **PHIL CHAPPLE**
Debut: v Rochdale, 4 April 1988
Farewell: v West Ham, 8 May 1993

Phil Chapple was another player whose Cambridge career both preceded and outlasted the first Beck era.

Philip Richard Chapple was born in Norwich on 26 November 1966 and joined his local league side on the government's Youth Training Scheme. He progressed from the youths to the reserves with much help from legendary centre-backs Dave Stringer and Dave Watson, but found the first team tantalisingly out of reach. During his last two years with the Canaries, Chapple's desperation became acute and he looked for a way out. Eventually, after five years at Norwich, he departed on a free transfer to Cambridge, signing in March 1988.

He tussled for a place with Lindsay Smith and Mark Crowe, displacing the latter and proving his worth by playing 70 consecutive games. Even as a youngster he seemed mature beyond his years, with a skill level way above the average Fourth Division fodder. He became captain during the 1988-89 season when Colin Bailie got injured, and proved his value in the diplomatic corps when he became United's representative on the PFA, although it must be said that the reason he got the job was that nobody else wanted it. He thus became the footballing equivalent of a shop steward, though a less militant one is hard to envisage.

Phil became captain and it was he who walked up the steps at Wembley to collect the play-off trophy in May 1990. In the autumn of that year his name went on to the transfer list, but thankfully the club kept hold of him. He was part of the rock-solid defence that meant that the free-flowing attack could operate in the knowledge that whatever goals were scored at the right end, would be shipped at a lesser rate at the other. Isn't football simple? It certainly looked that way with Phil. His 6ft 2in frame meant that nothing much would get past him via an aerial route, but on the ball he was composed and elegant, with a dainty, pigeon-toed running action that could cover ground surprisingly quickly. He appeared calm and unruffled, but wasn't afraid to voice his opinion to the players around him if he felt he had to.

In the maturity stakes he appeared to have a ten-year start on everybody else. He was happy to play a simple ball out of his defence if he was allowed to, or play a long ball out of defence to a man in space. In the Fourth Division it was unusual for a centre-half not to resort to the unthinking hoofed clearance to nobody in particular. Under John Beck's managership that was a hanging offence, but Phil was eventually able to adapt to life under the new regime. One aspect of his play that definitely found favour with Beck was his aerial mastery up front. United always put the fear of God into opposition managers at set pieces and the sight of Phil trotting forward to receive them was largely responsible. Often a neat, headed goal would result.

In August 1993 he joined Charlton Athletic for a £100,000 fee. At Christmas 1994 he gifted Wolves a goal when he stretched out his leg to clear a cross, then watched in horror as the ball hit the post and bounced in off his stomach. He helped Charlton to promotion in 1997-98 via the play-offs, saying he was playing the best football of his career, but left them in July 1998 to join Peterborough United on a free transfer.

Manager Barry Fry was chuffed with the signing, describing Chapple as the best central defender in the Third Division and Posh's most important ever signing, and making him captain to boot. Unfortunately he was stricken with a knee injury, then a back injury, which ended his playing days, but he became Posh's reserve-team manager, chief scout and head coach.

Magic Moment: *In a Littlewoods Cup-tie with Derby in September 1989, Chapple swivelled and fired an unstoppable 20-yard volley past Peter Shilton. It was the legendary keeper's first game as a 40-year-old.*

Worst Nightmare: *In the FA Cup quarter-final with Palace at the Abbey in March 1990, it was all-square with eleven minutes left when Chapple allowed Geoff Thomas's scuffed shot to pass between his legs and past the unsighted John Vaughan.*

CAMBRIDGE RECORD	Appearances		Goals
Football League	183	(+4)	19
FA Cup	23		1
League Cup	11		2
Play-Offs	5		—

No 75. **COLIN BAILIE**

Debut: v Grimsby, 27 August 1988
Farewell: v Bristol C, 14 March 1992

Colin James Bailie wouldn't have had a hope of making this book if I'd written it midway through his Cambridge career. He was playing poorly at right-back and was constantly barracked by a section of fans. The fact that he could turn around the situation in such a short space of time is testament to the astuteness of John Beck and the guts of Colin. Within a few months he had become a popular figure with his one-time taunters.

Colin is a native of Belfast, born on 31 March 1964, and he played well enough for a local boys' club to attract interest from across the water. With so few opportunities available to an ambitious footballer in Northern Ireland, it gave Swindon Town's youth-team manager a persuasive argument with which to lure Colin to the West Country in 1980.

Bailie spent two years as an apprentice before making the first team, playing as a right-back alongside the experienced pair of John Trollope and Ken Beamish. After 107 appearances and four goals in three seasons he decided to move on.

Ian Branfoot brought him to Reading for a tribunal-set fee of £22,500 in July 1985. To say he got off to a dream start with his new club is an understatement. His first eight League games for the club resulted in eight wins, and the club won all of their first thirteen League games to set a new record. Unsurprisingly, the championship was won at a canter. In 1987-88 Reading also enjoyed a run to Wembley in the Simod Cup, defeating QPR, Oxford, Bradford City, Nottingham Forest and Coventry on the way. They met Luton Town in the final and romped home to a 4-1 win in front of 61,000. Alas, it was a mere consolation for relegation from the Second Division.

Colin got married in the summer of 1988 and decided it would be a good idea to begin married life in a different part of the country. He was impressed with the straightforwardness of Chris Turner and John Beck at Cambridge and once more it was the League's tribunal that set the fee of £25,000.

Bailie got off to a reasonable start at the Abbey, his experience soon gaining him the captaincy and he put in some competent performances. He was actually quite an attacking right-back, in the sense that once he had the ball he would advance with a delicate twinkle-toed action, and after releasing the ball would try to support the midfield as the attack progressed, a trait which could leave him exposed when the move broke down. He was adept at spotting forward players in space and finding them with a good pass. He looked steady and was blessed with that Irish blend of grit and determination. He then had the misfortune to succumb to a nasty ankle injury in the spring of 1989 and things deteriorated from there on.

Quite why he played so badly on his return is a bit of a mystery. Lack of form and loss of confidence is one of those chicken and egg quandaries – which comes first? Either way, once that inner belief had gone, he was a shadow of his former self. Suddenly he was hesitant and prone to make appalling gaffes. This was demonstrated by a dreadful display at Lincoln on Boxing Day 1989, when he scored an own goal and helped the Imps win a game that was virtually lost with five minutes to go. When John Beck took over the reins from Chris Turner shortly afterwards, it looked a certainty that Colin would be soon on his way; compounded by the fact that United had a new right-back waiting in the wings, by the name of Andy Fensome.

Instead Beck switched Bailie into a midfielder and suddenly Cambridge had a new player on their hands. Showing true Irish passion, he became the cock of the roost as far as the centre of the pitch was concerned and the confidence came flooding back, helped by his strong character that knew that good times were around the corner. The crowd, which had got on his back before Christmas, now warmed to a player who showed guts in adversity. The change was probably the key element underlining the astonishing surge in performances under Beck, which lifted the team from mid-table mediocrity to FA Cup quarter-finalists and Wembley play-off winners in a few brief months.

Though his playing blossomed under Beck, he personally became bitter under the totalitarian regime of the dictator, which culminated in a dramatic walkout in the spring of 1992. After briefly appearing for Eynesbury Rovers, he became disillusioned with football in general and joined the Cumbrian Police. If John Beck ever ventures into that part of the world now, he had better be on his best behaviour. A professional meeting between the pair now might prove to be very interesting.

Magic Moment: *When he took the field at Wembley in the 1990 play-off final against Chesterfield, Bailie was the only player of the 22 to have played there before.*

Worst Nightmare: *Bailie cannot look back on his League debut with any fond regard. Swindon were crushed 0-5 by Oxford United.*

Cambridge Record	Appearances	Goals
Football League	104 (+15)	3
FA Cup	18	–
League Cup	10 (+1)	–
Play-Offs	3	–

No 76. **CHRIS LEADBITTER**
Debut: v Grimsby, 27 August 1988
Farewell: v West Ham, 8 May 1993

Sometimes playing alongside Bailie would be another tough, gritty player, this one hailing from Middlesbrough (born 17 October 1967). His name was Christopher Jonathan Leadbitter.

Not surprisingly for someone who revelled in the nickname of 'Leg Biter', Chris's childhood hero was the Leeds skipper Billy Bremner. Chris was brought up in Middlesbrough and played for his county side and also in the English Schools final. He had unsuccessful trials with Chelsea and Leicester City, but signed apprentice terms with Grimsby Town. He stayed with Grimsby for a year without making the first team, but enjoyed himself anyway.

In August 1986 he moved to Hereford and settled into the first team under John Newman. When Ian Bowyer replaced Newman, Chris fell out of favour and after a session of telephoning around various League clubs got invited down to Cambridge for a trial. He signed in August 1988, but after eight games on the left wing he was replaced temporarily by loan signing Doug Anderson. Along with Liam Daish, Chris was loaned out to non-League Barnet where he appeared as left-back. He was recalled to the first team following the departure of left-sided players Anderson and Brian Croft. His first goals for Cambridge both came in memorable games. He scored the fifth in the sensational 5-1 win over Peterborough at London Road and the first in the 6-0 record-equalling rout of Hartlepool. As a left-winger he was the complete opposite of Lee Philpott, whom he occasionally replaced. He would drift infield to midfield and relied on power and aggression to beat his man. At set-pieces Chris would lurk with intent on the edge of the area, waiting for the half-clearance that could be returned with venom. He used to take inswinging corners on the United right with that left foot.

It was at John Beck's behest that Chris moved into midfield and after a brief period of adjustment, gradually started enjoying himself more and more. Left-sided midfield proved to be his best position and it gave him more opportunity to unleash his favourite weapon – his fearsome left-footed shot. Chris had one of the hardest shots of any Abbey player and was responsible for some spectacular goals. Against Woking in the FA Cup in 1990 he casually rifled one into the top corner from 30 yards and a year later in the same competition he dispatched Wolves at Molineux with another blistering effort.

He went to Bournemouth in August 1993 for £25,000, before moving along the coast to join Plymouth in July 1995 on another free. After a brief drop into non-League footy with Dorchester Town, he moved to Torquay in November 1997. Despite being 30 years old he belied his age by proving to be a strong runner as well as a fierce tackler and he stood out in a very average Gulls midfield. In July 1999 he rejoined his old Torquay boss Kevin Hodges, who was now at Plymouth, on yet another free transfer, the Gulls apparently deciding he was too injury-prone. Hodges thought differently, thinking he added a bit of guile as well as experience in the centre of the park.

In early 2002 Leadbitter went from Gainsborough Trinity to Whitby Town (obviously he hankered for the seaside again).

Magic Moment: *At home to Scunthorpe in October 1989, in a gale, Leadbitter hooked the ball over his shoulder 58 yards out and saw the ball drop like a bomb into the net. Goalie Peter Litchfield would have needed to stand on the crossbar to save it.*

Worst Nightmare: *If footballers are valued by the total of their transfer fees, then Leadbitter has nothing to boast about. His nine moves added up to a combined value of £25,000. I hope he did better with the signing-on fees.*

CAMBRIDGE RECORD	Appearances	Goals
Football League	144 (+32)	18
FA Cup	16 (+2)	3
League Cup	12	3
Play-Offs	3	–

No 77. **JOHN TAYLOR**
Debut: v Gillingham, 30 August 1988
Final Farewell: Reading, 7 April 2001

If Leadbitter is a Golden Great, then you would have to find an even more valuable precious metal to describe John Patrick Taylor, who was once voted 'The Legend of the Abbey'.

John was born in Norwich on 24 October 1964, but was immediately adopted and brought up in Felixstowe on the Suffolk coast. He made the Suffolk county side and signed schoolboy terms for Colchester United aged fourteen after writing to a succession of clubs. He worked his way up to reserve-team level, but after leaving school at sixteen, he took a job as a clerk in a freight and shipping company. He still played on a part-time basis for Colchester and won a full-time contract when he was eighteen. His only appearance came in a Milk Cup-tie at Reading in September 1983 when he got off the bench to replace future Arsenal star Perry Groves. He was released at the end of the season, having been told that his beanpole figure wasn't strong enough for first-team football and returned to the shipping industry somewhat disillusioned.

Eventually Taylor's love of football returned and he played part-time for Sudbury in the Jewson League (the former Eastern Counties League). He played in both midfield and attack, but excelled up front, helping them to two championships and scoring a healthy 43 goals in his second season. Sudbury also reached the semi-final of the FA Vase, but the greatest achievement came when he was voted the Jewson League's Player's Player of the Year. He attracted the interest of Gary Johnson, once of Newmarket Town, and his recommendation to manager Chris Turner led to a signing in August 1988 for £1,000 and a set of shirts. He started off as a substitute, but soon earned his chance in the first team – at first playing along-side Gary Bull, Laurie Ryan and George Reilly, but in the latter half of the season teaming up with teenager Dion Dublin. That partnership provided the spark that ignited Cambridge out of five years of the Dark Ages.

John immediately earned the nickname 'Shaggy', his tall, gangly appearance and bushy haircut reminding fans of the hapless character from Scooby-Doo. The nickname stuck with him throughout his Cambridge career and he often signed off his manager's notes in the programme with his affectionate moniker. His playing gradually improved and in February 1989 John bagged a hat trick in a record-equalling 6-0 defeat of Hartlepool and finished as joint top scorer with Ryan when he netted with a spectacular overhead-kick in the last away game at York. In March 1989 rumours surfaced that West Ham were interested in signing him, along with speculation about a six-figure offer from another Fourth Division club.

It was the following season that everyone remembers. In the FA Cup, John scored in every round from first to fifth to set up a quarter-final tie with Crystal Palace. No Fourth Division side had ever gone further than this. In the League he again finished joint top scorer (fifteen, with Dublin), joining his partner on the list of the legends by scoring a hat-trick against Peterborough. The signing of Steve Claridge initially cost John his place, but the following season (1990-91) it was Claridge who was the frustrated sub as John kept tight hold of the No 10 shirt. Once again John helped Cambridge to the double of promotion and an FA Cup quarter-final.

The understanding that Taylor had with Dublin was almost telepathic. Each instinctively knew where the other one was, and because both players were unselfish they were continually setting up each other with easy goalscoring opportunities. John was a great header of the ball, but when on song had neat close control and an eye for a well-placed shot in the corner. He was a hardworking player, covering vast areas of the pitch. When he wasn't playing well, usually as the result of a debilitating migraine attack, or because he'd lost a contact lens in the mud, he could look gangly and awkward and was once described succinctly as 'looking like a lost giraffe'. The migraine attacks could persist for days. Suddenly without warning though, he would don the proverbial Superman cape and blow away the defenders who had been previously lulled into doziness by John's bumbling efforts. When in this mood he would confidently slot the ball home when on a one-on-one situation with the keeper, whereas before, the loss of confidence would be painfully obvious to everyone. He also played a couple of games as emergency goalkeeper when John Vaughan got injured and performed manfully in those situations as well.

Cambridge were within touching distance of the new Premier League when John Beck sold him to Bristol Rovers in a deal that brought Devon

White in the opposite direction. It was probably the worst transfer deal in United's history, especially as Cambridge had to pay £100,000 for the privilege. Apparently, Beck told his chairman that John's 'legs had gone'. In actual fact it was an unfit White who failed to make his mark at the Abbey, whilst John made a sensational start as a Pirate by bagging seven goals in his first eight games, and though his fourteen goals the following season couldn't keep Rovers up, he cracked in 23 League goals the season after that. Only the fact that no team-mate could even manage a quarter of that total cost Rovers a return to the First Division.

In July 1994 Taylor moved to Bradford City for £300,000 and bagged eleven goals for himself in a mediocre Second Division side, before moving to Luton in March 1995 for £200,000. Initially it looked a good move with three goals at the end of the season. But 1995-96 was a nightmare and John failed to find the back of the net in his 28 matches, hampered by a bad back.

It was Roy McFarland who rode to the rescue, bringing John back on board in January 1997. Initially he displaced Michael Kyd from the team, but as he got older and slower, and the quality of the strikers around him got better (Martin Butler and Trevor Benjamin), so his role changed. He was now used as an almost permanent substitute, able to turn things around whenever the mere mortals failed to deliver, or so it seemed. He created a sensation at Rochdale in April 1999 by coming off the bench to score the two goals that won the U's promotion. Eventually age caught up with him, but not before he had overtaken Alan Biley's record of 74 League goals in total for United. He became the reserve-team manager, but stepped up to replace John Beck midway through the 2001-02 season. Though he wasn't able to work miracles to keep United in the Second Division, you can never bet against him for long. 2002-03 is his testimonial season.

Magic Moment: *In an FA Cup second replay against Bristol City, Taylor created the first four goals before netting the fifth to keep up his record of scoring in every round.*

Worst Nightmare: *Against Reading in April 1991 Taylor chased the Royals' keeper Steve Francis to a ball. Francis grabbed it, then drew his knee up sharply into John's groin. United got the penalty (Dublin scored), but was it worth the agony?*

CAMBRIDGE RECORD	Appearances	Goals
Football League	236 (+89)	86
FA Cup	27 (+6)	11
League Cup	12 (+8)	4
Play-Offs	1 (+2)	–

No 78. **JOHN VAUGHAN**
Debut: v Gillingham, 6 September 1988
Farewell: v Peterborough, 10 April 1993

John Taylor was used as the emergency replacement for an injured or red-carded John Vaughan.

John (born Isleworth, 26 June 1964) was a Chelsea supporter as a boy, but he originally didn't want to be a footballer. He wasn't a very good runner and in true schoolboy tradition was forced in goal as a result. Much to his surprise he caught the eye in that position and progressed from his school team to the Middlesex county side. He moved to West Ham and spent six years as Phil Parkes' understudy. Parkes spent many hours coaching John at Upton Park and Phil later commented that John was a good shot-stopper. Vaughan kept goal in the 2-1 win over Spurs in the FA Youth Cup final, alongside Tony Cottee and Paul Allen. He worked his way up to third-choice keeper and was loaned out to Coventry City at the end of the 1984-85 season. The Sky Blues were suffering from an injury crisis, but John got injured himself before he could play for them. He appeared for a succession of League clubs between March 1985 and March 1986 in order to gain experience – Charlton, Bristol Rovers, Wrexham and Bristol City being the beneficiaries. Wrexham were interested in signing him and asked him what terms he would seek. John didn't like life in North Wales away from his London roots and named a ridiculously high figure to dissuade boss Dixie McNeil from signing him. To John's astonishment the figure was accepted, but the deal fell through when the club were obliged to upgrade the electrical supply at the Racecourse ground in the wake of the Bradford City fire.

In August 1986 he moved to Third Division Fulham for £20,000, in a youth-orientated side led by Ray Lewington. As is often the case with a young team, they took some fearful beatings and generally struggled. John suffered the unusual fate of being dropped, winning the Supporters' Player of the Year award, and being shunted into the reserves for the next season. His only first-team action in 1987-88 came in another loan spell with Bristol City. He had achieved little but learnt a lot, and knew that his best was yet to come. In June 1988 he was given the chance to prove it with Cambridge, when they signed him for nothing.

Vaughan proved to be one of the most popular keepers at Cambridge, earning the nickname 'The Legend' for his tales of goalkeeping derring-do, and inspiring the chant 'International Johnny Vaughan' in an affectionate mickey-take. Short for a goalkeeper at only 5ft 10in, he made up for that with agility and an excellent reputation as a shot-stopper. His lack of height meant he was disinclined to leave his goal-line, instead relying on excellent positioning and quick reflexes to save the day. He was stockily built, and in style was almost a Rodney Slack clone, although he decided which way to dive before any penalties were kicked. He was first-choice keeper throughout the meteoric rise from Fourth to the brink of the Premiership and during the Third Division championship season of 1990-91 he set a United record by keeping his goal intact for 648 minutes.

Under Beck he suffered greatly, as his boss insisted that his goal-kicks be aimed down the touchline to the wingers. Often they would go sailing into the crowd. 'It's the first time I have played rugby,' he mused. He did his best, practising goal-kicks dozens of times every day. When Beck's system finally collapsed, the Abbey let out a huge cheer when John threw the ball out of his area for the first time in two and a half years. By then his top dog spot was being challenged by Jon Sheffield, and Vaughan's days were numbered.

In August 1993 he moved to Charlton Athletic on a free, but after a frustrating season in which he played second fiddle to Mike Salmon he rejoined Beck, who was now Preston's boss. When Beck left to join Lincoln, once again John followed him. He says it wasn't a case of particularly wanting to be with Beck, but there weren't any other offers on the table. During his time at Sincil Bank he was relegated to the reserves. Beck had also signed Barry Richardson, largely for his ability to kick the ball to the edge of the opposition penalty area. John had a loan spells at Colchester and Chesterfield, who signed him as emergency cover, and he made his debut immediately against Cambridge. He was No 1 keeper at Lincoln in 1999-2000, but then let in five against Torquay and was dropped. He finally retired in June 2000.

Magic Moment: *In a crunch promotion game against Bolton in April 1991, Mark Seagraves powered in a close-range header. Though wrong-footed and at the wrong side of the goal, Vaughan somehow changed direction in mid-air, flung himself across goal and blocked the ball. Beck said it was a better save than Banks' against Pele in 1970.*

Worst Nightmare: *In September 1986, Vaughan's inexperienced Fulham were paired with Liverpool in the Milk Cup. In the first leg at Anfield, the Liverpool players ran riot and stuck ten goals past John, with Steve McMahon grabbing four (and missing a penalty as well). John feels he turned in a reasonable performance that night.*

CAMBRIDGE RECORD	Appearances	Goals
Football League	178	–
FA Cup	24	–
League Cup	13	–
Play-Offs	5	–

No 79. **LIAM DAISH**

Debut: v Gillingham, 6 September 1988
Farewell: v Wycombe, 4 December 1994

Liam Sean Daish added to the vocal outpourings from Vaughan in United's defence, and Daish was never afraid to put across his point of view to his colleagues.

Liam's father was a submariner – a career path Liam may well have followed if the football hadn't worked out. Liam was born in Portsmouth on 23 September 1968 and rose from the ranks of apprentice with his local club, Portsmouth, up to first-team level. Originally a midfielder at schoolboy level, he now moved into central defence. His only League appearance came in February 1987 at Ipswich, Liam only learning that he was playing two hours before kick-off. Although his contribution was praised, the true compliment of retaining his place wasn't forthcoming and he was back in the reserves.

Portsmouth were on their way to regaining a place in the old First Division for the first time since 1959, but Liam was at the edge of the action, just an onlooker. Inevitably this created tensions, and when you consider that the boss was the excitable and fiery Alan Ball, it was almost unavoidable that a major bust-up would occur with Liam, who shared many character traits with Ball. The manager was a complex and unforgiving man and there was only going to be one outcome – Liam was given the cold shoulder and, though he was offered a new contract, this was mysteriously withdrawn at the last minute.

Carlisle made an offer for Daish and Leicester and Bristol Rovers were also interested, but he signed for Cambridge in July 1988, having been impressed with the professionalism shown compared with Pompey.

He worked his way up from the reserves, and a loan spell with Barry Fry's Barnet, to take the permanent place of Lindsay Smith in the first team in December 1988. At the end of the 1988-89 season he represented the Republic of Ireland at Under-21 level in a tournament in France. He learned much on the trip from more experienced players and gained a hunger for further international honours. Although it was only through his Dublin-born father that he qualified to represent Ireland, he underlined his 'Irishness' by drinking Guinness and listening to 'The Dubliners' on his personal cassette player on away trips.

Liam not only took Lindsay Smith's shirt, he also took over the tough guy role in the Cambridge team. Playing alongside the more mild-mannered Chapple, it was Liam who showed the aggression and rolled-up sleeves to intimidate the less determined of the opposition strikers. Mind you, that's most of them at Fourth Division level. Daish couldn't claim to

be a great ball player. He was also undeniably slow and therefore an expo-
nent of the 'if in doubt, boot it out', school of thought. In fact, it caused
astonishment at one match when he gathered the ball in defence, beat his
man and strode purposefully forward. Though tall, he was inevitably the
player left behind on the halfway line at set-pieces near the opposition goal.
This meant that his first goal was a long time in coming. In his 63rd League
game he finally broke his duck by staying upfront after a corner had broken up and heading home Michael Cook's cross. He actually become a consistent goalscorer over time – one every season.

Liam's guts and drive were invaluable in Cambridge's meteoric rise
through the divisions. He was always the player with the clenched fist and
shouts of encouragement, whether United were winning or losing. Whilst
others appeared cautious about the U's chances in the Third Division in
1991, it was Liam who proclaimed that they were looking to 'Bosh – go
straight up.' The downside of this 'never-say-die' attitude was a tendency
to recklessness when the red mist descended over his eyes. Following a
fight with a Maidstone player in a League Cup-tie in August 1989 he
declared: 'I must bite my tongue and walk away.' Good intentions, but in
the final League game of the season at Aldershot he lost control and raced
across the pitch to deliver a wild tackle on David Puckett. That moment of
madness earned him a red card and a suspension that meant he missed the
Wembley play-off final.

Liam played half a dozen games for the Republic of Ireland's Under-
21 side and was then blooded for the full team as Jack Charlton started to
contemplate breaking up his team of ageing stars. He made his debut
against Wales in February 1992 and won five caps in total, including two as
a substitute. In June 1996, Ireland were competing in the final of a tournament in the United States against Mexico when Liam was sent off along
with Niall Quinn and Mick McCarthy. It later turned out that the referee
had a strong pro-Mexico bias.

Daish left Cambridge for Birmingham in January 1994 for £500,000
and soon became captain, though he won't thank me for revealing that
they nicknamed him Bert. He then when to Ron Atkinson's Coventry for
£1.5 million but in 1995 there was an unpleasant incident in a match in
Ancona, Italy, when a fracas in the tunnel led to an assault charge being laid
at Liam, amongst others, which was later dropped.

Sometimes Liam looked out of his depth in the Premiership, his sus-
pect ball control being a more obvious handicap in such company, but his
commitment still compensated for that weakness. In 1997-98 a cruciate lig-
ament injury kept him out for eighteen months, and in 1999 he quit the
professional game and joined Havant and Waterlooville. In April 2000 he
became player-manager, first as caretaker, then jointly with Mick Jenkins.

Magic Moment: *Barry Fry paid an unforgettable tribute to Daish's determination (or madness?). 'If the penalty box was being attacked by a squadron of F-111s, Liam Daish would jump up and try to head them away.'*

Worst Nightmare: *Birmingham were 3-0 up at Chester in December 1994, when Daish scored the fourth goal. A Brummie fan threw a toy trumpet onto the pitch and Liam picked it up and joyfully played it. The ref booked him for doing so, which took Daish over his points total for the season and earned him a three-match ban.*

CAMBRIDGE RECORD	Appearances		Goals
Football League	138	(+1)	4
FA Cup	16		–
League Cup	11		–
Play-Offs	2		–

No 80. **DION DUBLIN**

Debut: v Wrexham, 16 December 1988
Farewell: v Leicester, 13 May 1992

Another United 'Great' made his debut alongside Daish's – Dion Dublin.

Dion was born in Leicester on 22 April 1969 and joined Leicester City as a 10-year-old, but despite winning County honours he was released at sixteen. He spent three years working in a Leicester leisure centre, but with a supportive father (whose musical talent led to a spell with Showaddywaddy), he gained trials with Stoke, Birmingham and Norwich. All turned him down, but Norwich did give him a second chance, signing him from Oakham United in March 1988. He banged in five goals in nine games for the reserves, but it wasn't enough to get him a first-team place.

Luckily, Cambridge's youth team boss Graham Scarff spotted Dublin's potential and, after Norwich released him on a free transfer, he came to the Abbey for a pre-season trial in July 1988. He showed promise, but United already had four strikers and a fifth was a luxury they couldn't afford. Also there were questions about Dion's lack of work-rate. Reserve-team manager Gary Johnson suggested he should try his luck as a centre-half and when the reserve No 5 missed the bus after a prolonged dental appointment, Dublin had 90 minutes to prove his worth, which he duly did. He had a loan spell at King's Lynn in 1988-89 and also appeared for Barnet and Wycombe Wanderers.

Other people's health-related misfortunes provided another break for Dion, when George Reilly's young son poked his dad in the eye, causing him to miss the Sherpa Van Trophy game with Peterborough. Dion was named as a substitute, but were 0-2 down with time running out, when he stepped into the fray. The U's stormed back and it was left to Dion to grab the headlines by sliding in a dramatic late winner. That led to a League call-up and in his second start he created a sensation by scoring a hat-trick in the 5-1 demolition of Peterborough at London Road. That made Dion an instant legend amongst the U's fans, a status that never deserted him.

Dublin was a footballing enigma. So casual and laid-back, that some (i.e. the author) initially assumed he was lazy. He was nothing of the sort: in fact, he was amongst the hardest-working strikers at the club. Like a cat, though, he never took an unnecessary step, only moving when he judged it in his best interests to do so. Against Chester on one occasion, he chased a lost cause to the bye-line, forced the ball out of the goalkeeper's desperate clutches and set up John Taylor with the easiest of tap-ins. Sometimes Dion hung around up front, looking for a ball to be played towards him, but at other times he would race back into defence and snuff out any impending threats at that end. His ability to defend was better than the good-intentioned efforts of most strikers, and he could probably have carved out a career in central defence.

But the quality that Dublin possessed was something nobody could miss, namely his one-touch ability. Without exerting himself in the slightest, he could flick a ball with either foot or head into the path of a better-placed colleague, usually John Taylor. His knack of knowing where a ball was going also led to the countless numbers of gentle tap-ins that he scored. Almost all of Dublin's goals came from within the six-yard box, and even when he struck from further afield, it was all about timing rather than ultimate power. Dion insists his weaknesses are lack of skill, ball-holding and shooting. He may not have a long-range shooting ability and obviously prefers a quick pass or flick to prolonged possession, but there's certainly no lack of skill. His early nickname was 'Dizzy' and Beck once earned himself a chiding in some quarters for calling him a 'Black Pearl'.

When Dion was transferred to Manchester United in August 1992 the fee was a U's record £1,000,000 plus £300,000 if the player earned an England cap. He made substitute appearances in his first three games, but was then deemed good enough by Alex Ferguson to take the place of Andrei Kanchelskis. Dublin had a wonderful full debut, scoring the only goal of the game at Southampton, but in his third full game (and his first at Old Trafford) he broke his leg. The recovery was long and he never appeared in a United shirt again. Had it not been for that cruel injury, it is easy to speculate that he might have gone on to be a legend at Old Trafford. Certainly the United fans recognised his ability, and even today they regard him with much affection.

In September 1994 Dublin moved to Coventry City for around £2 million and justified their gamble by a string of superb displays in both attack and defence that kept Coventry in the top flight. In 1997-98 he finished joint top scorer in the Premiership, a fact that seemed to accelerate the already feverish transfer rumours that were surrounding him.

His eye-catching displays for the Sky Blues earned him a surprise England call-up from Glenn Hoddle in February 1998 and he made his international debut in a 0-2 defeat against Chile. He linked up well with Ian Wright and seemed as though he might make the World Cup squad, but it wasn't to be. He did start for England in the 2-0 win over the Czech Republic and impressed greatly, but Kevin Keegan didn't seemed to like him as much as Hoddle did and his England career looks to have finished on four caps.

It was a major blow to Coventry fans to lose their star man to John Gregory's Aston Villa in November 1998 for £5.75 million, though Dion had rejected a move to Blackburn a month earlier, preferring to stay in the Midlands with his family. Gregory felt he could be a real 'big club' player – a 1998 version of Peter Withe. Dublin continued his trait of making an instant impact by bagging seven goals in his first three games, bringing out the best in Stan Collymore. When Collymore's off-field problems became too much for his manager, Dion then forged a link with Julian Joachim and for several months Villa were serious title contenders. Dion's form (and Villa's) dipped at the end because he was carrying a hernia injury, which required surgery. A more serious operation was needed in December 1999 when he crushed a vertebra in an accidental collision – an injury that could easily have confined him to a wheelchair. Thankfully, moving some bone from his hip to his back fixed the problem and he was able to return alongside his new strike partner Benito Carbone just four months later. He also scored the decisive penalty in the FA Cup semi-final shoot-out with Bolton that sent them to the final, though they played poorly on the day and lost 0-1 to Chelsea. In Euro 2000, Dion even became a pundit, but a lack of incisiveness meant that was never going to be a long-term career path. He had a poor playing season in 2001-02 and, with his first-team opportunities restricted by the signing of Peter Crouch, ended up going to Millwall on loan, temporarily rejoining his old Cambridge colleague Steve Claridge.

Magic Moment: *Against Newcastle in 1997, goalkeeper Shay Given held the ball in his outstretched palm then looked incredulously as Dublin raced back from behind the goal-line to knock it out of his hand and score one of the most bizarre goals.*

Worst Nightmare: *Dublin was in the Cambridge United reserve team's minibus when the engine caught fire. Somebody shouted out that the engine was going to blow up, which prompted Dion to sprint up the M11 at a rapid rate of knots, far outstripping any of his team-mates..*

CAMBRIDGE RECORD	Appearances	Goals
Football League	133 (+23)	52
FA Cup	21	10
League Cup	8 (+2)	5
Play-Offs	5	2

No 89. John Filan

No 90. Micah Hyde

No 91. Carlo Corazzin

No 92. Jody Craddock

No 93. Matt Joseph

No 94. Danny Granville

Chapter Nine

Beckism

No 81. **DANNY O'SHEA**
Debut: v Grimsby, 19 August 1989
Farewell: v Leyton Orient, 21 March 1995

Danny O'Shea was another versatile United player readily identifiable by his first name.

Daniel Edward O'Shea was born in Newington on 26 March 1963 and played for Staines Town Juniors and Surrey County before joining his favourite club – Arsenal – as an apprentice. He worked hard at his game and after three years was good enough for the first team, making his debut wearing the No 2 shirt previously worn by John Hollins. He made nine first-class appearances for the Gunners in the autumn of 1982, mostly as a midfielder, before dropping back into the reserves. In 1983-84 he went to Coventry on loan, but didn't get a game and soon afterwards he briefly turned out for Charlton (where Alan Kimble was his boot-boy). In the summer he was released by Arsenal on a free transfer and joined Exeter.

O'Shea played in almost every game of 1984-85, despite appearing under three different bosses, but at the season's end he was once more on the move, this time joining Southend for a £5,000 tribunal-fixed fee. He settled at Southend with ease under the stewardship of Bobby Moore, and became a Roots Hall regular for four years, making 118 League appearances and scoring twelve goals. In 1988 he picked up a serious injury and was released from his contract a free man.

At Cambridge, Chris Turner was forever metaphorically rummaging through the dustbins of clubs, looking for discarded treasure in Womble-like fashion, and he signed Danny in August 1989. Initially O'Shea found it difficult to break into the first team, a situation probably exacerbated by the fact that he was considered a midfielder or defending utility player. Inevitably, he was the one player who would be kept on the bench or in reserve, ready to fill in for injuries and suspensions. When he did play, he showed that it wasn't a case of 'Jack of all trades and master of none', but more a case that he was a master in more than one position. Although naturally a midfielder, lacking the sheer physical presence of a stopper, he surprised most people by making more than an adequate replacement for the suspended Liam Daish in the 1990 play-off final against Chesterfield. O'Shea used his brain to good effect, reading the game to a degree that was virtually unheard of at that level and thus ensuring that he was always in the right place at the right time. Allowing his partner, Chapple, to take care of the high balls, United didn't miss Daish on the day and Chesterfield were effectively neutralised up front, which left them vulnerable to Dublin's killer blow at the other end.

Danny also replaced Daish the following season, though this was due to injury. It was his versatility that proved invaluable to Beck. Able to play anywhere in defence or midfield, he was the man who gave Cambridge strength in depth, the key to a successful side. The one overlooked aspect of the Beck style was the tenacious tackling. As soon as an opposition player dwelt on the ball, two ferocious tacklers would bear down upon him and inevitably Danny was one of them. Although generally speaking a mild-mannered player, occasionally he would allow his high level of commitment to go to his head and he would get carried away with a rash challenge. He was never noted for goalscoring and would rarely venture beyond the halfway line. Nor was he inclined to try his luck from long distance, but his first goal was dramatic – the winner in a 4-3 victory at Grimsby in United's first Second Division game for seven years.

When Gary Johnson became manager he made Danny player-coach, a role he also fulfilled at Northampton Town in March 1995 when he left Cambridge. He subsequently played for Rushden & Diamonds, Aylesbury United and Canvey Island and is currently the assistant coach with Arsenal Ladies with Vic Akers. He has also played for Arsenal in a 'Masters of Britain' indoor football tournament for the Over-35s.

Magic Moment: *O'Shea proudly led Cambridge out at his old stomping ground Highbury in the FA Cup quarter-final of March 1991, though U's lost narrowly.*

Worst Nightmare: *O'Shea was sent off with David Speedie in a promotion clash at Blackburn. Although undeserved (my opinion) it cost United dear. They lost 1-2.*

CAMBRIDGE RECORD	Appearances		Goals
Football League	186	(+17)	1
FA Cup	16	(+3)	–
League Cup	18	(+1)	–
Play-Offs	3	(+2)	1

No 82. **LEE PHILPOTT**

Debut: v Maidstone, 30 August 1989
Farewell: v Portsmouth, 7 November 1992

Dancing down the left wing, often alongside O'Shea, was the ladies' favourite, Lee Philpott.

Although born in Barnet (on 21 February 1970) Lee's family moved to St Neots when he was small. His father worked for the BBC in Shepherd's Bush and on Saturdays they would travel together and watch neighbours QPR in the afternoons. Lee can proudly claim that he played a part in the first all-Merseyside Cup final of 1986 – he was a ball boy.

Lee's footballing career started with Cambridge Crusaders, progressing to Luton Schoolboys and then on to Peterborough United. Although some at Peterborough were helpful (manager Noel Cantwell, for instance), Lee felt that the club never brought out the best in him and help him to develop as a player. He only played four League games over two seasons and three of those were as a substitute. Salvation came in May 1989 when rivals Cambridge offered him a one-year contract following a successful trial. In contrast to his time at Posh, he found more encouragement at the Abbey, especially with John Beck, who gave him the confidence to take the ball past defenders and, just as importantly, to try again if it didn't work out first time around. He was a good old-fashioned winger in the sense that he hugged the touchline and never ventured infield, unless an attack had developed on the opposite wing, when he would appear in front of goal, sliding in low crosses and spectacularly dispatching others, usually with his left foot, because he was a heavily one-footed player. He wasn't strong and could easily be pushed off the ball and he wasn't a great tackler either, but instead relied on the drop of the shoulder, nifty footwork and moderate pace to bamboozle the full-backs. This Stanley Matthews-like ability to weave past defenders is perhaps the one thing that is sadly lacking from lower-division football and Lee showed what we were missing. This daintiess, combined with his longish, well-groomed hair, delicate physique and unmanly running action, occasionally earned the taunts that he was a bit of a girlie, but his ability silenced most of the critics.

In common with most of his colleagues, a big-money move was always on the cards. It came in November 1992 when Lee signed for Leicester City for £350,000. He was at Filbert Street for just over three seasons, making 75 League appearances (eighteen of them as substitute) and scoring three goals. He played a part in lifting Leicester into the Premiership, and their subsequent relegation, but left in March 1996 before he could celebrate another promotion.

He joined Blackpool for £75,000 after his pace (which was never great) had inevitably dropped off as he approached footballing middle age. Two years later he was at Lincoln on a free transfer, but suffered a double whammy of a pulled stomach muscle and damaged hamstring. Playing against the lesser abilities of Third Division defenders, a fit Lee was able to resurrect his dizzy dribbling skills to weave his way past them once more, though by then he was fed up with being stuck out on the wing, patiently waiting for the ball, preferring to play on the left of a three-man midfield. His contract wasn't renewed and in the summer of 2000 he rejoined his old Leicester boss Brian Little at Hull City.

Philpott returned to form at Boothferry Park, now playing in his preferred role in midfield and scored his first goal for the club on the 450th appearance of his career in March 2001. The following season was disappointing as it was decimated by injury, but by the February he had recovered. He was transfer-listed in the summer of 2002.

Magic Moment: *In an FA Cup-tie with Sheffield Wednesday in March 1991 Philpott scored what was voted as the best goal ever seen at the Abbey. A right-wing cross came over and he volleyed it in the top corner with his usually unreliable right foot.*

Worst Nightmare: *Philpott's Blackpool manager John Reames described Lee as the best player in the Third Division, but then kept dropping him from the side.*

CAMBRIDGE RECORD	Appearances	Goals
Football League	118 (+16)	17
FA Cup	19	3
League Cup	10	1
Play-Offs	5	—

No 83. **MICHAEL CHEETHAM**
Debut: v Torquay, 13 October 1989
Farewell: v Huddersfield, 26 April 1994

Whilst Lee Philpott was dancing down the left wing, it was usually Michael Cheetham who was causing havoc on the other.

Michael's father Les served in the British Army, which explains why Michael Martin Cheetham was born in the Netherlands on 30 June 1967. At the age of eight, young Michael was living in Belgium and started playing for the Army's school team. He was uprooted four years later to West Germany, where he impressed Borussia Moenchengladbach, who invited him to train with their junior squad. He played for various local German sides and then at the age of sixteen joined the Army himself, training as a technician at Harrogate. He completed his training and joined the Signals Regiment, playing for the Army and Combined Services. Afterwards he signed for Basingstoke Town in the Vauxhall-Opel League Division One, but his breakthrough came whilst playing in the British Army Centenary Cup final, where he was voted Man of the Match by England Manager Bobby Robson, who tipped the wink to his old club Ipswich. After a successful trial, the Blues paid the Army £400 to release him from his contract in October 1988. He made his debut for Town against Blackburn, but only made one full and three substitute League appearances after that.

In October 1989 he was brought to Cambridge on loan, to help boost a team next to bottom of the League. Michael took Tony Dennis's place on the right wing and made an instant impact in the 5-2 win over Torquay. He did so well, that his first five games all resulted in victories and he can take credit for helping to awaken a slumbering team that went on to win promotion via the play-offs and reach the FA Cup quarter-finals.

Cheetham set up countless goals through his mastery of the right wing. A more direct player than Philpott, he tended to beat his full-back using pace, rather than trickery, knocking the ball past him and racing through. A succession of crosses towards the ever hungry Dublin and Taylor was always going to result in a goal feast, but Michael was a more than useful goal-poacher in his own right. In an early game at Hartlepool he struck a dramatic late winner from 30 yards to provoke the memorable newspaper headline 'Cheetham Cheats-'em'. In fact, only the aforementioned strikers would better the eleven League and Cup goals he bagged in his first season. This tally was boosted when Alan Kimble went off injured in the home match with Colchester in April 1990. Deprived of their regular penalty-taker, it was Michael who confidently converted two spot-kicks to add to his earlier goal from open play, and effectively send the Essex side into the Conference. He bagged another penalty in the final game at Aldershot that confirmed a place in the play-offs, and then scored a spot-kick in each of the play-off semi-finals with Maidstone, that earned the U's a trip to Wembley. He also became a free-kick specialist – a vitally important role in a Beck side.

Michael mostly kept his right-wing place in the Third Division championship-winning side, but suffered anxious moments when the Gulf War was announced, fearing an imminent recall into the Army, because he was a reservist. That scare proved unfounded. When the U's went up into the Second, Michael found life tougher. The wingers were always the most important players on the pitch as far as Beck was concerned and any deficiency in the crossing department was ruthlessly punished. Michael's orders were strict. Race down towards the corner flag, use pace to beat the full-back (always on the outside, never cut inside) and send over a quality ball into the penalty area. Michael lost his place to a succession of other players that season – Taylor, Dennis, Claridge, Rowett and Wilkins were all tried – but few could match his ability on the right wing. Beck's dreadful start to the 1992-93 season led to him placing Cheetham in various makeshift attacks, but playing men out of position rarely works, especially when it's done out of desperation. Cheetham was an attacking winger – not a striker.

Most of Beck's dream team were quickly jettisoned after the doomed attempt at Premiership status, but Michael was amongst the last to go, though he was handicapped by both thigh and back injuries. He finally went in July 1994 to join Chesterfield, but that wasn't a success and after a handful of appearances he joined Colchester in March 1995.

At last Cheetham could revel once more in his favoured position, with more freedom to operate under the watchful eye of boss Steve Wignall and he made 37 League appearances over two seasons. He moved to the non-League giants of Suffolk soccer – Sudbury Town – and was part of the side that dumped Brighton out of the FA Cup in November 1996 in a penalty shoot-out. He had a short spell at Cambridge City, but in 2000 rejoined Sudbury as a player and as assistant manager. He also trained to be a driving instructor, though presumably he was hampered by a tendency to always veer to the right.

Magic Moment: *In the big derby game at Peterborough in April 1990, Cheetham scored from a half-clearance after just 21 seconds.*

Worst Nightmare: *After making his debut for Ipswich, Cheetham forced the team coach to drive all the way back through Oxford so he could fetch his car keys in the hotel.*

CAMBRIDGE RECORD	Appearances		Goals
Football League	123	(+9)	17
FA Cup	17		1
League Cup	8	(+1)	1
Play-Offs	5		2

No 84. STEVE CLARIDGE

Debut: v Southend, 25 February 1990
Farewell: v Fulham, 3 January 1994

Cheetham's rival on the right wing was often an out-of-position Steve Claridge, though Steve was a recipient of his crosses when playing as a striker.

Stephen Edward Claridge was born in Portsmouth on 10 April 1966 and says that he only went to school to play football. Being a fan of his local club Portsmouth, he was naturally delighted when they took him on as an apprentice. Though Pompey (under Bobby Campbell and Alan Ball) were passionate and demanding, Steve admits that he didn't respond in the same manner and he was released after three years.

The following season he broke his ankle playing for the Hampshire County side and after recovering joined Fareham Town. In September

1984 he moved to Bournemouth and once again learned much from a couple of willing and experienced tutors – this time it was Harry Redknapp and Archie Styles. After fourteen months (and a handful of games) he transferred to Weymouth for £12,000. No longer a professional, he had to supplement his wages by selling fruit and veg on the roadside and doing the odd gardening job. He stayed at Weymouth for two seasons, but found the financial strain of commuting from Portsmouth three times a week crippling and in August 1988 he was released on a free transfer. A number of clubs showed a willingness to take Steve on, but Crystal Palace were Steve's chosen club. Still living in Portsmouth and attempting to commute every day, Steve got caught up in a traffic jam on the M25 in his first month and was fined for being late for training. The following month he was loaned to Aldershot and soon settled into the side, becoming a regular up front with Dave Puckett. He was signed full-time for £14,000 and in 1988-89 he won a clean sweep of the Player of the Year trophies.

Claridge was a star in a struggling team and as Aldershot teetered on the brink of financial ruin, they were forced to unload their assets to survive. Cambridge had been led a merry dance on the pitch by Steve many times, and they came in with a £75,000 offer – a figure that looked a bargain, even without the benefit of hindsight. That was in February 1990 and immediately he gave his new boss selection problems. Dublin and Taylor were playing too well to be dropped, so Steve was used as a substitute in his first five games, a role in which he would become all too familiar. As United set off on their backbreaking run of matches – due to fixture congestion caused by the FA Cup run (Steve was ineligible for these) – so the presence of Steve became essential. Beck was forced to include him in the starting eleven, alongside Dublin and Taylor if necessary, and he helped lift the team towards their play-off destiny. Though he played in both semi-finals, he was once more only a substitute at Wembley.

The Third Division championship season led to poor Steve making the bench more often than the starting eleven. Again, this was more due to the prowess of Dublin and Taylor up front and Cheetham on the right, rather than any deficiencies on Steve's part. Indeed, he was by then a crowd favourite, a role earned by his insatiable desire and hunger to take a starring part in any game he played in.

Claridge was someone who loved to take on defenders and weave his way round them. It was a joy to watch a player terrify the opposition, his opponents often not having a clue how to deal with him, except by fouling, which resulted in a glut of penalties. Often, this determination would result in blinkered vision, when Steve would ignore the fact that other players were better placed. Very frustrating for the unselfish Dublin and Taylor, but the crowd understood. You can't tame a free spirit.

Steve was unconventional in other ways as well. He would turn up at the club in a shabby car, full of clutter, and his own appearance tended to match that of his transport. This gave him the nickname 'Worzel', and he received more than one booking from officious referees for having his socks rolled down to his ankles.

He joined Luton in July 1992 for £160,000, but found it impossible to replicate his form at Cambridge – something he publicly apologised to manager David Pleat for – and he moved back to Cambridge in the November. With no Dublin or Taylor at the Abbey, he was at least guaranteed a first-team spot, but his partnership with Steve Butler never really gelled, which was probably more down to Butler's problems. Having said that, Steve had exorcised his game of his old selfishness and had gone too far the other way, often passing when shooting was a better option, but still showing his magical ability at holding a ball up.

In January 1994 he moved to Barry Fry's Birmingham for £350,000, when the board needed to make some money, then continued his career as a journeyman, signing for Leicester in March 1996 for £1.2 million, Wolves for £400,000 in March 1998, and then Portsmouth. At Fratton Park he became a legend. He was originally a loan signing from Leicester in January 1998, but signed on a permanent basis from Wolves for a bargain £200,000 in August 1998. He was helping to keep Pompey in the First Division, whilst ploughing a lone furrow up front. His appearance led to a nickname of 'Gypsy' by the Pompey players.

In October 2000 he became football's most unlikely boss when taking over his relegation-threatened team. Steve was astute enough to surround himself with knowledgeable ex-colleagues and this, coupled with his infectious enthusiasm, lifted the team into mid-table. Then in February 2002 came a jolt. Chairman Milan Mandaric appointed Graham Rix as manager, claiming Steve's appointment was only temporary. Steve hotly disputed this, and understandably rejected an offer to go back to his playing duties.

He joined Millwall in April 2001, initially on loan, but three goals in six starts led to a permanent move and he helped his new side to the Second Division championship.

Magic Moment: *Claridge contributed to the goal that clinched victory in United's 1990 play-off final. Coming off the bench he told Dublin he was out of position at the far post for a corner. Dion went to the near post and dispatched the vital header.*

Worst Nightmare: *In a promotion tussle with Ipswich in March 1992, Claridge was substituted after 22 minutes for the crime of cutting inside the full-back, instead of going round the outside. At half-time he got involved in a fight with Beck, allegedly giving his boss a black eye. Feel free to call this a Magic Moment if you so desire.*

CAMBRIDGE RECORD	Appearances		Goals
Football League	109	(+23)	46
FA Cup	5		–
League Cup	6	(+4)	5
Play-Offs	4	(+1)	–

No 85. **RICHARD WILKINS**

Debut: v Birmingham, 25 August 1990
Farewell: v Rotherham, 5 March 1994

It might be thought that Richard Wilkins' views on John Beck would be no less charitable than Claridge's, especially as the long hoof from defence inevitably sailed over the central midfielder's head, but this is not the case.

Richard John Wilkins was born in Lambeth on 28 May 1965, but he was playing for West Suffolk Schoolboys when he was detected by Ipswich who signed him up on schoolboy terms. They released him at the age of sixteen after saying he was too small to make the grade at 5ft 4in. Had they never heard of Steve Spriggs? Also, weren't they aware that teenagers are liable to grow, because Richard went on to be a six-footer? He dropped down several levels to play for Haverhill Rovers for three years before moving to Colchester United after impressing them in a match against their reserves in November 1986. A couple of good games led to a professional contract and he had to quit his job as a window installer.

He started off in their midfield, but in 1987-88 he switched to centre-forward. That season was a momentous one at Layer Road. Top of the table at Christmas, but all downhill from there, as one disastrous managerial appointment followed another. Colchester just survived relegation to the Conference the following season, but in 1989-90 they were doomed. Ironically, it was a 0-4 reverse at Cambridge that confirmed it.

Richard wasn't desperate to leave Colchester, but Third Division Cambridge United had been after him for a while and weighed in with £65,000 that was tempting to both club and player. Richard was the only new signing Beck made at the start of his first full season in charge (1990-91), although it appears that Chris Turner too had been after him at an earlier date. Though Richard had the reputation of being a cultured player, that wouldn't have been too much in evidence as this was the time that Beck's 'Route One' footballing system really started. Richard's job was to spray the ball out to the wings, and this certainly limited the range of talents he could display. He was forbidden from passing through the middle, or from setting off on surging runs on his own. Nevertheless, he showed a composure on the ball in midfield that hadn't been seen since Beck himself had hung up his boots. Having said that, Richard got on well with

Beck and was quick to defend the system from critics, especially Glenn Hoddle, 'who hit more 70-yard passes than anybody else.' Wilkins believes firmly that it was only the high quality of personnel that Beck had available to him that made the system work – hence its failure at Lincoln. He thinks Beck also deserves credit for turning many of the team from Fourth Division fodder into Premiership class players, but admits that the too-rigid application of the system proved to be its undoing.

Wilkins also gave Beck another weapon with which to bludgeon his way through the divisions – a long throw. Richard could hurl the ball into the opposition penalty area with ease, well in excess of the distance generated by Fensome and Kimble. Suddenly, the safe option for opposition defenders of clearing the ball into touch was negated. A throw-in was as good as a corner-kick. An enthusiastic cricketer, there is no doubt that Wilkins' fielding practice paid off on the football pitch.

Undoubtedly, Cambridge never saw the best of Wilkins. By the time Beck left, Richard was handicapped by a succession of injuries and was a rare sight on the pitch in his last two seasons with the club. At the beginning of the 1992-93 season he fractured his femur at a time when Derby County were expressing an interest. Richards also got on well with Beck's replacement, Ian Atkins, but barely played a game for him. By the time he was fit, Gary Johnson was in charge and Richard was frozen out.

In July 1994 he joined Hereford, soon after U's rejected an offer from Peterborough. Hereford were prepared to wait for Wilkins to regain fitness and they got two seasons out of him. Cambridge made a half-hearted bid to re-sign him, but instead he rejoined Colchester for £18,000. He featured in their play-off triumph in 1998 and filled just about every defensive and midfield role, despite repeated injuries. It was a neck injury that finally ended his professional career in March 2000. The following season he joined Bury Town in the Jewson League and became their player-manager.

Magic Moment: *Wilkins' full Colchester debut came in a Freight Rover tie at Aldershot. Although they lost 2-4, he headed both goals and soon made his League debut.*

Worst Nightmare: *In a vital promotion game against Portsmouth in April 1992, Wilkins stormed down the middle and scored to put Cambridge 2-0 up. Beck was absolutely furious with him for defying team orders and not passing to the wing.*

CAMBRIDGE RECORD	Appearances		Goals
Football League	79	(+2)	7
FA Cup	8	(+1)	–
League Cup	6		–
Play-Offs	2		–

No 86. **GARY ROWETT**
Debut: v Millwall, 7 September 1991
Farewell: v Port Vale, 22 February 1994

Unlike the previously mentioned 'Golden Greats' of the Beck era (all cheap discards from other clubs), the emergence of Gary Rowett was a landmark for the club, he being the first player to emerge from United's rebuilt youth system

Gary was born in Bromsgrove on 6 March 1974, but grew up on the Isle of Wight. It was whilst playing as a centre-forward for his school team in a national tournament in Norfolk that a United scout spotted him. He came through the Cambridge ranks as an apprentice and showed enough promise to win a professional contract. Originally Gary played as a striker, but after a bit of experimentation it was discovered that he was better on the right wing, though he always preferred to play in central midfield. His game came on in leaps and bounds and, aged just seventeen, he came on as substitute in a Division Two match at Millwall in September 1991. He marked his debut with a winning headed goal at the far post that showed commendable panache. Beck used him sparingly, but he will never forget his first two starts for the club. The first was in a Rumbelows Cup-tie with Manchester United and the second was in the match at Ipswich that put United on top of the Second Division. Gary scored the opening goal that day, showing a cool head in a crowded penalty area and displaying his composure once more with a laid-back goal celebration.

He was usually played as a straight up-and-down right-winger, though he was also used as a striker, a right wing-back and a right-back. He was quick and his height gave him an advantage over Cheetham when meeting over-hit left-wing crosses at the far post. He was a strong player, but always seemed more comfortable when in a more attacking role at Cambridge, though he didn't work hard enough to make things happen as an out-and-out striker.

A £300,000 move to Everton in May 1994 came out of the blue (sorry) for many U's fans, but he couldn't play for toffee (ouch) at Goodison and was released after appearing in just four League games. He had been loaned out to Blackpool in the latter half of 1994-95, but in the close season it was Derby County who signed him permanently for another £300,000 fee. It was here that he regained his earlier form and came to everybody's attention.

After a century of League games for the Rams he joined First Division Birmingham City for £1 million in August 1998 and made his debut at right-back soon afterwards. He was a strong, athletic defender who could either make great early balls to the attackers, or set off on surging runs himself. He impressed as an emergency centre-half and kept up his prolific goalscoring record, especially with headers. His manager, Trevor Francis, suggested he was good enough to play for England.

At the start of the 2000-01 season Rowett returned to the Premiership, when he became Peter Taylor's first major signing at Leicester City. He was an ever present that season, playing in his favoured attacking right full-back position, though also using his 6ft frame to good effect in the centre of defence when required.

He joined Charlton in May 2002 for an initial £2.5 million, manager Alan Curbishley being impressed by his defensive versatility – an important asset for a relatively small club. He was now comfortable in the centre of defence or on the right, which made it easy for Curbishley if he ever wanted a back three instead of a back four.

Magic Moment: *Against Premiership Oldham in the Coca-Cola Cup in December 1992, Cambridge manager Gary Johnson gambled by playing Rowett as a striker. He repaid his boss's faith by scoring the only goal of the game, from a Paul Raynor cross.*

Worst Nightmare: *A crippling knee injury blighted Rowett during the 2001-02 season, just as he was being touted by some for a possible England call-up.*

Cambridge record	Appearances	Goals
Football League	51 (+12)	9
FA Cup	5 (+2)	–
League Cup	7	1

No 87. **MICK HEATHCOTE**
Debut: v Leicester, 29 September 1991
Farewell: v Wrexham, 6 May 1995

Another cultured defender, though different in style, was Mick Heathcote, who was a Newcastle fan as a youngster, but ended up playing for their two greatest rivals – Middlesbrough and Sunderland.

Michael Heathcote hails from Kelloe in County Durham and put in his first appearance on 10 September 1965. He played for Spennymoor United Juniors, before joining Malcolm Allison's Middlesbrough at the age of eighteen, where he clawed his way up to reserve level. His reserve-team manager, Willie Maddren, professed that although lacking the ability of first-choice defender Alan Kernaghan, Mick would run through a brick wall if you asked him to. He also predicted that he would never make the top grade, but that he was good enough to make a living at the lower levels. After a year Mick was released, along with fourteen other players as

Boro lurched in the grip of financial ruin. He returned to Spennymoor, where he knuckled down for another three years, playing in a variety of positions, including striker, before realising that he was better equipped to be a central defender. He was originally targeted by Hartlepool, but they baulked at the £5,000 fee. Southampton also expressed an interest, but his value was now placed at £20,000 by the Northern League side and that too fell through. Then one day, Mick's father happened to bump into Sunderland's chief scout in a pub and complained that his son hadn't been given a fair chance to prove himself. Denis Smith had just taken over as the Rokerites new boss and was on the lookout for fresh talent, so Mick took a week off his day job – as a delivery driver for the Spennymoor chairman – and after a couple of successful appearances in the reserves signed for the Roker club in August 1987 for £15,000 – a move that caused much ribbing amongst his mates who, like Mick, were dedicated Newcastle fans. He certainly won't forget his debut for Sunderland, coming on as sub in a 7-0 whipping of Southend. He had a loan spell with Halifax in December 1987, scoring on his debut, but a year later he was laid low with a back injury that kept him out for nearly a year. After that he only played a handful of games for Sunderland, but had loan spells with Halifax Town and York City.

Desperate for first-team football, Heathcote looked set to join Fourth Division Burnley, but in July 1990 he moved to Third Division Shrewsbury for £55,000. He stayed for a year at Gay Meadow, which coincided with a famous run to the FA Cup fifth round and a game against Arsenal, which the Gunners just sneaked with a 1-0 win to set up a quarter-final tie against Cambridge United. Several clubs were alerted by Mick's form, but John Beck managed to convince Mick that Cambridge were a better proposition than Wolves and he signed in September 1991 for a club record £150,000, as Liam Daish was injured. With Chapple, Daish and O'Shea already there, it was the first indication that United's board were going to bankroll a serious push for promotion to the Premiership. He scored on his debut in the 5-1 leathering of Leicester that emphasised that Cambridge meant business in the old Second Division. Mick found it difficult to adapt to the Beck style of football and made the mistake of trying to alter his game to suit it. He failed to break the stranglehold on the central defensive berths that Chapple, Daish and O'Shea held so tightly, but broke into the team in the unlikely position of right-back when Andy Fensome got injured.

He made the No 5 shirt his own the next season and for a while it was the other three defenders who couldn't dislodge him. The downfall for him was sustaining a pelvic injury at the beginning of the 1994-95 season. Though he fought back to regain his place, he was now the old-timer amongst kids and his days were numbered.

He was a ball-playing centre-half, and under Atkins and Johnson he was allowed to bring the ball out of defence. His earlier incarnation as a striker meant he was very useful up front and was used as an emergency striker in April 1995. His weakness was a lack of pace, which had been evident even when he was younger. This languidness was a minor quibble compared with the commanding presence he gave at the heart of defence. His huge physical bulk made it nigh on impossible for any attacker to barge his way through him and he possessed enough nous not to be bamboozled by fancy footwork either. He was strong in the air and reasonably proficient with the ball at his feet. He was always a popular figure with the fans and was never aloof when meeting them.

He joined Plymouth in July 1995 for £100,000 and helped them to promotion, winning their Player of the Year trophy at least twice. In 2001 a local Plymouth bookie gave him a free £100 bet for charity. Mick duly put it on Argyle to win the championship at 16-1. Though he subsequently joined Shrewsbury in July 2001 (and played against Argyle), the bet was allowed to stand. At the season's end, the Devon Air Ambulance and the St Mary's Hospice were each £800 better off. He has started coaching and is an inspirational figure to the youngsters.

Magic Moment: *Heathcote had tattoos of cartoon characters on his backside and when asked why, he replied that he couldn't afford a TV and it kept the kids occupied.*

Worst Nightmare: *Heathcote's crippling back injury kept him out of contention for the best part of a year and Mick described it as the loneliest time of his life. The problem was never completely cured and was an irritation throughout his career.*

CAMBRIDGE RECORD	Appearances		Goals
Football League	123	(+5)	13
FA Cup	5	(+2)	2
League Cup	7		1
Play-Offs	2		—

No 95. Trevor Benjamin

No 97. Ian Ashbee

No 96. Paul Wanless

No 98. Martin Butler

No 99. Andy Duncan

No 100. Alex Russell

No 101. Lionel Perez

Chapter Ten

Young Guns

No 88. **STEVE BUTLER**
Debut: v Watford, 28 December 1992
Farewell: v Torquay, 25 November 1995

Stephen Butler was a similar looking player to Heathcote, but was usually to be found at the opposite end of the pitch.

Brummie-born (on 27 January 1962) Steve started his career in the Army, during which time he obtained his coaching certificate at Lilleshall. He began his playing career with two Berkshire sides – Windsor & Eton, then Wokingham Town. He joined Brentford on a free transfer in December 1984, scoring three goals in 21 games, before joining Conference side Maidstone United in August 1986. He helped put them into the League in 1989 and helped them get off to a cracking start with 41 goals in 76 League games.

The only question was when he was going to leave the hapless Kent side. The answer came in March 1991 when he joined Watford for £150,000, but a third of his 62 League games for the Hornets came from the subs bench and he only managed nine goals. He was part of a group of strikers that Steve Perryman had 'littering the bench', according one fan. He played alongside the legendary Luther Blissett, but was criticised for having a powder-puff shot and poor heading ability due to poor timing of his jumps. He was also deemed to be slow and a poor reader of the game, but was praised for his ability to lay the ball off with his back to goal and his concerted effort. He earned himself the nickname 'The Golden Eagle', due to his lanky frame, which was topped off by a mass of blond hair.

In December 1992 he was loaned out to Bournemouth, but he only got to play one game before Ian Atkins signed him for Cambridge for £75,000. Atkins had wanted him for a long while, having tried to sign him for his old club Colchester when Steve was at Maidstone. He replaced the unloved Devon White, but for a long while he was equally unpopular. He lacked aggression and didn't impose himself physically. The problem turned out to be a physical one rather than a mental one. Gary Johnson's father was a sports osteopath and diagnosed a skeletal imbalance. Once he had corrected this, his son (now United manager) gained a new striker. But Johnson thinks it might be that he didn't like the style of play under Atkins, and Johnson's tactics suited him better. Steve was now in a position to make the critics eat their words. In one of the most devastating goalscoring spells in United's history he tucked away thirteen goals in seven games. Prior to this he had managed eight goals in twenty League games.

Undoubtedly the surge in confidence from being fully fit was a factor in his new form, but another was his partnership with Carlo Corazzin. Steve was the master in the air, and possessed good close control and a sharp brain to lay the ball off if his partner was better placed. He was also deadly from the penalty spot, scoring from ten out of the eleven that he took, not including penalty shoot-outs. When on form he looked a totally natural striker who could bang the ball in the back of the net for fun. He could dominate the penalty area and the only real regret is that he never maintained this form for long periods.

Steve was still living in Maidstone, so when Gillingham wanted to buy him for £100,000 in December 1995 it was natural that he went there. He linked up with Leo Fortune-West and Dennis Bailey, but in August 1998 found himself frozen out by the signing of Carl Asaba. In October he moved to Peterborough briefly as player-coach. In March 1999 he was loaned out to Stevenage Borough, but returned to Gillingham, where he scored the second goal as they came from behind to beat Wigan 3-2 in the 2000 Division Two play-off final. He then went to Leicester City as coach, before rejoining the reformed Maidstone and helping them to the Kent League title in April 2002.

Magic Moment: *At Exeter in April 1994, Butler scored all the goals in a 5-0 win, the first time a U's player had gone nap for 35 years, and only the ninth time a United player had done it. He had scored a hat-trick three days earlier against Orient.*

Worst Nightmare: *One Watford fan described Butler as one of the most inept players that the Hornets had ever bought.*

CAMBRIDGE RECORD	Appearances		Goals
Football League	107	(+2)	51
FA Cup	6		5
League Cup	4	(+1)	–

No 89. **JOHN FILAN**
Debut: v Newcastle, 3 April 1993
Farewell: v Bournemouth, 5 November 1994

United followed the 1990s trend of importing foreign talent by capturing John Filan, an accomplished goalkeeper who was never destined to stay at the Abbey for too long.

John Richard Filan was a native of Sydney in Australia and was born on 8 February 1970. He became a goalkeeper at the age of twelve and idolised Pat Jennings as a youngster – Australian soccer fans being especially keen on watching English football. He played for two sides, Budapest St George and Wollongong Wolves, but was desperate to play football full-time, which meant a move to the motherland. His agent (who also represented Carlo Corazzin) organised trials at Southampton and Peterborough, but it was Ian Atkins at Cambridge who was sufficiently impressed to give him a contract in March 1993. He was scheduled to replace John Vaughan, who was on his way out, United paying £40,000 for Filan's services. John found the game in England to be much faster and physical than in Australia, where teams tended to play with a sweeper system.

It's not easy settling down in a new country when you have no family, but John found the friendliness of the club reassuring. Initially he shared digs with colleague Mick Danzey and the local takeaways did a booming business. John then moved to the altogether more amenable Jolly Waterman pub in Chesterton Road. This enabled him to play more darts, which he found aided his goalkeeping as it is all about hand and eye co-ordination, well that's his excuse anyway.

John proved to be the sort of keeper who was competent and reliable. Although this probably makes him less interesting than some of the more flamboyant keepers in United's history, he was less prone to the appalling gaffes that seem to befall the more spectacular wearers of the green jersey. John was a competent shot stopper, but was unafraid to go venturing outside his area to nullify any threat from marauding attackers. Like Vaughan, he wasn't a great kicker of the dead ball. Unlike his contemporaries – Vaughan and Jon Sheffield – he was a genuine six-footer, and was a better physical specimen than either of them. He was stronger than the slight Sheffield and not as podgy as Vaughan. His short brown hair may not have been entirely fashionable, but he certainly made a statement with some lurid goalkeeping jerseys, including a mauve, light green and dark blue one with eye-straining asymmetric stripes.

He was one of the few players Cambridge ever signed who was a current international. He made the Australian squad for the 1992 Olympics in Barcelona, but when they lost the opening game 1-3 to Ghana he was dropped in favour of Mark Bosnich. In the semi-finals the Aussies were crushed 1-6 by Poland, and John was recalled for the Bronze Medal match, also against Ghana, which they lost 0-1.

He was United's regular No 1 from April 1993 to November 1994, but Sheffield was now emerging from the shadows and in March 1995 United took the money and Filan joined Coventry City for £300,000 but struggled to establish himself in the side against the old warhorse Steve Ogrizovic.

After just sixteen League games he moved to Blackburn for £700,000 in July 1997. He was locked in a battle for a first-team place with Tim Flowers and in November 1998 got his chance when Flowers was injured. He turned in brilliant displays against Leeds and Arsenal, and kept his place when Flowers was fit again. He was regarded as being agile on the line, and was decisive when leaving it to punch clear. He was Rovers' Player of the Year in 1998-99, but later suffered a hamstring injury. He regained his place but in November 2000 was dropped by Graeme Souness to enable American Brad Friedel to get a work permit as first-choice keeper. Piqued at being dropped when playing well, he put himself on the transfer list and eventually signed for Wigan Athletic in December 2001.

Magic Moment: *Australia needed to beat Holland to reach the 1992 Olympics in Barcelona but a 1-1 draw in Sydney left Holland as favourites. A 2-2 draw in Utrecht, with Filan at his best, led to the Aussies winning through on the away-goals rule.*

Worst Nightmare: *Filan faced nine penalty-kicks during games whilst at United, but never managed to save any of them. He did save a couple for Blackburn though.*

CAMBRIDGE RECORD	Appearances	Goals
Football League	68	–
FA Cup	3	–
League Record	6	–

No 90. **MICAH HYDE**
Debut: v Bournemouth, 20 September 1993
Farewell: v Fulham, 3 May 1997

Like Filan, classy Micah Hyde seemed destined to play at a higher level, though he hasn't (yet) achieved the heights that his ability deserves.

Micah Anthony Hyde was born in Newham, East London on 10 September 1974 and he played in the same schoolboy team as David Beckham. He was spotted by Cambridge's Gary Johnson at the age of sixteen, but was told he was too small and frail and that he should come back in a year's time. This he did, and Johnson was impressed to see he had grown from 5' 5" to 5' 8" (he was to add another couple of inches to that soon afterwards). He progressed through the youths and the reserves and was rewarded with a two-year contract in May 1993. He broke through into the first team in 1993-94 where he caught the eye as an untypical U's midfielder. He revelled in making delicate touches and sensuous dummies and indulging in swift interplay with his more workmanlike colleagues. His superb off-the-ball movement provided effective link-up play with the attackers. He was also a good tackler, when he was so inclined, and end-lessly harried opposition midfielders into mistakes. At United it was his ability to maintain possession which was his greatest asset and which most lower division midfielders don't seem to be able to do. He was creative, but wasn't a goalscorer, and was also inconsistent. He tended to do too much with the ball on occasions. Tommy Taylor didn't seem to like him as much and in 1995-96 he was dropped for long periods as inferior players came in, and he nearly went to Peterborough, but the two clubs couldn't agree terms. Things were resolved the following season, and Micah was made skipper before he was 23. Elegantly built with a sharp short haircut, he famously sported a pair of bright yellow 'banana-boots'.

He joined Watford on a pre-season trip to Finland, and signed perma-nently in July 1997 for £225,000, which was convenient as he still lived in East London. At first he was too inconsistent, making bad errors through carelessness. He improved considerably when he linked up with Richard Johnson, as his colleague was able to be the 'weighty midfield anchor' that Micah could never be. It was then that Micah's star qualities could shine.

Hyde's parents hailed from Jamaica and Trinidad, which led to both Caribbean countries pursuing him, but he decided on Jamaica and made his debut for the 'Reggae Boyz' in a World Cup qualifier in April 2001, when a mixture of injuries and suspensions led to his acceleration into the team. He has since impressed Jamaica with his good vision and ball con-trol, and looks set to become a long-term member of the team.

Magic Moment: *Hyde received criticism at Watford for his lack of goals, which was put down to a lack of belief in his shooting ability. He regained his scoring touch after a year-long goal drought, two days after the birth of his first son in April 1999.*

Worst Nightmare: *United were 1-0 up against Wigan in injury-time. Rather than keep possession, Hyde naively launched an attack. He lost the ball and Wigan levelled.*

CAMBRIDGE RECORD	Appearances	Goals
Football League	89 (+17)	13
FA Cup	7 (+2)	–
League Cup	3	–

No 91. CARLO CORAZZIN
Debut: v Stockport, 11 December 1993
Farewell: v Mansfield, 23 March 1996

Striker Carlo Corazzin completes a trio of international players for United. Giancarlo Michele Corazzin was born in New Westminster in British

Columbia, Canada, on Christmas Day in 1971. He started his career with Italian sides Giorgione and Pievigina in the lower divisions, this coming about after he decided to stay with his grandmother after a family holiday (both his parents are Italian). On his return to Canada he played for Winnipeg Fury in the Canadian Soccer League before joining Vancouver 86ers in August 1992. He yearned to try his luck in the more football orientated climate of England, and his agent put him in touch with Gary Johnson at Cambridge United who signed him for £20,000 in December 1993. He had nearly signed for Stoke, but fortunately for Johnson a managerial change had scuppered that piece of business.

At first, Corazzin was very much in the shadow of Steve Butler, and this has led to him remaining one of the most underrated U's players. He was a 'sniffer', most goals coming from inside the six-yard area. Although only of medium height, he was quite springy and useful in the air. He formed one of United's greatest ever attacking partnerships, the two players feeding off each other in a display of telepathy and unselfishness. In the two seasons between 1993 and 1995 they bagged 64 League goals between them, which eclipsed even the more famous Dublin-Taylor partnership. A fine goal-creator, Carlo's greatest talent must be holding the ball up for his colleagues, but he was much underrated as a goalscorer. He has a powerful shot and was a workaholic, but needed to be braver in the area and maybe another ten goals a season may have resulted. He did manage nineteen in a season in 1994-95, which has only been bettered by Biley, Crown, Butler and Benjamin in United's League era.

In June 1994 Corazzin made his debut for Canada in a friendly and has gone on to make over 50 international appearances, scoring ten goals. He played in the CONCACAF Gold Cup, which is a tournament for Central and North American countries, as well as Caribbean nations. He helped his team win through to the final, despite them not playing particularly well. 'We're like the bad news bears', declared Carlo, which apparently means the same thing. He rounded off the tournament nicely by scoring in the victorious final match against Colombia and won the top scorer award as well. He also apparently had the women swooning over him for his boyish good looks. He played in all Canada's World Cup qualifiers and was unlucky against Mexico when he hit the crossbar twice.

He had a trial with Derby County in the summer of 1995, but they remained unimpressed and it was left to Plymouth Argyle in March 1996 to make a £150,000 successful bid for him. He did well enough to make Argyle's '101 Golden Greats' list, but after their relegation to the Third in 1997-98 they couldn't afford the wage demands of their out-of-contract star and he escaped to Northampton Town in July 1998 on a free transfer, thanks to the notorious Bosman ruling, though Watford had also shown an interest. He made an instant impression with Cobblers fans by cracking home a stunning 25-yard free-kick and went on to dominate the scoring lists that season, becoming the club's regular penalty-taker. He won the Player of the Year award, but had to collect the trophy on crutches due to a leg injury.

He joined Oldham Athletic (on another Bosman) in July 2000, manager Andy Ritchie having pursued him for two years. He was transfer-listed by Oldham's new boss, Mick Wadsworth, in December 2001, but Wadsworth then had a change of mind.

Magic Moment: *In the summer of 1994, Corazzin played in the Canada side that gained a creditable 1-1 draw with soon-to-be World Champions Brazil.*

Worst Nightmare: *Corazzin fell out with the Cobblers when they insisted he had to give up his international career that was causing them so much disruption. He naturally refused and left the club in dismay.*

CAMBRIDGE RECORD	Appearances		Goals
Football League	104	(+1)	39
FA Cup	5		–
League Cup	4		2

No 92. **JODY CRADDOCK**
Debut: v Stockport, 11 December 1993
Farewell: v Fulham, 3 May 1997

Although it's starting to look unlikely that Jody Craddock will gain full international honours, at least he has eclipsed Corazzin by playing regularly in the Premiership.

Though born in Bromsgrove in Worcestershire (on 25 July 1975), Jody was brought up in Dorset, where he played for his local schools team. He had a trial with Yeovil, but was rejected in size-obsessed footballing fashion for being too small. If they had been more patient they would have had a strapping 6ft 2in player on their books.

Christchurch (of the Wessex League) weren't so fussy and it was while he was there that he attracted the attention of Gary Johnson's uncle who recommended him to his nephew. Johnson couldn't believe it when he first saw Jody. He had a ginger ponytail, great big knees, but no thighs or legs to speak of. He thought his uncle was tacking the mickey. He changed his mind when he saw him play though, because he had so much aggression and determination to succeed that it overrode the physical shortcomings, and he signed for them on a free transfer in August 1993.

A lengthy spell in the youth team and reserves looked likely, but in the autumn Craddock was loaned out to Conference side Woking. Expecting to be there for three months he was surprised to be suddenly recalled and thrown into United's first team by Gary Johnson who dropped Liam Daish to accommodate him. Wearing a head bandage as the result of an earlier injury, he put in a competent display against Stockport's 6ft 7in Kevin Francis. Craddock retained his place and, despite his inexperience, was good enough to be awarded the honour of being voted into the PFA's Third Division Team of the Season. He kept his place throughout his four seasons with the club, which was no mean feat as he played under three different managers (Johnson, Tommy Taylor and Roy McFarland) and in a bewildering variety of systems. At first he had the experience of Mick Heathcote and Danny O'Shea to guide him, but when they left he was suddenly expected to be the 'wise head on young shoulders' – a daunting prospect. He struggled at first, and Johnson reckoned that he tended to make all his mistakes in the first team instead of the reserves, but his commitment was again strong enough to overcome that.

His youth obviously gave him pace, but he eventually gained an athletic build, which should stand him in good stead for his later years. He was a good reader of the game, seeing where the danger was coming from and putting himself into the right position to deal with it, usually with a timely tackle. This made up for the fact that he had hopeless ball control, and his tactic was to release it quickly via a simple pass or an inelegant hoof. Also his physique was more height than bulk and he could get shouldered aside in a physical battle. Interestingly, his idol was Vinny Jones – the complete opposite of Jody in so many ways. Roy McFarland praised Craddock's heading ability and his attitude, and stated that his passing was improving all the time. These attributes earned him a clean sweep of all the Player of the Year awards in 1995-96.

By the spring of 1997 United were having one of their frequent player purges to earn some money. A move to Preston was rejected by Jody (it was a sideways transfer) and later he spurned a move to Oxford too, though apparently he changed his mind later in the day, only for the deal to be called off. Eventually United received an offer of £350,000 plus bonuses from Sunderland, an offer too good to refuse by club or player.

Craddock coincidentally joined the Black Cats on the same day that the Stadium of Light was opened. He got off to a shaky start in his first season before establishing himself in the side by playing 30 consecutive games from October 1997, but in 1998-99 he lost his place to Paul Butler, following an injury. In the 1998 First Division play-off final, Jody was led a merry dance by Charlton's Clive Mendonca, who helped himself to a hat-trick. Sunderland lost on penalties after drawing 4-4, and this unhappy experience and a subsequent injury led to him losing his place to Paul Butler.

Craddock was loaned out to Sheffield United, but he soon managed to fight his way back into the Sunderland side. To Peter Reid's credit he kept faith with his somewhat inconsistent central defender who was now fast approaching 200 League games, despite being only in his early twenties. Jody has developed into a stronger player (both physically and mentally) and the number of errors he makes has been reduced greatly, a fact confirmed by his high rating in the OPTA statistics. He dealt comfortably with Holdsworth and Hughes in the two big promotion battles of March 1999 against Bolton and West Brom, and only his lack of ball control has prevented him being touted for an England place, though he is a consummate header of the ball. In 2000-01 he played alongside four different partners, but lost his place to Andy Melville after another injury. He has since regained his place once more and partnered Emerson Thome.

Magic Moment: *Craddock's Player of the Year trophy awarded by Sunderland's Internet fans in 2001-02 was a fitting tribute to his dedication to improve over the years.*

Worst Nightmare: *In August 2002, Craddock's four-month old son Jake died. Jody and his wife Shelley were inconsolable. He was very touched by all the condolences expressed by fans, including several from United supporters.*

CAMBRIDGE RECORD	Appearances		Goals
Football League	142	(+3)	4
FA Cup	6		–
League Cup	3		1

No 93. **MATT JOSEPH**

Debut: v Blackpool, 19 December 1993
Farewell: v Scunthorpe, 4 November 1997

If Jody Craddock was displaying cool maturity in the heart of the defence, then it was Matt Joseph who was showing youthful aggression.

The youngest of six, Matthew Nathan Adolphus Joseph was born in Bethnal Green on 30 September 1972. He played in a schoolboy team for Islington-Camden, as well as Inner London Schoolboys, showing enough promise to join the FA School of Excellence at Lilleshall. He progressed from there to win three England Youth caps.

Whilst his brother Steve was playing schoolboy football with Spurs, it was Matt who joined their north London rivals Arsenal as a youth trainee in 1990. Although helping the youth team to a couple of trophies, he was considered too small and inexperienced to seriously challenge Nigel Winterburn and Lee Dixon for a first-team place and was further hampered by the diagnosis of a double hernia. Joseph was given a free transfer in the summer of 1992.

Matt struggled to locate a secure berth for himself in 1992-93, having brief stopovers with Enfield, Watford and Gillingham, but failing to win a contract with any of them. He moved across to Finland to play for Ilves in the summer of 1993, but in November 1993 was given another crack at English football when Gary Johnson brought him to Cambridge, at the recommendation of Mark Flatts, who had also come across from the Gunners. Although Flatts is one of the players that didn't show any promise at Cambridge, he deserves some credit for finding Joseph.

Matt was able to play as either right-back or right-sided midfield, which was useful as Johnson struggled to decide whether to play with a flat back four or with a wing-back system. He was in contention with Junior Hunter, but whereas Hunter was equipped with a self-destruct button, Matt was more reliable. Either way, Matt was a player who loved to come forward, admitting that he didn't like defending. Johnson's side was certainly attack-minded and Joseph was a useful creator of goals as he raced down the right-hand side in search of opportunities. It was such a young side that at the age of 22 he could never work out whether he belonged to Young Cambridge or Old Cambridge during five-a-side training matches. He did, however, have the opportunity to become one of United's youngest ever captains.

Though modest about his defending abilities, it was as a right-back that Matt really shone. It had long been a problem position for United, and Matt was easily the best the club had seen since Ian Measham. Opposition left-wingers didn't seem to trouble Matt much, they were usually too busy trying to stop him racing past them on the overlap. He also played as a sweeper, and his tenacious tackling ability and lightning pace were often demonstrated to good effect. His lack of height did cause a problem in a match against Colchester though, when ex-Abbey legend John Taylor easily beat him to a header to plant the ball into the net.

Joseph joined a number of ex-United men at Tommy Taylor's Orient in January 1998 for a paltry £10,000. Whilst excelling in his more normal right-back and sweeping roles, he has displayed remarkable versatility at Brisbane Road. Although only 5ft 8in tall, he has had spells as a centre-forward, and even at centre-half, demonstrating that a combination of spring heels and good timing can outwit much taller opponents His enthusiasm has earned him two consecutive Player of the Year awards for Orient, and helped them to two reach two (unsuccessful) Third Division play-off finals.

Joseph's many talents attracted the interest of his parental homeland, Barbados. Though touted by the *Sport First* newspaper as a possible future England player, the Barbadians made sure he was going to represent them instead. They were battling for a place in the 2002 World Cup finals, and had already qualified out of the Caribbean Zone and won through to the CONCACAF semi-finals. Matt played in two games against Guatemala and the USA, though ultimately the Barbadians weren't strong enough to earn a place in Japan.

Magic Moment: *Joseph astonished Orient fans on his debut at centre-forward by outjumping a much taller defender and planting a header in the back of the net.*

Worst Nightmare: *It caused enough confusion at Cambridge – where there was a Matt Joseph and a Marc Joseph in the same team. It was worse at Orient, where they had two Matthew Josephs on the books.*

CAMBRIDGE RECORD	Appearances		Goals
Football League	157	(+2)	6
FA Cup	7		–
League Cup	6	(+1)	–

No 94. **DANNY GRANVILLE**
Debut: v Swansea, 15 March 1994
Farewell: v Wigan, 15 March 1997

Daniel Patrick Granville was another schoolboy who, like Joseph, also had connections with Islington (his birthplace on 19 January 1975) and who also played on the fringes of Tottenham Hotspur's youth team.

Granville began his career in the schoolboy team of Charlton Athletic, though he trained briefly with Tottenham Hotspur. It was whilst playing for Chapel Market in a Sunday League that he was spotted by the sharp eyes of youth team boss Gary Johnson.

He came to Cambridge in 1991 with a group of Islington youngsters, namely John Fowler, Junior Hunter, Micah Hyde and Kofi Nyamah. He worked his way through the youth system, including a loan spell with Saffron Walden Town, signing professional terms in May 1993. Towards the end of the following season he made his debut in an attacking midfield position, where he made a great impression on the fans. In only his second start he nabbed a couple of goals at Brentford and was undoubtedly a factor in United's incredible goal-glut during April 1994. His five goals from ten starts was promising indeed, and he loved to have a crack at goal from distance. He was a consistent player, who loved to get forward on the overlap and harry the full-backs. This led to him being converted to a left wing-back at the beginning of the 1995-96 season, and he later played on the left side of a three-man defence.

Despite his potential, he surprised many by going to Chelsea for £300,000 (or £500,000 depending on appearances and England caps etc) in March 1997, becoming one of the few English-born players at Stamford Bridge, let alone London-born. He did well at left-back and was tipped to be an England star of the future (he had already won Under-21 caps).

Granville moved to George Graham's Leeds in June 1998 for £1.6 million (Cambridge receiving a £280,000 sell-on fee), but had a difficult start as a combination of a thigh strain and the good form of Ian Harte kept him out of the side. He struggled to establish himself at Elland Road, not helped by getting sent off within 31 minutes of his debut.

He went to Manchester City in 1999 and made his debut on the opening day of the season against Wolves, but tore his hamstring. He came back in October, scoring a winner against Port Vale, but lost his place to Danny Tiatto in the last two months of that season. He was loaned to Norwich in October 2000, making six appearances, and there was speculation that Norwich wanted him permanently. He rejoined Manchester City, though, and regained his place as a left wingback where he used his pace more effectively. He also developed into a free-kick specialist.

After 70 League games for City he joined Crystal Palace for £500,000 in December 2001, but couldn't get them into the Division One play-offs.

Magic Moment: *Granville's first touch of the ball for Leeds was in a penalty shoot-out against Maritimo in the UEFA Cup. He scored to help Leeds progress.*

Worst Nightmare: *When Granville first went to Cambridge, youth manager Gary Johnson used to send him home for being dopey on the pitch. His dad queried this, thinking he wasn't wanted, but it was Johnson kidology, trying to sharpen up his alertness.*

CAMBRIDGE RECORD	Appearances	Goals
Football League	89 (+10)	7
FA Cup	2 (+2)	–
League Cup	3 (+2)	–

No 95. **TREVOR BENJAMIN**
Debut: v Gillingham, 3 February 1996
Farewell: v Wycombe, 6 May 2000

Trevor Junior Benjamin was another United YTS boy who reached the Premiership.

Cambridge had failed to make an impact during the 1995-96 season, briefly appearing in the promotion places early in the season, before falling backwards. In February 1996 they came up against master-defenders Gillingham, who had already kept nineteen clean sheets that season. Despite only playing against nine men, their attack failed to penetrate the Gills' solid shell. It was time for something completely different. Off the bench came Trevor Benjamin, still five days short of his seventeenth birthday. He may have been a baby, but he certainly didn't look like one. He was 6ft 2in and weighed 14st. He was huge, clumsy, but even in those few minutes, the new centre-forward gave the Gills' defenders problems they had rarely encountered that season. He nearly scored when he stuck out a giant leg to steer a Danny Granville shot just wide of the post. Even with that brief glimpse, it was clear that his awkwardness would be both his biggest asset and his greatest handicap.

Trevor was born in Kettering on 8 February 1979, but was brought up in nearby Wellingborough. He started playing for Wellingborough Colts in his familiar striking position and was then selected for the Northampton district side. This brought him to the attention of Kettering Town, who signed him up as a 14-year-old apprentice. He only played once for the first team, and that was in a friendly, but then moved to Rushden & Diamonds, thereby joining his brother Richard. The Diamonds, who were then just starting the charge that would eventually take them to the Football League, bankrolled by businessman Max Griggs. Benjamin progressed from the youths to the reserves, but when Cambridge came knocking with the lure of League football it was an offer too good to resist. Trevor had been on an extended trial, which meant playing for United's Under-16 side, but at the end of it he was awarded a YTS contract.

Manager Tommy Taylor resisted the temptation to burn out this bright prospect; instead he gave him brief outings from the substitutes bench. He scored his first senior goal in September 1996 against Scarborough in this way. He wasn't entrusted to start a game until May 1997, and that was a meaningless (for Cambridge) match against promoted Fulham. He saw more action the following season, but was fighting to claim a striking berth ahead of the more established forwards – Martin Butler, John Taylor and Michael Kyd. Benjamin was often stuck out on the left wing when two of the others were used up front, but this was a weak position for him which never brought out his strengths.

It wasn't until the 1998-99 season that Trevor was used regularly in a three-pronged attack with Butler and Taylor, which produced 44 of United's 78 League goals that season – fifteen from Trevor. It was the perfect combination. Taylor had the guile, Butler the speed and the finishing, and Benjamin the muscle. Watching him lumber towards goal was like

watching an elephant saunter from one end of its enclosure to the other..
Opposing defenders would scatter or be brushed aside with contempt, and
the goal would open up invitingly. Often he would display similar ball control to a pachyderm, regularly showing an uncanny ability to miss an open
goal, but gradually the finishing improved. United won promotion from
the Third, but it was in the Worthington Cup where he really shone. He
scored the winner at home to First Division high flyers Watford, and then
won the penalty at Vicarage Road.to seal the victory. He got an early winner at Premiership Sheffield Wednesday, then equalised in the second leg
to create another upset. Bruno (his inevitable nickname) also played a
prominent part in the third round tie at Nottingham Forest (for details, see
below).

When Butler was sold to Reading in February 2000, Trevor really came
to the fore, banging in goals in eight consecutive appearances to set a new
club League record and keeping his side in the Second Division. Having
also scored in three consecutive FA Cup-ties against Palace, Wrexham and
Bolton in their march to the fifth round, it was now inevitable that Trevor
was going to go for big money.

Trevor was on holiday in Cyprus when he heard that Leicester had
come in with a £1 million offer in July 2000. Initially, he made a bright start
with the Foxes, scoring a headed goal against Middlesbrough, but when the
team started to pick up injuries Trevor's form dipped along with that of his
team-mates. He seems to be affected by a lack of confidence even more
than most players. It proved impossible to get him to regain his Cambridge
form, though he was capped for England Under-21s against Mexico at the
end of the season. He was loaned out to Crystal Palace, Norwich and West
Brom as he struggled to get into the Leicester side.

Magic Moment: *Punching the irritating Stan Collymore in the dressing room after
a reserve game endeared Benjamin to many, especially after Stan was alleged to have hit
Ulrika Jonsson. Trevor was an incredibly gentle giant, so the provocation must have been
immense, but fancy Stan picking on someone with the build of a heavyweight boxer.*

Worst Nightmare: *In a Worthington Cup-tie against Premiership Nottingham
Forest, United were 0-3 down with 22 minutes left. Benjamin scored to spark a come-
back to 3-3. The match went to penalties, but Trevor's weak kick was easily saved and
Cambridge went out.*

CAMBRIDGE RECORD	Appearances		Goals
Football League	96	(+27)	35
FA Cup	9	(+1)	5
League Cup	7	(+3)	4

No 96. **PAUL WANLESS**

Debut: v Plymouth, 9 March 1996
Farewell: still with United

Unlike Benjamin, who soon departed for pastures new, Paul Wanless is a rare example (in recent years) of a talented player who has remained at the Abbey.

Paul Steven Wanless was born in Banbury on 14 December 1973. It was Paul's dad and big brother who steered him into a love of football. At the age of five he was playing alongside kids three years older than himself, which helped teach him to take care of himself. Originally Paul was a goalkeeper, but when he moved to a local youth team he moved into midfield and has stayed there ever since. He was then spotted by Oxford United, who were smart enough to bag him for their youth team.

Paul was seventeen when he made his debut in a Rumbelows Cup-tie against Portsmouth in October 1991. He almost created a sensation by heading the equaliser, but the keeper tipped the ball over the bar. He did well enough to earn his first start as Oxford fought to lift themselves off the bottom of the old Second Division. They were playing away that day, against the top side – Cambridge United. He accredited himself well in a 1-1 draw, and, though used sparingly over the next four seasons was still confident of becoming an established Ox. It wasn't to be and he was made aware of the fact that he wasn't included in the team's long-term future plans.

In July 1995 Wanless joined Lincoln on a free transfer and at once settled into the side. Just as at the Manor Ground though, his dreams were dashed by the arrival of a new manager – John Beck. Beck had arrived in October 1995 with the job of lifting the Imps off the bottom of the League. He instantly made it clear that Paul wasn't going to assist him and he only played once under the controversial boss – out of position at right-back. In March 1996 he gladly joined Cambridge on loan – a move that was made permanent at the end of the season, though he was sad to leave Lincoln – 'A lovely club and a lovely city'.

Paul is a box-to-box player, aided by his excellent heading ability, but he remained economical in movement. He became a noted goalscorer with a wicked shot. He was totally committed, he never shirked a tackle (which tended to be bone-crunchers) and he was an inspirational captain, leading by example. Though his huge 6ft and 14st frame literally adds its weight to his natural air of authority, he is soft enough to gently dish out words of comfort to the disheartened, when to bellow would be the wrong thing to do. He showed his ability as a stand-in goalkeeper and could probably have made a career out of it if he wasn't so good as a midfielder. He had played in goal for Oxford in a Youth Cup semi-final and also for Lincoln City reserves. He has a huge physique for a midfielder, and plays as the anchorman. It seems inevitable that in the future he will be groomed into becoming a more than useful centre-half as his pace gradually tails away.

In March 1997 Orient boss Tommy Taylor made a cheeky £10,000 bid for him that McFarland thankfully rejected. When John Beck replaced McFarland, it could have caused problems for both of them, but Paul's gutsy attitude won respect from Beck and the two managed to form a reasonable working relationship.

Wanless intends to take up coaching and possibly management when he finally retires, and nobody would be surprised if he eventually took over the helm at United.

Magic Moment: *Against Orient in May 1996, an injury to keeper Scott Barrett meant Wanless had to play in goal for 86 minutes. He kept a clean sheet and won the Man of the Match award. Weirdly, he had told his dad earlier that this would happen.*

Worst Nightmare: *Undoubtedly this is the serious illness to Wanless's daughter that touched the hearts of everyone at Cambridge United and led to a massive fundraising effort for the hospital where she was treated. Thankfully, she has now recovered.*

CAMBRIDGE RECORD	Appearances		Goals
Football League	237	(+8)	39
FA Cup	13	(+2)	1
League Cup	12		–

No 97. **IAN ASHBEE**
Debut: v Torquay, 28 December 1996
Farewell: v Tranmere, 13 April 2002

Frequently dominating the midfield alongside Wanless was the equally tall and chunky figure of Ian Ashbee, though at first his hairstyle was considerably longer than Wanny's.

Ian Ashbee entered the world on 6 September 1976 in Birmingham and was therefore faced with the usual Brummie dilemma of choosing between City and Villa. He compromised by supporting the Blues, but modelling his defensive game on Villa's Paul McGrath. Not that he was heavily into football in his pre-teens. His family were in the carpentry business, and for a long while it seemed more likely that he would be building goalposts rather than defending them.

He started taking his football more seriously at thirteen, and progressed quickly enough to join Birmingham City as a trainee. The Blues weren't showing much interest in bringing him towards the first team though, and Ian realised that a move was needed to give his career a jolt. Both Villa and Derby took an interest in him, but it was the warmth and friendliness shown to him by manager Arthur Cox and his assistant Roy McFarland at Derby that showed him that the Baseball Ground was the place to be.

After serving his apprenticeship for one year, Ashbee signed professional terms in November 1994 at a time when the Rams looked more likely to be dropping down into the new Second Division than joining the Premiership. By this time Roy McFarland was the manager and he gave Ian his chance in the first team against Southend in April 1995. The Rams lost 1-2 — a result that cost Roy McFarland his job. Jim Smith replaced him, but Ian was unable to make the first team again, so he went on loan to Reykjavik in Iceland for three months. He enjoyed it, despite having to wear gloves for the games like the other 'Southern softies', whilst the natives would run around on the coldest days in the normal skimpy footballing attire.

By the time of his return, Derby were heading towards the Premiership, which scuppered Ian's chances of making a breakthrough into the first team. From a selfish point of view, Ian would have preferred the Rams to struggle and therefore change the team. Once more it was time to make a move.

Ian's old team-mate David Preece had informed Cambridge manager Tommy Taylor about this promising youngster, but before anything developed Taylor had jumped ship to Orient. Whilst there, Taylor did bid for him, but the chance to rejoin his mentor Roy McFarland (the new manager at Cambridge) clinched the deal in United's favour. He arrived in December 1996, just in time to witness United's typical mid-season collapse that saw them blow their chances of promotion out of the Third.

By this time, Ian preferred playing in midfield, but his strength and bulk (6ft 1in and 13st 7lb) meant he was equally adept at slotting in anywhere in defence, including centre-half. Being a part of a small squad and lacking anyone else to fulfil that role, Ian became 'Mr Versatile'. In one three-game spell in the autumn of 1999 he played consecutive games in midfield, centre-half, then left-back. Good for the team, but frustrating for Ian, who preferred the centre of the park, because he liked to muscle his way through defenders and show off his shooting prowess. He could use either foot, and was one of the few United players who were prepared to shoot from distance. The thing that hampered his ambition was the fact that Wanless was already established in that position, and they both play a similar hatchet-man style of game. Ashbee was used in midfield during the promotion season, and the fact that the two players crushed any opposition attempts to control operations in the middle was a factor in the success of the team. That aggression and hard tackling are also good defensive qualities, so inevitably Ian was often employed as a full-back (on either side), though that couldn't prevent him surging forward at every possible opportunity.

At the end of the 2001-02 season he turned down impoverished United's new contract proposal, and was signed by Hull City, where he managed to get himself sent off on his debut.

Magic Moment: *Ashbee was hardly a prolific goalscorer but he bagged a couple in a 5-1 win in February 1999 at what was a bogey ground for United – Scarborough.*

Worst Nightmare: *In February 1995 Ashbee represented England Youth against Denmark. The Danes won 6-5, a result that did defenders no favours whatsoever.*

CAMBRIDGE RECORD	Appearances	Goals
Football League	192 (+11)	11
FA Cup	13	–
League Cup	6	–

No 98. **MARTIN BUTLER**
Debut: v Scarborough, 9 August 1997
Farewell: v Bolton, 29 January 2000

Unlike Ashbee, there was no doubting where Martin Butler's true position at United was. He was an out-and-out striker, but it wasn't always like that.

Martin Neil Butler was born in Wordsley in the West Midlands on 15 September 1974 and he was a trainee at nearby Walsall. He made his debut as a substitute in October 1993 against Gillingham, but it wasn't until the end of the season that he managed a run in the side as a striker, scoring three times. The rest of his time at Walsall was frustrating. Unable to break into the team for long spells, when he did get in he was played out of position in midfield, on both wings, and finally as a left-back. It was during one of his many stints in the reserves that he was spotted by Cambridge's player-coach David Preece. When Butler's contract was up for renewal in August 1997 he opted for regular football at Third Division level as a striker, rather than occasional Second Division football as a stopgap. The fee was £22,500.

United's problem at the time was too many strikers, with Martin vying for a place with three other players. His workaholic attitude, combining strength, pace and a clinical finish, soon marked him out as a first-choice striker, but who to play with him was the question. He didn't link well with Michael Kyd, because they played too similar a game. Although Butler is a six-footer, he wasn't a great header of the ball and neither player posed an aerial threat. Trevor Benjamin was too callow at this early stage, so it was with John Taylor that Butler found his perfect partner. With Taylor's aerial ability and guile able to compensate for the weaknesses in Martin's game, his fair, handsome partner was ready with the speed and the power that the old man was now lacking. It was the classic master-apprentice relationship. Martin was also used as the penalty taker, but whilst he converted most of them, he blotted his copybook by missing four spot-kicks whilst at Cambridge. Later, as Benjamin gained more experience, the pair of them could usually be relied upon to cripple most opposition defences, with Taylor used as an emergency substitute. It all came to glorious fruition in 1998-99 when United marched to promotion, with Martin leading the way with his 21 League and cup goals. As an extra reward he won the Player of the Year award and was voted into the PFA's Division Three select team.

Though he accelerated his strike rate in the Second Division by scoring more than a goal in every other game, the defence was letting in even more at the other end. With United stuck near the bottom and short on readies, it was no surprise that they cashed in on their most valuable asset. The shock came because it was the club that occupied twentieth place – which United coveted, as 21st place spelled doom – who splashed out £750,000 for him in February 2000 – Reading.

Butler certainly rejuvenated the Royals' attack. He scored in his first two games and brought out the best in Nicky Forster, whose loss of form had been instrumental in their woes. Reading survived (along with Cambridge) and the following season the Berkshire side were amongst the pacesetters in the Second Division, helped by an incredible partnership between Martin and Jamie Cureton who had replaced the injured Forster. They bagged 50 League goals between them, and though they just missed out on automatic promotion, they did make the play-offs. The final against Walsall went to extra-time, but though Martin netted in the 91st minute he ended up on the losing side as Walsall stormed back. His one consolation was winning the Supporters' Player of the Year vote by a considerable margin. Reading did succeed in 2001-02, but at a cost to Butler, who was injured early in the campaign.

Magic Moment: *With four minutes of the 2001 semi-final play-off against Wigan left and a goal down on aggregate, it required a late goal from Butler to save Reading from heartache, before Cureton scored a last-minute winner to send them to Wembley.*

Worst Nightmare: *At Walsall's 1996 Christmas party Butler and fourteen others turned up dressed as Elvis Presley. Anyone at Cambridge catching him in party mood was also likely to hear the 'King of Rock and Roll' sung in a Black Country accent.*

CAMBRIDGE RECORD	Appearances		Goals
Football League	100	(+3)	41
FA Cup	9	(+2)	5
League Cup	9		5

No 99. **ANDY DUNCAN**
Debut: v Shrewsbury, 17 January 1998
Farewell: still with United

Unlike all the others in this book, Andy Duncan is included as much as for what I believe he will achieve as opposed to what he has already done for the U's.

Andy follows in the footsteps of the early 1980s United superkids by hailing from Geordieland, having been born in Hexham on 20 October 1977. Coming from that part of the world, where a baby's first pair of boots are equipped with studs, it was no wonder that Andy was an enthusiastic player in Sunday football from an early age. He was twelve when Manchester United's extensive scouting web caught him and steered him into a local school of excellence. It is perhaps this desire to pounce on pre-teenagers and teach them good footballing habits whilst they are still malleable that shows the greatest change in English football in recent years. Mind you, at twelve Andy was a late starter compared to some.

Throughout his teenage years Duncan followed the well-trodden path that leads to success, managing to avoid the mines that explode under most youngsters as they wander off course. At fourteen he signed schoolboy forms and two years later he stepped up to youth training scheme level. He had already played for England Schoolboys and when he was made a full-time professional at eighteen and started playing in the reserves he looked as though he was on the brink of the big time. That's when the train came off the track. There is an almighty gulf between reserve-team football and first-team football at any club, but especially so at Manchester United, whose massive squad could easily be augmented at any time by signing ready-made talent using little more than petty cash. For Andy it was evident that he was not going to go any higher and when Roy McFarland offered to take him and team-mate Grant Brebner on a month's loan in January 1998, Duncan jumped at the chance.

Initially, it was midfielder Brebner who looked the most promising, but once Andy got into the side in place of the ageing centre-half Colin Foster it was he who had his loan period extended for three months. Playing alongside fellow rookie Marc Joseph, he continued to perform well and was rewarded with a permanent contract that cost the U's £20,000 in transfer fees.

All the other central defenders in this book seemed to have been able to develop with a senior partner to help guide and develop them, but Andy had to be a man from day one. Of course, he was greatly helped by manager Roy McFarland, and who better than to have as your mentor and father figure than the consummate England defender of the 1970s? Roy wasn't on the pitch though, and it speaks volumes for Andy that he has lasted so long without burning himself out like so many others. In playing style he is perhaps closer to Danny O'Shea than anyone else. His excellent reading of the game and subsequent good positioning helps to nullify his lack of pace in defence. He is a whisker under six feet and is consequently not an aerial master, but he is confident and able with the ball at his feet and is a useful barrier to hard-charging attackers. His precociousness led to him being made captain at a very young age, when Wanless was injured, and even before Duncan reached his mid-twenties he was being looked upon as a senior pro.

A broken leg in October 1999 was a major blow, but he came back strongly and regained his form. It looked as though he might leave in the summer of 2002, having been sidelined by John Beck, but he re-signed for John Taylor and carried on the good work. His best is yet to come, I feel.

Magic Moment: *When asked by their careers teachers what they are going to do when they leave school, the stock answer is 'I don't know'. How gratifying it must have been for Duncan to reply: 'I've already signed a contract to play for Manchester United.'*

Worst Nightmare: *At Rochdale in September 2002, ten minutes had gone when Andy tackled an opponent by attempting to separate him from his neck. A yellow card was shown, but a minute later he was similarly clumsy and earned himself a red. United went on to lose the match when they had been 3-2 up with a minute to go.*

CAMBRIDGE RECORD	Appearances		Goals
Football League	135	(+5)	3
FA Cup	4		–
League Cup	9		–

No 100. **ALEX RUSSELL**

Debut: v Torquay, 8 August 1998
Farewell: v Wrexham, 10 March 2001

Although arguably as talented as Duncan, it seems as though Alexander Graham Russell will forever be known as a lower-division player.

Alex's father (also called Alex) was a midfield legend at Southport (and also appeared for three other Lancashire clubs), where he made nearly 400

League appearances in two spells, scoring 75 goals. It was during the second of these spells at Southport that Alex junior was born on 17 March 1973, in Crosby.

Alex junior was originally on Liverpool's books, but was released at the end of his YTS period in 1993. He also failed to make the grade at Morecambe and Stockport County and he joined Burscough Borough. He was given another bite at League football when Rochdale splashed out £4,000 for him in July 1994, but his first couple of seasons at Spotland were frustrating too, and he found himself in and out of the side. At Rochdale he played as an attacking midfielder, slotting in just behind the front two strikers, and he scored fifteen goals in his 115 League appearances (though he came on as a substitute in 23 of them). He appeared to lack motivation at times, though, and this led to a four-game loan spell to Glenavon in November 1995, though it wasn't long enough to prevent him from being Dale's leading scorer that season.

He went to Cambridge United in the summer of 1998 and impressed greatly in a 6-1 pre-season victory over Cambridge City. His movement was excellent; he had great vision and touch; and had a degree of self-belief that was almost arrogant. Not surprisingly, United snapped him up on a free transfer. He became a star in United's midfield, winning the Supporters' Player of the Year award in the promotion season of 1998-99. He was one of the few lower-division players who was capable of 'bending it like Beckham', and his free-kicks were eagerly anticipated by the fans. He was quite tall and gangly, but despite this physical handicap (for a midfielder) he was an adept passer and crosser of the ball, and much thought was put into most of his passes.

In August 2001 Russell went with Roy McFarland to Torquay United on a free transfer, which was an easy decision for Alex to make, as he is a great admirer of Roy's management and coaching ability. Alex goes to the USA each summer and coaches in their summer schools, and when he quits professional football he wants to coach full-time in the United States.

Magic Moment: *Russell being voted United fans' Player of the Year in a promotion season is an accolade worth boasting about.*

Worst Nightmare: *Russell found himself shunted from lower division club to lower division club, when advancement seems far more deserving.*

CAMBRIDGE RECORD	Appearances		Goals
Football League	72	(+8)	8
FA Cup	6		–
League Cup	7	(+1)	–

No 101. **LIONEL PEREZ**

Debut: v Oxford, 25 Mar 2000
Farewell: v Tranmere, 13 April 2002

And last but not least we come to the most expensive player in United's history (in terms of wage demands) and one who made an instant impact on the Abbey fans.

Lionel Perez was born on the 24 April 1967 and brought up in Bagnois Ceze in the South of France. He played in goal for his local side, before playing alongside Eric Cantona at Nimes from the 1989-90 season. He then moved onwards and upwards to Bordeaux in 1993, where he rubbed shoulders with a galaxy of future French stars, including Zinedine Zidane, Christopher Dugarry and Laurent Blanc. He finished his French career in 1995-96 by spending a loan season with Laval.

In August 1996 he was signed by Sunderland for £250,000, where a lengthy spell in the reserves looked likely. A broken leg for Tony Coton in October proved to be a lucky break for Lionel though, and he put in a couple of scintillating performances in his first couple of games for the club. The Wearside fans fell in love with him instantly. He certainly made a physical impression on them with his long, flowing blond hair and rolled-up sleeves. He also stood out from the average English keeper in action. At just under six feet, he was comparatively small, but made up for that by a willingness to use just about every part of his body to block the ball. In fact, at times it seemed as though he used his legs to save more than he did his hands.

Though Sunderland were relegated from the Premiership that season, the fans knew that Lionel's presence delayed their inevitable fate. He performed even more capably the following season. With his place in the team secured by the departure of Shay Given to Newcastle, he improved his ability to deal with crosses, while his commitment was never in doubt. His distribution also improved, though he always preferred throwing the ball to kicking it. Lionel, too, fell in love with the club, preferring the passionate atmosphere at the Stadium of Light to the quieter, emptier French stadiums. He fell out with manager Peter Reid though, and in the summer of 1998 he went to Newcastle, just after playing on the losing side in the play-off final against Charlton. The score was 4-4, but the Black Cats lost 6-7 on penalties.

Ironically, Perez was stuck behind Shay Given (and one or two others) in the Toon pecking order and he never got to play for them in two seasons. In desperation he was loaned to Scunthorpe in October 1999 (eleven games), then to Cambridge in March 2000. It is rumoured that Newcastle had to subsidise the U's, other they could never have afforded his wages.

It is arguable whether anyone has ever become an Abbey legend so quickly. With his long shaggy permed hair and short-sleeved shirts, he would bawl at defenders in an impenetrable French accent (though they soon got the gist of what he meant. He was always keen to rush out of his area in gung-ho fashion, which was always spectacular if not always successful. Perhaps he was Cambridge's first sweeper-keeper. In desperate moments he would come up for corners and free-kicks, and in his final U's game he took a penalty and missed. If he conceded a goal it obviously hurt and if it meant the U's were losing he would pick the ball out of the net and run up to the halfway line to put it on the spot. He was agile, therefore good on the line and a good shot-stopper, but poor on crosses, just like most of the ex-U's keepers who were under six feet tall. Perez's many howlers were forgiven as part of his eccentric charm.

He played a big part in the miraculous escape from relegation at the end of his first season, by keeping four clean sheets in his last nine games, but surprised everybody by taking a big cut in wages to stay at Cambridge permanently, though he undoubtedly earned a far higher wage than any other United player ever did – £2,000 a week being the reputed figure. Though United did succumb to the drop the following season, conceding over 90 goals in the process, most fans were aware that it could have been far, far worse without Lionel's Gallic flair to shore up the porous defence. This was also apparent in the LDV final against Blackpool, where he performed heroics to keep the score down to 1-4. To underline this, many fans put him as their all-time favourite United keeper, even several long-standing fans who can remember Malcolm Webster and Keith Branagan in their prime.

Inevitably, relegation meant Lionel was a luxury United couldn't afford and he was released in the summer of 2002. He once said that if offered the job of manager at the Abbey, he would take it. The mind boggles.

Magic Moment: *In the Leyland Daf Trophy semi-finals against much-fancied Bristol City, Perez made a string of stunning saves over the two legs to earn United a place in the final at the Millennium Stadium.*

Worst Nightmare: *In a match at Tranmere, Perez was sent off after eleven minutes for handling the ball outside the area. Cambridge went on to lose 1-6. He later did the same thing against Wycombe, and received the same punishment.*

CAMBRIDGE RECORD	Appearances		Goals
Football League	87	(+1)	–
FA Cup	4		–
League Cup	3		–

Martin Addison	Dion Dublin	Anders Kankfelt	Dion Dublin
Peter Anthony	David Stringer	Debbie Lamb	Lionel Perez
William Arnold	Steve Spriggs	Lionel Lambert	Dion Dublin
Nick Aves	David Crown	Michael Langran Jnr	Lindsay Smith
Amie Barber	Tom Youngs	Michael Langran Snr	Steve Spriggs
Nigel Barber	Steve Claridge	Neal Lawrence	Liam Daish
Paul Barry	Lindsay Smith	John Lincoln	Dion Dublin
Barry Benton	Brendon Batson	Jason Lucas	Devon White
Bob Bishop		Christopher Mallows	Michael Danzey
David Bonnett	Dion Dublin	Chris Marsh	John Taylor
Graeme Bridges	John Taylor	Peter Marsh	John Taylor
Steven Broomfield	Steve Spriggs	Peter May	John Taylor
David H J Brown	Alan Biley	Kevin McGann	Alan Biley
Peter Brown	Dion Dublin	E McKenzie-Boyle	Trevor Benjamin
Nigel Browne	Dion Dublin	Martyn Melvin	Dion Dublin
Alan Burge	Alan Biley	Paul Mitton	Dion Dublin
John Butler	Steve Claridge	Barry M Moore	Dion Dublin
Scott Conway	Tom Horsfall	Mark Mumford	David Crown
Rob Cook	Alan Biley	Kevan Murphy	Dion Dublin
Denis Cooper	Rodney Slack	Peter Nagy	Paul Wanless
Simon Cousins	David Crown	Simon Pike	Adam Tann
Pete Coveney	Dion Dublin	James Prime	John Taylor
Martin Coxall	Alan Biley	Dave Radmore	Paul Wanless
Keith Crown	Dion Dublin	Dennis Rawlings	Tom Finney
Paul Davies	Alan Biley	Christopher Ray	Alan Biley
Peter Day	Steve Fallon	Andy Salton	Alan Biley
Steve & Max Dighton	David Crown	Ian Scarr	Dion Dublin
Kane Dingley	Steve Claridge	Mr J Scurr	
Andy Dresback	Alan Biley	Jonathan Sell	John Taylor
David Edson	Shane Tudor	Douglas Shulman	Steve Claridge
Sylvia Emmerson	Len Saward	Aidan Slater	Tom Youngs
Paul F Facer	Steve Fallon	Mark Slater	Alan Biley
Graham Fairweather	Rodney Slack	Ticker Smith	Steve Fallon
H M & I R Fletcher	John Taylor	Nicholas & Christopher	
Jevan & Isaac Gill	Alan O'Neill	Smithson	Shane Tudor
Bob Green	Alan Biley	Duncan K Stanley	Dion Dublin
Marcus Gynn	Dion Dublin	Richard Stocken	
Marilyn Hardy	Robin Hardy	Michael Strupczewski	Lionel Perez
Tony Harradence	John Taylor	Peter Sulston	Micah Hyde
Robert G A Hart	Jody Craddock	Ian S Taylor	Alan Biley
Phil Hayes		Mark Taylor	Steve Claridge
Gary Hicks	Paul Wanless	Alan Declan Turner	John Taylor
Ian Howell	Steve Fallon	Ashley Whiskin	Dion Dublin
Neil Hudson	David Stringer	Henry White	Shane Tudor
Andy Ivy	Dion Dublin	Michael Roy Williams	John Taylor
Simon Jarvis	Dion Dublin	James Willis	Alan Kimble
Kevin Jeeps	Alan Biley	Garry Wright	Dion Dublin
Andy Jennings	Steve Claridge	David York	Steve Fallon